JESUS IN MUSLIM-CHRISTIAN CONVERSATION

JESUS *in* MUSLIM-CHRISTIAN CONVERSATION

Mark Beaumont

CASCADE *Books* • Eugene, Oregon

JESUS IN MUSLIM-CHRISTIAN CONVERSATION

Copyright © 2018 Mark Beaumont. All rights reserved. Except for brief quotations in critical publications or reviews, no part of this book may be reproduced in any manner without prior written permission from the publisher. Write: Permissions, Wipf and Stock Publishers, 199 W. 8th Ave., Suite 3, Eugene, OR 97401.

Cascade Books
An Imprint of Wipf and Stock Publishers
199 W. 8th Ave., Suite 3
Eugene, OR 97401

www.wipfandstock.com

PAPERBACK ISBN: 978-1-5326-1354-8
HARDCOVER ISBN: 978-1-5326-1356-2
EBOOK ISBN: 978-1-5326-1355-5

Cataloguing-in-Publication data:

Names: Beaumont, Mark. | Singh, David Emmanuel, foreword writer

Title: Jesus in Muslim-Christian conversation / Mark Beaumont, with a foreword by David Emmanuel Singh.

Description: Eugene, OR: Cascade Books, 2018 | Includes bibliographical references and index.

Identifiers: ISBN 978-1-5326-1354-8 (paperback) | ISBN 978-1-5326-1356-2 (hardcover) | ISBN 978-1-5326-1355-5 (ebook)

Subjects: LCSH: Christianity and other religions—Islam | Islam—Relations—Christianity | Jesus Christ—Islamic interpretations | Jesus Christ—Person and offices

Classification: BP172 B218 2018 (print) | BP172 (ebook)

Manufactured in the U.S.A.   FEBRUARY 22, 2018

Biblical quotations are from New Revised Standard Version Bible, copyright © 1989 National Council of the Churches of Christ in the United States of America. Used by permission. All rights reserved.

Table of Contents

Foreword vii
Preface ix

Chapter 1. Born of Mary 1
Chapter 2. Miracle Worker 23
Chapter 3. Teacher of Love of God and Neighbor 44
Chapter 4. Proclaimer of the Kingdom of God 65
Chapter 5. Word and Spirit of God 86
Chapter 6. Son of Mary—Son of Man 107
Chapter 7. Son of God 128
Chapter 8. Messiah and Redeemer 149
Chapter 9. Raised from Death 171
Chapter 10. Returning in Power 192

Bibliography 215

General Index 221
Bible Index 227
Qurʾan Index 231

Foreword

OFTEN THE SIMPLEST AND the most obvious points are easily missed or ignored. Mark avoids both errors: firstly, by acknowledging the absolute centrality of Jesus in the future of Muslim-Christian relations; and secondly by providing an engaging exposition on the topic by choosing to employ the creative means of imaginative dialogues. The scope of his work is comprehensive in starting with Jesus' birth and ending with the theme of his return in power. His fictional protagonists are believable and true to life. The voices of their equal and honest exchanges promise to extend far beyond their, arguably, "marginal" affiliations. This book is a fine new addition to works by Mona Siddiqui (*Christians, Muslims and Jesus*) and Carl Medearis (*Muslims, Christians and Jesus*) and undeniably innovative in making the topic of his previous monograph appealingly accessible.

David E. Singh
Oxford Centre for Mission Studies

Preface

JESUS IS A REVERED messenger of God for Muslims and Lord and Savior for Christians. How can Muslims and Christians relate to each other when this figure from the past simultaneously attracts them yet drives them apart? Jesus is the very center of the Christian faith, but he is of great significance for Muslims too, a faithful witness to God who is central to Islam. In the twenty-first century, is it possible for Muslims and Christians to relate to each other around him?

This book is an attempt to bring together two representative voices, one Muslim and one Christian, to talk about Jesus. They come from particular strands of Islam and Christianity. Ibrahim is a Sunni Sufi Muslim who has studied Christianity and has been active as an academic in the Western world. Paul is an Evangelical Protestant who has lived in the Muslim world and has been engaged in teaching religious studies in the West. They sum up the experiences I have had in my life so far as someone who is close to Paul but not identical to him. Ibrahim is like many Muslims I have met, but not a replica of any one person. As such, Ibrahim and Paul are my imaginary friends, whose conversation I hear and report.

I wanted to follow up my 2005 book, *Christology in Dialogue with Muslims* (Oxford: Regnum), which analyzed the writing of Christians who had attempted to use Muslim foundations to explain Christian convictions in Islamic terms. In that work, Muslim voices were heard in response to these Christians, but they were responding rather than taking the initiative. In this new book, I have brought together a Christian and a Muslim as equal partners in conversation about Jesus to explore points of agreement and tension.

The conversation begins with the conception of Jesus and ends with his return from heaven, dealing with his earthly work in between. His miraculous activity, his teaching, and the titles he has been given are considered in detail. Differences over the ending of Jesus' life are debated.

I hope that Christians and Muslims might find this exchange of views helpful, even when the opinions expressed do not match those of the readers.

one

Born of Mary

IBRAHIM GETS THE CONVERSATION started on the belief shared by Muslims and Christians that Jesus was conceived in Mary when she was still a virgin. Ibrahim presents the teaching of the Qur'an, the sayings of the Prophet Muhammad, and the interpretation in Qur'an commentary. Paul follows up with the presentation of the virginal conception in the Gospels, the apostolic writings, and later interpretation. The theme of the miraculous conception of Jesus is followed by discussions of the birth stories in the Qur'an and the Gospels, and the qur'anic story of Jesus speaking as a newborn child. The beginning of Jesus' life occupies a very significant place in the Qur'an, and seems to be more important than stories about his adult work. Paul points out the way that legends about the birth of Jesus and his speaking as an infant from some of the apocryphal gospels have resurfaced in the Qur'an. He challenges the Muslim view that the Qur'an was revealed directly from heaven without any influence from previous writing.

The final section of the chapter is an exchange of views between Ibrahim and Paul on the significance of the virginal conception of Jesus for Muslims and Christians. They both acknowledge that some Muslims and Christians no longer believe in the miraculous conception without the involvement of a human father, but they seek to maintain the traditional account. Paul argues that since some of the apocryphal gospels portray Mary as perpetually a virgin even after the birth of Jesus that Muhammad heard such stories and reacted against them. Thus, the Qur'an criticizes Christians for elevating Mary to a divine status by reporting Jesus denying that he told people to worship him and his mother Mary. Ibrahim agrees that Christians are being warned not to give to Mary what belongs to God. They both discuss the tradition of offering prayer to

Mary, especially for healing. While Paul thinks this is misplaced, Ibrahim makes allowance for appeals to the saints who have walked closely with God as long as believers do not ascribe divinity to them.

The Conception of Jesus in the Qur'an

Ibrahim: The story of Mary and the conception of Jesus is told in Q3:45–47:

> The angels said, "Mary, God announces the news of a word from Him: his name is the messiah, Jesus, the son of Mary: he will be honored in this world and in the next life, and he will be among those who are near to God. 46 He will speak to people as a young child and as an adult and will be among those who are righteous." 47 She said, "My Lord, how can I have a son when no man has touched me?" He said, "In this way God creates what He wills. When He has decided to do something He simply says, 'Be,' and it exists."[1]

The conception of Jesus by the creative power of God without the involvement of a human father is clearly presented in Q3:45–47. Mary's shock at hearing the angelic announcement of a boy to be conceived in her womb is vividly shown in her protestation of her sexual purity, in her absolute certainty that she has never become intimate with a man. The Qur'an interprets the momentous event of the coming of Jesus into the world as a sign of God's decision to create in a way that is unexpected, unusual, and unprecedented. Prophets come and go by God's will but they are conceived by normal means through the sexual union of a father and mother. This prophet is different.

Mary is addressed by name, and the son conceived in her is to carry her name. The fact that this woman is honored by her name being embedded in the life of the prophet who comes from her makes Mary unique among women mentioned in the Qur'an. Of the four book-bearing prophets, Abraham, Moses, David, and Jesus, who came to their people with revealed books, only Jesus is connected so closely to his mother. Although Abraham's wife is part of the narrative of the first Muslim to bring a revealed text, she is not named. The families of Moses and David, who both brought books to the children of Israel, are not mentioned by name.

---

1. Translations from the Qur'an are my own.

The narrative of the angelic visit to Mary does not introduce the background to her story, so her own family life and circumstances are left in the shadows of the dazzling brightness of the messengers of God arriving suddenly in her private experience. There is no need to know where she was and who was with her, for the reality of the encounter need only be personal to her. This family narrative does come in Q19:16–17, where it is said that Mary "withdrew from her family to a place in the east to screen herself from them." In that place of separation, she received a visit from an angel who appeared to Mary "in the likeness of a well-built man." Thus, the encounter is a very private one with no witnesses among her family. But her sense of family honor is just as vivid in this version of the story as in Q3:45–47. In Q19:20, when the messenger announces the conception of a "pure son" in her, she protests her virginity, "I have not been unchaste." The conception took place by God's ordination (v. 21), and Mary "went away with him to a distant place" (v. 22). The sense of Mary being led away from her family is very much at the center of this narrative, emphasizing the depth of Mary's commitment to the will of God. How dedicated she was to the divine call on her life, to the extent that she was willing to put her future well-being as a woman at risk by consenting to becoming pregnant outside the normal conventions of her society. She represents all those who hear the call of God to submit to his plan without holding back out of fear of human rejection.

Mary's submission to God's decision that Jesus be conceived in her without normal human means is told twice in the Qur'an, showing the importance of this woman in the history of the Creator's dealings with humankind. She symbolizes all other female believers who have the courage to obey the message that God sends despite the consequences for the disrespect in which they might be held in their family life. The honor of God comes before the honor given by human relationships. Mary obeys God rather than her parents.

The sharpness of this choice of obedience to God is seen in the narrative of Mary's return to her family after giving birth to Jesus in 19:27–28. "She returned to her people with him in her arms. They said, 'Mary, you have done something unheard of. Sister of Aaron, your father was not an evil man nor was your mother unchaste.'" The full force of Mary's breaking of moral laws according to the rules of her culture is heard in the language of her family. The good moral character of her father and mother has been put under suspicion by Mary's reckless behavior. The implication of the outburst is that Mary would be thought by the surrounding community to have inherited evil actions from her parents. People in the neighborhood might interpret Mary's rebellion either as copying her mother's bad behavior or as fulfilling a curse put upon her in punishment for her father's wrongdoing.

According to some traditions, the choice of Mary to carry the miraculous son is linked to the prayer of her mother Anna, who asked God to protect Mary and her son from the attack of Satan. As a result, neither Mary nor Jesus were pierced by Satan at birth, something which all children experience.[2] Yet her mother was horrified at the way the conception occurred. Other traditions speak of a young man named Joseph, son of a carpenter, who was Mary's cousin on her mother's side, who served with Mary in the temple. He was the first to notice that Mary was pregnant and asked her "whether a crop could grow without seeds, and a child without a father? Mary answered yes, since God had created the first crop from nothing, just as He had created Adam without father or mother."[3] Some traditions say that Mary withdrew to a secluded place to avoid gossip among those who might accuse her of becoming pregnant through Joseph or Zechariah, who was her guardian as a temple leader.[4]

Qur'an commentators have emphasized the power of God in the conception of Jesus beyond normal means. Few have assumed the involvement of a human father. Sayyid Ahmed Khan (d. 1898) thought that Mary had sexual intercourse with her husband, and Ghulam Ahmed Parwez (d. 1886) held that since the angelic announcement of the conception of John to Zechariah in Q3:40 is identical to that given to Mary in Q3:47, then Jesus is the fruit of the union of Joseph and Mary in the context of their married state.[5]

Given that most interpreters of the Qur'an have held that the conception was by miraculous means, their attention has focused on the role of the angelic messenger in the process of conception. Most have identified the angel as Gabriel who appeared to Mary as a handsome, beardless young man with curly hair, but some have thought that this was actually Joseph, Mary's companion in the service of the temple.[6] When he says that he has come to give Mary a pure boy in Q19:19, this has generally

---

2. See Ibn Kathir, *Qisas al-anbiya'*, 2:370, and 461.
3. See Stowasser, *Women in the Qur'an*, 74.
4. Ibn Kathir, *Qisas*, 2:390.
5. See Baljon, *Modern Muslim Koran Interpretation*, 69–70.
6. So Zamakhshari, *Al-Kashshaf*, 3:7, and Razi, *Al-Tafsir al-Kabir*, 2:197.

been understood to mean that he breathed on Mary, and that his breath entered Mary through her garment or mouth.[7] That Gabriel had no power to create life is taken for granted, since Q21:91, "We breathed Our spirit into her and we made her and her son a sign for all people," demonstrates that "the divine breath caused Mary to conceive."[8]

The Conception of Jesus in the Gospels

Paul: The narrative of the visit of the angel Gabriel to Mary is found in the Gospel of Luke 1:26–38:

> 26 In the sixth month the angel Gabriel was sent by God to a town in Galilee called Nazareth, 27 to a virgin engaged to a man whose name was Joseph, of the house of David. The virgin's name was Mary. 28 And he came to her and said, "Greetings, favored one! The Lord is with you." 29 But she was much perplexed by his words and pondered what sort of greeting this might be. 30 The angel said to her, "Do not be afraid, Mary, for you have found favor with God. 31 And now, you will conceive in your womb and bear a son, and you will name him Jesus. 32 He will be great, and will be called the Son of the Most High, and the Lord God will give to him the throne of his ancestor David. 33 He will reign over the house of Jacob forever, and of his kingdom there will be no end." 34 Mary said to the angel, "How can this be, since I am a virgin?" 35 The angel said to her, "The Holy Spirit will come upon you, and the power of the Most High will overshadow you; therefore the child to be born will be holy; he will be called Son of God...." 38 Then Mary said, "Here am I, the servant of the Lord; let it be with me according to your word." Then the angel departed from her.[9]

The story relates a young woman called Mary who was engaged to be married to a man named Joseph in a town in Galilee. Nothing is mentioned about her family. Joseph is said to be a descendent of the famous king David, whose legendary power is to be re-enacted by the son conceived in Mary by God's Spirit. The promise of an eternal rule for this son recalls the word of God through the prophet Nathan to David in 2 Samuel 7:16; "Your house and your kingdom shall be made sure forever

---

7. So Tabari, *Jami' al-Bayan*, 16:48.

8. Stowasser, "Mary," 293.

9. New Revised Standard Version. All Bible references are taken from this translation.

before me; your throne shall be established forever." Mary protests the impossibility of such a conception happening at that moment since she is a virgin not yet married. Gabriel reassures her that God can do the impossible through his Spirit acting within her. Thus, the child is holy, and is to be given two names, Jesus and Son of God. Mary immediately assents to this angelic proposal, calling herself servant of God.

This narrative is supplemented by a version of the story told from Joseph's perspective in the Gospel of Matthew 1:18–25. He discovered that Mary was pregnant while engaged to be married to him. After Joseph decided to sever the relationship without exposing Mary to public shame, an angel appeared to him and told him to marry Mary because the child was conceived by God's Spirit. He should name the boy Jesus because "he will save his people from their sins" (v. 21). Matthew quotes from the prophet Isaiah 7:14; "The virgin shall conceive and bear a son, and they shall name him Emmanuel," and says that the name means "God is with us" (v. 23). Joseph did not repudiate Mary, but had no sexual relations with her until she had given birth to Jesus.

The apostolic writers pay little attention to the conception of Jesus. The only interest is in the descent of Jesus from the line of David. Luke, like Matthew, understands this Davidic line to be via Joseph not Mary (Luke 3:23). Paul writes of God's Son "descended from David according to the flesh" in Romans 1:3. The role of Mary as the obedient servant of God is confined to Luke's presentation in the New Testament. He has her sing a song of praise before the birth of Jesus in 1:46–55, in which she calls God her Savior because he has favored her in her lowly state. She says, "Surely, from now on all generations will call me blessed: for the Mighty One has done great things for me, and holy is his name" (vv. 48–49).

Christians have normally understood that Jesus was conceived by the Spirit of God in the virgin Mary without a human father being involved. Only since the Enlightenment in the eighteenth century have some preferred to think that Jesus was the product of the union of Joseph and Mary. The earliest narrative of Mary beyond the New Testament is found in *The Protevangelium of James* from the second century, in which her family background, marriage to Joseph, an older widower with children, and her perpetual virginity are presented. Mary is glorified by the narrative that the birth of Jesus "preserved Mary's virginity," by the "Davidic descent of Mary," and by Mary being seen "as an instrument of divine salvation in her own right."[10]

---

10. *The Protevangelium of James*, 50–51.

Devotion to Mary developed in the Eastern and Western churches. Severian (c. 400), bishop of Gabala in Syria, mentions that Mary was praised daily. Feasts of Mary were held in the Eastern churches by the fifth century and in the Western churches by the seventh century. The decision of the Council of Ephesus in 431 to call Mary *theotokos* (God-bearer) led to a stress on "Mary's transcendent role in the present as heavenly lady, queen, and intercessor."[11]

The Romantic movement of the nineteenth century in Europe resulted in a renewed interest in the veneration of Mary. In 1854, Pope Pius IX made the immaculate conception of Mary a church dogma, which provided an environment for visions of Mary at Lourdes in France in 1858 and Fatima in Portugal in 1917. In 1950, Pope Pius XII declared the dogma of the bodily assumption of Mary. The popularity of pilgrimage sites such as Lourdes and Fatima demonstrates that Catholic Christians seek spiritual help from Mary. "Votive offerings are for special needs and for giving thanks for the help received."[12]

Interaction of Islamic and Christian Accounts of the Conception of Jesus

Ibrahim: Muslim traditions of Mary have taken a special interest in her family background based on the narrative in Q3:35–37:

> 'Imran's wife said, "My Lord, I dedicate completely to you what is in my womb. Please accept him from me. You hear and know everything." 36 When she gave birth, she said, "My Lord! I have given birth to a girl." (God knew what she had given birth to: the male is not the same as the female.) "I name her Mary and I entrust her and her children to Your protection from the accursed Satan." 37 Her Lord fully accepted her and caused her to develop well by entrusting her to the care of Zachariah. Each time Zachariah went to see her in the place of prayer, he found she had food. He said, "Mary, how do you have this food?" She said, "It's from God, because God provides food without measure to whoever he wishes."

Ibn Kathir (d. 1373), in his *Stories of the Prophets*, adds detail to the qur'anic account. Mary's mother is named Anna, though the Qur'an

---

11. Petri, "Devotion to Mary," 439.
12. Ibid.

only names her father as 'Imran.¹³ Anna and 'Imran hoped and prayed for a child and after she conceived, Anna consecrated her child to the service of God in the temple. She duly brought Mary to the temple after she had been weaned. Zechariah looked after her in the temple where he locked her into a room. She was miraculously provided with fruit out of season.¹⁴ On attaining puberty, Mary was removed from the temple and taken by Zechariah to his home to be looked after by Mary's aunt, who was his wife. It was while she served in the temple that Mary met her cousin Joseph, who served under Zechariah.¹⁵

Paul: The naming of Mary's mother as Anna is found in *The Protevangelium of James*. She had been unable to bear a child and prayed earnestly for God to intervene. An angel appeared to her saying that God had heard her prayer and would grant her a child. Anna offered to dedicate this child to God's service. Anna called the girl Mary. When she was three years old Anna took Mary to the temple and left her with the priests. After Mary reached puberty at the age of twelve, the priests were anxious that her bleeding would defile the temple. Zechariah, the high priest, was commanded by God to assemble the widowers and he would show which one should marry Mary. Joseph, a widower with sons, was chosen, but protested that he might be a laughing stock if he married such a young girl. After agreeing to marry her, Joseph left her in the temple where an angel appeared to her to announce the conception of Jesus.¹⁶

The marks of this narrative are found both in Q3:35–37 and in the traditions reported in interpretations of the qur'anic passage. The way that the angelic announcement comes to Mary in *The Protevangelium of James* is also reflected in Q3:42; "Mary, God has chosen you and purified you. He has chosen you above all women." In *The Protevangelium of James* the angel says, "You are blessed among women,"¹⁷ a phrase not found in the narrative in Luke 1:28.

This Islamic interpretation of the significance of Mary has drawn on traditions emanating from a much older milieu of storytelling, and has woven them into a coherent narrative of Anna the mother of Mary and Mary's husband Joseph who was not the father of Jesus. The basic story

---

13. Ibn Kathir, *Qisas*, 2:349.
14. Ibid., 2:369–71, 373–74.
15. Ibid., 2:385, 388.
16. *The Protevangelium of James*, 58–59.
17. Ibid., 61.

of Mary in Luke's Gospel was added to in *The Protevangelium of James* out of a desire to locate Mary in a wider family setting. The first-century story became embellished in a second-century Christian context. This second-century narrative emerged later in the telling of Mary's story in the Qur'an 3:35–42, and more fully in the subsequent Islamic interpretation of that story.

The Birth of Jesus in the Qur'an

Ibrahim: The birth of Jesus is recounted in Q19:23–34:

> 23 The labor pains brought her to the trunk of a palm tree. She said, "If only I had died before this and had been completely forgotten." 24 Then a voice called out to her from below, "Don't be sad. Your Lord has provided a stream beneath you. 25 If you shake the trunk of the palm tree towards you it will let ripe dates fall on you. 26 Eat, drink, and be happy. If you see anyone say, 'I have vowed to the Merciful to fast, so I will not talk to anyone today.'" 27 She returned to her people with him in her arms. They said, "Mary, you have done something unheard of. 28 Sister of Aaron, your father was not an evil man nor was your mother unchaste." 29 She pointed to him. They said, "How can we talk to a child in the cradle?" 30 He said, "I am a servant of God. He has given me the Book and made me a prophet. 31 He has made me blessed wherever I may be. He commanded me to pray and give alms as long as I live. 32 He has made me devoted to my mother and not haughty or nasty. Peace was on me the day I was born, and will be on me the day I die and the day I am raised to life." 34 Such was Jesus the son of Mary.

In the context of Mary's withdrawal to a secluded place, she gave birth to Jesus alone, and then returned to her mother and father with the newborn child. The voice that spoke to her "from below" is not named as an angel. The fact that the newborn Jesus spoke to Mary's family suggests that perhaps it was he who also spoke to his mother to reassure her that God was providing food and drink for her in her isolation. The furious reaction of her family is met by silence from Mary, who keeps her vow to abstain from conversation. She passes the task of replying on to Jesus, who she knows is quite capable of defending her honor. Her faith in Jesus' capabilities is not matched by the faith of her family who are incredulous that a baby should be asked to speak. Jesus' testimonial that he would cherish his mother vindicates her obedience to God. But the response of the family is not mentioned.

Ibn Kathir gives traditional interpretations of this narrative. The date palm provided dates out of season, and this not only nourished her but also demonstrated a proof of her purity before God who made the miraculous provision. She stayed there for forty days until her physical condition had become pure. When she returned to her family they were angry that the child should speak on behalf of his mother.[18] He also reports that the king of Persia sent ambassadors with gifts of gold, myrrh, and frankincense, after having seen a star rise which was understood to mark the birth of an important person. However, the local king of Syria wanted to kill the baby. When Mary was told of this she went down to Egypt with Jesus and stayed there until he was twelve years old.[19]

Commentators have noted the important role of the infant Jesus in vindicating his mother's chastity before her angry family. For example, Zamakhshari (d. 1143) pointed out that the family considered stoning Mary for her fornication but were persuaded not to by the infant Jesus, who stopped nursing, propped himself up, and wagging his finger at them supported his mother against their accusations.[20]

The Birth of Jesus in the Gospels

Paul: The events of the birth of Jesus are told in Luke 2:1–21. Mary gave birth to Jesus in Bethlehem while visiting the hometown of Joseph to whom she was engaged to be married. He had not been able to find accommodation there, and so the baby was laid in an animal feeding trough. Shepherds were visited by angels who told them to go and see the child in the town, because he was to be their Savior, Messiah, and Lord. After eight days, the baby was circumcised and named Jesus after the angelic command. Matthew 2:1–12 adds a story about wise men from the East coming to Jerusalem to find a newborn king of the Jews as a result of their observations of the stars. They found Mary in a house in Bethlehem and offered the baby gifts of gold, frankincense, and myrrh.

The apostolic literature of the New Testament does not comment on the birth stories. But there was a considerable interest in elaborating

18. Ibn Kathir, *Qisas*, 2:390, 393, and 395–96.
19. Ibid., 2:411–12.
20. Zamakhshari, *Al-Kashshaf*, 3:11.

details of the birth narratives in Christian writing beyond the first century. The second-century *Protevangelium of James* elaborates the Lukan narrative of the birth at Bethlehem by mentioning that Joseph was not sure how he should enrol Mary in the census called by the ruler Augustus:

> I shall enrol my sons, but shall I do with this child? How shall I enrol her? As my wife? I am ashamed to do that. Or as my daughter? But all the children of Israel know that she is not my daughter. On this day of the Lord the Lord will do as he wills.[21]

Before they reached Bethlehem, Mary went into labor and Joseph found a cave in a desert place and left her in the care of his sons to go and look for a midwife in Bethlehem. The midwife, Salome, discovered that Mary was still a virgin even after giving birth to her son. However, due to her unbelief in that possibility, her hand became inflamed and an angel appeared telling her to touch the child to receive healing. Then the wise men from the East arrived at the cave and offered the baby their gifts.[22]

The motive for filling in aspects of the birth story was presumably that Christians wanted a more complete account of the amazing events already narrated in the Gospels of Luke and Matthew. However, the discrepancies between *The Protevangelium of James* and the two Gospels show that the former attempted to smooth over differences in the location of the birth by choosing a cave outside Bethlehem rather than an animal shelter or a house in Bethlehem. The internal debate within the mind of Joseph is a sign of the desire to make his dilemma of trust in God more acute than the Gospel accounts allowed. The addition of Salome the midwife and her discovery of the intact hymen of Mary emphasizes the belief in the perpetual virginity of Mary, which had obviously become important by the second century in some Christian circles.

Interaction of Islamic and Christian Accounts of the Birth of Jesus

Ibrahim: The qur'anic interest in the birth of Jesus lies especially in the vindication of Mary's purity of character in the face of the angry rejection by her family, which contrasts markedly with the confidence her mother had in Mary when she was born. The disappointment of her mother in

---

21. *The Protevangelium of James*, 63.
22. Ibid., 64–65.

the manner of the conception and birth of Jesus casts a dark shadow over the miraculous arrival of the prophet Jesus. Faith in the creative power of God is not always easy for human beings when God chooses a way of creating that goes beyond the normal.

Paul: There is a shared concern with Christian traditions here. The Matthean narrative indicates Joseph's anxiety with the reputation of Mary if he were to divorce her publicly and thus bring shame on her. The angelic command to Joseph to take Mary as his wife demonstrates the difficulty that faced Joseph in accepting the divine creative work in her. This concern is highlighted in *The Protevangelium of James*, where Joseph argues with himself aloud about how he should refer to Mary for the purposes of the census. Will she be put to shame in the process? However, the Christian focus in the birth of Jesus is not on the shame of Mary's assumed fornication but the contrast between the humble situation of the coming of Jesus into the world far from home in the most rudimentary conditions and the singing of the angelic choir, along with the visits of the shepherds and the wise men to the newborn Savior, Lord, and King.

Ibrahim: Islamic interpretation of the birth has sought to add detail to the qur'anic account by adopting the Matthean story of the wise men and their gifts and the flight of Joseph and Mary to Egypt. There has been no similar concern to add the singing of the angelic choir or the visit of the shepherds, probably because the birth takes place beside a palm tree in the Qur'an, a context in which hill shepherds would not naturally fit. There has been no interest in the perpetual virginity of Mary in Islamic commentary, given that Muslims have seen Mary as a woman who displayed remarkable faith in God and persistent obedience to his command. They have not been drawn to imagining Mary as a woman whose virginity needed to be preserved by miraculous means. For Muslims, the miracle of the conception of Jesus without a human father has not required a further miracle to keep Mary's virginity intact after giving birth to Jesus.

Jesus the Child Prodigy in the Qur'an

Ibrahim: The story of the newborn Jesus speaking in defense of his mother to her angry family has already been referenced from Q19:30–33. Not only does he vindicate his mother's purity by saying that God commanded him to cherish his mother, but he also speaks of his future activity as a prophet who has been given the Scripture. Q3:46 includes a prediction that Jesus will "speak to people as a young child" in the angelic message to Mary before Jesus is conceived in her. Q5:110 mentions that God will one day remind Jesus that he spoke to people in his infancy. Therefore, the speaking infant is emphasized in the Qur'an as part of the miraculous creative work of God with respect to the coming of Jesus. His speaking in such an unexpected way is an indication of the boundless freedom of God to create as he will, and for humans to be aware that the normal manifestation of human capabilities does not confine God to operating with typical methods.

Commentators have tended to point out the significance of the infant's claim to be under the command of God as a prophet. The earliest evidence of this comes from *The Life of Muhammad* by Ibn Ishaq (d. 787), when Muhammad was attempting to convince a deputation of Christians who had come to him in Medina from Najran that Jesus was a prophet but that he was not divine. Ibn Ishaq reports that the leaders of the deputation said that they believed in Jesus as Son of God because "he spoke in the cradle and this is something that no child of Adam has ever done."[23] Muhammad argued to the contrary that, "God marked him out by speech in his cradle as a sign of his prophethood and to show mankind where his power lay."[24] Barbara Stowasser sums up the subsequent repetition of this tradition in the history of Qur'an commentary; "The effectiveness of Jesus' defense is seen in the fact that his (Qur'an-recorded) words concerned himself as God's prophet and thereby established Mary's virtue within the parameter of prophetic veracity."[25]

Paul: There is no mention of the baby Jesus speaking in the canonical Gospels, but a speaking infant Jesus is found in *The Gospel of Pseudo-Matthew*. Mary was on the way to Egypt with Joseph and his three sons and a daughter. Having decided to rest in a cave, Mary was sitting with Jesus on her lap when a host of dragons came out of the depths of the cave. The others were terrified, but Jesus stood on his feet before them and the dragons worshipped him. Jesus commanded them not to hurt anyone. His parents were afraid for Jesus, but he said to them, "Do not be afraid, and do not consider me to be a child, for I am and always have

---

23. Ibn Ishaq, *The Life of Muhammad*, 271.
24. Ibid., 275.
25. Stowasser, *Women in the Qur'an*, 75.

been perfect; and all the beasts of the forest must needs be docile before me."[26]

The story of Mary being fed dates is narrated in this work. Mary rested under a palm tree on the third day of the journey and said to Joseph that it would be good if she could eat some dates. Joseph was surprised at her request since the dates were so high up. He was more concerned to find water for them and the cattle. Jesus then spoke to the palm tree, "O tree, bend your branches and refresh my mother with your fruit." So, the tree bent down and Mary could pick dates. Jesus then commanded the tree:

> Raise yourself, O palm, and be strong and be companion of my trees which are in the paradise of my Father; and open from your roots a vein of water which is hidden in the earth and let the waters flow, so that we may quench our thirst.[27]

The water that poured forth satisfied both man and beast and they all gave thanks to God. John Elliot mentions that this writing "seems to have been compiled in Latin, possibly in the eighth or ninth century, although the oldest manuscript extant is of the eleventh century."[28] However, a similar piece of writing may have been referred to in the sixth-century Gelasian Decree of sixty-one apocryphal works, which would date the traditions contained in it to at least the sixth century, if not before.[29]

Another work entitled *The Arabic Infancy Gospel* has a story of Jesus speaking as an infant. Mary and Joseph were travelling to Egypt across a desert, when two robbers confronted them. One, called Titus, said to the other, called Dumachus, that they should leave Mary and Joseph alone, and Mary said that God would forgive them their sins as a result of their kindness. Jesus spoke up:

> Thirty years hence, O my mother, the Jews will crucify me at Jerusalem, and these two robbers will be raised upon the cross along with me, Titus on my right hand and Dumachus on my left; and after that day Titus shall go before me into Paradise.[30]

---

26. *The Gospel of Pseudo-Matthew*, 95.
27. Ibid., 95–96.
28. Ibid, 86.
29. Ibid.
30. *The Arabic Infancy Gospel*, 105.

Elliot believes that this work is based on "a Syrian archetype, which could be of the fifth-sixth century."[31] Neal Robinson thinks that *The Gospel of Pseudo-Matthew* and *The Arabic Infancy Gospel* both post-date the rise of Islam, but "Christians in Muhammad's audience were probably familiar with the episodes to which they refer."[32] Therefore, the story told by Ibn Ishaq of the Najran Christians believing that Jesus' capacity to speak as an infant was a sign of Jesus' divine nature could well have been an accurate assessment if they knew the stories in these works.

Interaction of Islamic and Christian Accounts of Jesus the Child Prodigy

Paul: It appears likely that the Christian traditions of Jesus speaking as an infant and of him providing dates for his mother and water for the family were reflected in the Qurʾan in support of Islamic beliefs. The speaking infant Jesus in the Qurʾan proves that he is called to be a prophet of God who will bring a Scripture to his people. The prophetic prediction comes true in his adult life and confirms his calling as a baby to his prophethood. The bending date palm reappears in the Qurʾan, not as a result of the command of the infant Jesus, but as the result of an unnamed voice, which reassured Mary in Q19:24–26, "Don't be sad. Your Lord has provided a stream beneath you.25 If you shake the trunk of the palm tree towards you it will let ripe dates fall on you.26 Eat, drink, and be happy." Some commentators held that indeed the voice belonged to the infant Jesus, but others thought an angel gave the directions. Whichever was the source of the voice, the story confirms in the Qurʾan that God made miraculous provision for Mary in her time of weakness and need, having given birth to Jesus in a remote place far from the comforts of home and the attention of her family.

Jesus Born of Mary in Muslim-Christian Conversation

Ibrahim: The stories in the Qurʾan relating to the birth of Jesus teach the incomparable power of God in creation. He only has to say, "be," and something will come into existence. When God chooses to create a prophet who will bring his word in a Scripture he does not need to

31. Ibid., 100.
32. Robinson, "Jesus," 13.

confine his creative energy to the normal processes he has devised for the bringing into existence of a new human life. However, the Qur'an does acknowledge that prophets are usually born by normal processes. Q3:37–40 tells the story of Zechariah, the guardian of Mary in the temple, who found that God provided food for her miraculously without human intervention. He asked her, "Mary, how do you have this food?" She said, "It's from God, because God provides food without measure to whoever he wishes" (v. 37). So, Zechariah asked God to give him a child. While he was praying, angels came to him and said, "God gives you news of John, confirming a word from God. He will be honorable, chaste, and a prophet among the righteous" (v. 39). But Zechariah protested that he was too old and his wife was barren. When the angel said, "in such a way God does whatever he wishes" (v. 40), Zechariah asked for a sign. The angel said that the sign would be that he would not be able to speak for three days.

There is no hint here that the child John would be born in an exceptional way, like Jesus without a human father. But the Qur'an does indicate that at least one other prophet was born by exceptional means. Q3:59 states that "With God Jesus is equivalent to Adam. He created him from dust then He said to him, 'Be', and he came into existence." The meaning of this comparison is that just as Jesus had no human father, Adam had no human parents. The point of the comparison is to confirm that miraculous conception does not allow Christians to infer that the virginal conception of Jesus, popularly known as the virgin birth, automatically confers divine status on Jesus. This has always been understood by Muslims to be the correct way to interpret the comparison made between Adam and Jesus. For example, Ibn Ishaq reports that Muhammad argued with the Christian delegation from Najran that if Christians say that Jesus was created without a male being involved they should hear from God that "the likeness of Jesus with God is as the likeness of Adam whom God created of earth," which means, "I created Adam from earth by that same power without a male or a female. And he was as Jesus was: flesh and blood and hair and skin." Thus the "creation of Jesus without a male is no more wonderful than this." Muhammad concluded the argument by saying that he had brought them the true story of Jesus, and invited them to worship only God and not associate anything with him, or take other Lords beside God.[33] It is clear from the testimony of the Prophet Muhammad himself that he interpreted the comparison between Adam

---

33. Ibn Ishaq, *The Life of Muhammad*, 276–77.

and Jesus as a denial of the Christian tendency to elevate Jesus to a status which only God has. Christians take Jesus as Lord, but deny the exclusive Lordship to God by so doing.

Paul: The narrative of Zechariah and Elizabeth having a child out of season, because she was barren up till that point, and the story of Mary having a child outside the normal means because she had no sexual relations with a man are faithfully reported in the Qur'an from the Gospel of Luke. It is heartening to see the way the genuine history of Jesus' birth is recognized here. It is also interesting to note that in recent times some Muslims have believed that Mary did conceive Jesus with her husband Joseph, a belief held by liberal Christians nowadays. Geoffrey Parrinder believed that the Qur'an announces the divine decree "be" "without indicating whether the birth is to be by normal channels."[34] He was reflecting the post-Enlightenment view that miracles do not happen, and that it is necessary to rewrite the miracle stories in the Bible to bring them into line with normal occurrences. He was an ordained Methodist Minister, who like many other twentieth-century Protestants felt that Christian faith in Jesus no longer required a belief in the virgin birth.

Catholics have tended to uphold the virginal conception because they honor Mary much more than Protestants do. However, the Catholic theologian Hans Küng came into conflict with Pope John Paul II over his reworking of traditional doctrines. He advises Christians to think about Jesus from his death rather than his birth:

> Belief in a virgin birth does not belong at the centre of the Christian message. Hence we can understand that even those in the early church who knew nothing or thought nothing of virgin birth could be convinced, like Mark, Paul or John, that Jesus was the "Messiah" or could confess him "Son of God," the centre of the Christian message.[35]

More conservative Catholics, such as Gerald O'Collins, believe not only that Matthew and Luke held that Jesus was conceived by the Holy Spirit without the intervention of a male, but also that contemporary Christians should uphold this:

> Traditionally the major value of his virginal conception has been to express Jesus' divine origin. . . . There never was a moment in his history when Jesus was not Son of God. . . . The event of the

---

34. Parrinder, *Jesus in the Qur'an*, 74.
35. Küng, *Islam*, 491–92.

virginal conception plays its part in revealing and clarifying that central truth: from the beginning to the end there is a Trinitarian face to the story of Jesus Christ. His total history discloses the God who is Father, Son, and Holy Spirit.[36]

From my perspective as an Evangelical Protestant, the virginal conception is an important indication of the status of Jesus as from God in a way that is unique among human beings. While he may be compared to Adam as having an origin that is unusual in not having two human biological parents, Matthew 1:23 testifies to the coming of "Emmanuel" meaning "God with us," and Luke 2:11 to the arrival of the "Lord" (Gk. *Kurios*), a title used of God in the Greek translation of the Old Testament read by the early church. Adam could never be named in these ways! He may be the progenitor of humanity in both the Bible and the Qur'an, but he is exactly that, the beginning of the human race. Jesus, by contrast, is the beginning of a new race of people who are saved from their self-centered lifestyle by his coming and called to follow his radical purity and love. His virginal conception is the indicator of the newness of creation at that point in the history of humanity. So, the apostle Paul can speak of Christians as a new creation in Christ (2 Cor 5:17), because Christ has the power, which belongs to the Creator, to create a new people.

Ibrahim: Maybe Christians have elevated Jesus' status beyond being a prophet who was called to challenge his people to a pure life of love for God and neighbor. We can talk about this later. But as an Evangelical Protestant surely you will agree with me that many Christians have been too ready to elevate Mary's status beyond her being an obedient servant of God to being the Queen of Heaven who sits on some heavenly throne! Since Christians developed the traditions about Mary's perpetual virginity, which are not found in the oldest documents, the Gospels of Luke and Matthew, then it follows that those closest to the events did not believe that Mary was any more than a devoted woman who submitted voluntarily to the will of God. The fact that Protestants rejected the perpetual virginity of Mary as an innovation that was not supported by the New Testament documents demonstrates that it is not essential to all types of Christianity to believe in this. Martin Luther (d. 1546) attacked the veneration of Mary because seeking her mediation interfered with the role of Jesus Christ as a mediator between human beings and God.[37] Yet the

---

36. O'Collins, *Christology*, 276–78.
37. Petri, "Devotion to Mary," 441.

widespread veneration of Mary in the Orthodox and Catholic churches shows how tenacious this exalted status remains for a vast crowd of the world's Christians.

The Qur'an explicitly refers to this elevation of Mary to a divine status in Q5:116–17:

> God said, "Jesus, son of Mary, did you say to people, 'Take me and my mother as two gods alongside God'?" He replied, "May You be exalted! I would not have said what I had no right to say. If I had said such a thing You would have known about it. You know what is in my inner being, but I do not know what is in Your inner being. You know what is hidden. 117 I only said to them what You commanded me to say: 'Worship God, my Lord, and your Lord.'"

Here Jesus denies telling people to worship him or his mother, but this proves that there were Christians who had been guilty of doing just this, venerating Jesus and Mary in an inappropriate way, and that God was warning them to stop doing it. The advent of Islam, in the will of God, was in part to put an end to this false veneration of Mary, the mother of Jesus. It was as if the patience of God had run out after centuries of Christians taking a wrong direction with the amazing event of the miraculous conception of Jesus. Just because Jesus was conceived in a different way Christians built all kinds of beliefs around it about Jesus being God and Mary being the Mother of God.

Paul: This criticism of the worship of Mary in the Qur'an does seem to demonstrate that Muhammad encountered significant numbers of Christians, whether in Mecca or on his trading travels to Syria or Ethiopian Christians, to whom he sent the persecuted Muslims from Mecca. There is the tradition that there were images of Jesus and Mary in the Ka'ba in Mecca among many representations of divine beings. Ibn Ishaq records that the Quraysh had placed pictures of Jesus and Mary in the Ka'ba, and that after Muhammad's triumphant return to Mecca toward the end of his life, he ordered that the 360 idolatrous statues standing in the Ka'ba be removed and burnt, but that the pictures of Jesus and Mary be preserved.[38] Presumably these pictures did not show Mary with a crown as Queen of Heaven, but rather Mary with the baby Jesus on her lap. Perhaps we can see that Muhammad was trying to purify the way Mary was venerated among the Christians he had encountered, seeking

---

38. Ibn Ishaq, *Life of Muhammad*, 552.

to remove any taint of divine power from her by bringing her back to an appropriate respect as the one who had willingly submitted to the strange will of God to have Jesus conceived without human intercourse.

It is interesting too, that the Qur'an and many of the traditions used in the interpretation of the Qur'an, reuse stories about Mary and her family developed from post-New Testament Christian traditions that sought to fill in details left unspoken in the Gospels of Matthew and Luke. To me this suggests that Muhammad met Christians who had absorbed this developed tradition and that his message was partly oriented toward correcting the false assumptions embedded in these stories. I know that almost all Muslims believe that the mind of Muhammad was not creatively engaged in the language or content of the Qur'an, but it is very difficult for the objective observer to think that the Qur'an was created by God before he created anything else, and that he preserved the book entire in heaven so that he could send it down when the time was right to the Arabs in a language only they could understand. The very complex contextuality of the narrative details in the Qur'an and the Traditions passed down by his companions of the oral teaching of Muhammad leaves the firm impression that the Qur'an was very deeply related to the interaction of Muhammad with his audience over a period of twenty or so years.

Naturally, I am happy that Muhammad challenged the veneration of Mary in his time, since I believe he was right to challenge Christians he encountered to keep their attitude to the mother of Jesus within strict bounds. When the Qur'an warns Christians in Q4:171, "Do not exceed the proper bounds in your religion" this certainly applies to excessive attention to Mary as a channel for God's mercy to reach the believer. Mary was not capable of performing creative activity herself. She was the willing vessel for the conception of Jesus by the Spirit of God, but that did not convey to her the spiritual powers that some Christians seek, especially the crowds that seek her healing power at Lourdes every year. The BBC reported on the 6th December, 2007:

> Pope Benedict XVI authorised special indulgences to mark the 150th anniversary of the Virgin Mary's reputed appearance at Lourdes. Catholics visiting the site within a year of 8 December will be able to receive an indulgence, which the Church teaches can reduce time in purgatory. Lourdes has drawn pilgrims since Mary was said to have appeared in 1858 to shepherdess

Bernadette Soubirous. The waters of the French shrine are said to have miraculous healing powers.[39]

Despite the overwhelming numbers who have sought healing, the Catholic Church has only recognized sixty-nine healings through Mary's intervention at Lourdes. What these Catholic Christians should be doing is seeking healing *from God*, especially through Jesus, the one who came to heal. Mary had no healing ministry, according to the historical Gospels, and seeking her help only distracts Christians from looking to the one who has the power to heal.

Ibrahim: I wholeheartedly agree with you here. *God* is one who heals, no matter the human healer who is involved. It is right to give God the glory and the praise for all healing, for that is the result of his bountiful mercy and compassion. We should seek for healing from him while looking to human means that he has ordained. Muslims, like Christians, can be led astray looking to other sources of healing power, so that they forget to thank God, their Creator, for healing received. There is always the danger that Muslims pay good money to human healers whom they credit with divine powers, and then give them the praise that is due to God. God, out of his mercy and compassion, grants healing to whoever he wills. He gives some human beings the skill to heal and they are his servants in the healing process. Perhaps we should turn to the subject of the healings of Jesus recorded in the Qur'an to further investigate this truth. For Jesus was no ordinary medical doctor, but was able, by God's permission, to heal those who were sick and even raise the dead back to life.

Paul: The fact that the Qur'an commends Jesus as a healer is a very significant line of agreement between Muslim and Christian portraits of Jesus. After all, the Gospels are full of stories of Jesus healing people who were not capable of being healed by conventional means. I suppose the surprise for me as a reader of the Qur'an is that none of these accounts from the Gospels are repeated there, even though the Qur'an repeats aspects of the Gospel of Luke in telling the story of the conception and birth of Jesus. There is the mere summary that Jesus healed the lepers, opened the eyes of the blind, made the lame walk, and even raised the dead to life. Why Muhammad neglected to include any of the wonderful stories from the Gospels puzzles me. Was it perhaps because Christians attributed his healing power to his divine status? Maybe you will be able

39. BBC News, 6 December 2007.

to shed light on this. Is it linked to Jesus denying that he told people to worship him, and that if they looked to him for healing they might see him as carrying the nature of God? That could explain the reticence of Muhammad in retelling those healing stories. But he could not deny that Jesus was a remarkable healer, according to the oral testimony of Christians that he heard. So let's make the healing work of Jesus the focus of our next study.

two

Miracle Worker

IBRAHIM AND PAUL TURN to the theme of the miracles performed by Jesus. Ibrahim begins by presenting the teaching of the Qur'an and the way these actions are interpreted by Muslims. He points out that Moses was granted miraculous powers by God, according to the Qur'an, and that the miracles performed by Moses and Jesus are signs of God for people. However, Christians see Jesus' miracles as signs of his divine nature and this is contested by Muslims. Paul contributes an exposition of the miracles of Jesus in the Gospels. He recognizes that modern Christians sometimes doubt the authenticity of Jesus' miraculous activity, but even very skeptical Christian scholars accept that Jesus had a reputation for healing. Paul outlines the performance of miracles by the apostolic community and shows that Jesus expected his followers to heal in his name. He raises the issue of the use of the New Testament by the Qur'an, and wonders why the bare mention of Jesus' healing activity was not developed into recounting stories of healing from the Gospels.

Ibrahim likes the more modern approach of Christians to Jesus' miracles. He thinks that seeing Jesus as a healer brings Muslims and Christians closer together so long as the older view that the healings prove Jesus' divinity is discounted. The newer opinion that Jesus was a man exercising the gifts that God gave him is far more conducive to harmonious relations between Christians and Muslims. Paul argues that the Fourth Gospel, especially, shows the miracles of Jesus as signs of the presence of God in him. Therefore, an honest assessment of the Gospel testimony includes the view that Jesus healed because he represented the love of God for people in a way that is also to be practiced by Christians in the power of God's Spirit. Ibrahim agrees that Jesus had a special spiritual nature that marked him out as the most important saint in history, the one who was closest to God without being divine.

They both dialogue on the contemporary understanding of Muslims and Christians concerning miracles occurring today. Paul emphasizes that Christians can be channels of healing today. He recounts stories of Christians seeing remarkable healings through the power of the Holy Spirit after prayer for those who were addicted to drugs. Ibrahim accepts that saints still have spiritual power granted to them by God for healing of those who seek their help. He is critical of Muslims who deny the intervention of saints today when Muslims call on them for aid. However, he chooses to turn the discussion to more everyday miracles of transformation of people's lives using financial investment in poor farming communities. Muslims who heal the needy by the strategic use of financial resources are reflecting the power of God to lift up the weak who are subject to illness as a result of poverty. Prevention of illness is as much part of the miraculous activity of God as curing it through prayer.

The Miracles of Jesus in the Qur'an

Ibrahim: One of the purposes of the coming of Jesus was to demonstrate the power of God through the performance of miracles. According to Q3:49, God will send Jesus as a messenger to the children of Israel. He will say:

> I have come to you with a sign from your Lord. I will make the shape of a bird for you out of clay. Then I will breathe on it and it will become a bird by the permission of God. I will heal the blind and the lepers, and raise the dead to life by the permission of God.

The context of this declaration is the announcement of the conception of Jesus by God's power without normal human means. The outcome of that miraculous conception is an unusual ability to perform powerful actions that are signs of God's presence. This messenger will carry the miracle of his beginning into his work, demonstrating that God has called him to be the vessel for the creative energy of God in bringing to life that which has no life or has lost life. He will also be able to bring defective and wasted life into full functioning capacity, showing how God desires to restore people who are damaged by illness and social ostracism.

Jesus is not the only prophet with miraculous powers. Moses was granted such capability when he confronted the ruler of the Egyptians in Q26:10–68. God sent Moses and his brother Aaron to Pharaoh, the ruler of the Egyptians who had enslaved the children of Israel, to bring a message from God, "Send the children of Israel out with us" (v. 17). Pharaoh questioned who their God was, and when he heard the reply, "Lord of the heavens and the earth and everything between them" (v. 24), he said, "If you take any god except me, I will put you in prison" (v. 29). Moses responded, "Even if I show you something convincing?" (v. 30). Pharaoh bid him show it, and Moses threw down his staff, which became a snake, and drew out his hand, which became white. Pharaoh declared, "This man is a clever magician" (v. 34), and urged his counselors to send for the best magicians in Egypt. After they arrived and threw down their ropes and staffs, Moses threw down his staff, which swallowed up "their fakery" (v. 45), and the magicians fell on their knees and cried out, "We believe in the Lord of the Worlds, the Lord of Moses and Aaron" (vv. 47–48). When Pharaoh threatened to kill them for treachery to him they said, "That will not harm us. We will return to our Lord. We hope that our Lord will forgive us our sins, so we will be foremost among the believers" (vv. 50–51).

The subsequent flight of the children of Israel led them to the sea, which parted after Moses obeyed the command of God, "Strike the sea with your staff" (v. 63). The children of Israel were saved by walking between the walls of water while the Egyptians were drowned. Verses 67–68 say, "Truly there is a sign in this, but most of them are not believers. 68 Truly only your Lord is the Almighty, the Merciful."

Both Moses and Jesus brought signs of God's power to act in ways that were unexpected. Therefore, the actions of Moses in changing a staff into a snake, in changing his hand to white, and in parting the sea were signs of the work of God on behalf of his people, who were enslaved by the great power of their time, the Egyptians. They may have been the most powerful nation at that time, but God demonstrated that he was the unseen power in the world, defied by Pharaoh, who arrogated to himself all power and majesty. While human beings can claim the power and authority for themselves, the truth is that only God grants power to human beings. This is the truth that he proved in sending Moses to this arrogant man, Pharaoh, who rejected the truth in his pursuit of power and his love of human worship.

Thus, the actions of Jesus in giving life to birds made of clay, in giving sight to blind people, in curing lepers, and in raising the dead back to life, were signs of the work of God on behalf of his people in the time of Jesus. Just like Moses, Jesus was granted that power to show that to God belonged the creative energy to give life, to restore life, and to make life better when it is not fully developed or blighted by illness.

There is another miraculous action performed by Jesus, according to Q5:112-15. Jesus' disciples asked him, "Jesus, son of Mary, can your Lord send down a table of food to us from heaven?" (v. 112). They wanted to have their hearts reassured that Jesus had told them the truth, and to witness such a miracle. Jesus prayed, "God our Lord, send down a table of food to us from heaven so that we can have a festival, (the first and last of us), and a sign from You. Provide for us for You are the best provider" (v. 114). God replied, "I will send it to you, but whoever does not believe after this I will punish with a punishment that I will not inflict on anyone else in the world" (v. 115). Here the action of Jesus is indirect, since he does not produce the feast himself, but simply asks God to send it down without normal human means. His prayer is the action. In the other instances, Jesus commands the clay bird to fly, the blind man to receive sight, the leper to be clean and the dead person to rise to life. Now he asks God to command the feast into reality. He seeks a sign from God for his disciples so that they will have confidence in God, which they as yet had not developed. The miraculous feast should enable them to trust in God who provides.

The Miracles of Jesus in Islamic Interpretation

Ibrahim: Ibn Ishaq recounts how the leaders of the Christian deputation to the Prophet Muhammad told him that Jesus was divine because of his miraculous powers:

> They argue that he is God because he used to raise the dead, and heal the sick, and declare the unseen; and make clay birds and then breathe into them so that they flew away. This is one of the assertions of the Christians about which the Qur'an came down.[1]

When Ibn Ishaq reports Muhammad's response to them, Muhammad includes the miracles of Jesus as proof of Jesus' prophethood, but *not* of his divinity. According to Muhammad, Jesus spoke of his coming to the children of Israel with a sign from their Lord confirming that he

1. Ibn Ishaq, *Life of Muhammad*, 271-72.

was a prophet and apostle. He would create from clay the likeness of birds and breathe into them so that they would become birds by the permission of God, who had sent him to them, "He being my Lord and yours," and that he would heal the blind and the leper and raise the dead by God's permission.[2] Muhammad later repeated to the delegation that Jesus brought signs from God, but that these very signs proved that he was a messenger of God and not what the Christians believed about him. Jesus said to his people, "I bring you signs from your Lord, so fear God and obey me. God is my Lord and your Lord." In other words, argued Muhammad, Jesus was "disowning what they say about him and proving that his Lord (is God)."[3] Ibn Ishaq testifies that the mention of Jesus' miracles in the Qur'an came because of the Christian belief that his miracles were a proof of his divine status, since no human being could perform them. The Qur'an announces that the miracles Jesus performed do not prove his divinity, but rather prove his prophethood and being sent as a messenger of God. This has been the accepted view in the history of Islamic commentary on the miracles of Jesus.

There has been discussion of the miraculous power that Jesus exercised. What did God permit him to do? Jesus announced in Q3:49, "I will make the shape of a bird for you out of clay. Then I will breathe on it and it will become a bird by the permission of God." The verb "to make" is *khalaqa,* usually preserved for the action of God elsewhere in the Qur'an. Zamakhshari points out that the verb *khalaqa* can be used of human creativity, as in "making a sandal."[4] Razi emphasizes that only God creates in the sense of "causing to be" (*takwin*), and "originating" (*ibda'*), so *khalaqa* means "determining" or "arranging." For Razi, when Jesus blew on the clay birds, God caused them to come to life.[5] Jesus was also able to bring dead humans to life. Zamakhshari mentions the story that Jesus raised Sam b. Nuh.[6] Razi includes this story with two other raisings attributed to Jesus, that of 'Adhar, and of the son of an old woman who was in the process of burying him.[7] In these instances, Jesus was granted the power to raise the dead to life, just as he was given the

2. Ibid., 276.
3. Ibid.
4. Zamakhshari, *Al-Kashshaf,* 1:228.
5. Razi, *Al-Tafsir al-Kabir,* 2:451–52 and 3:468–69.
6. Zamakhshari, *Al-Kashshaf,* 1:431.
7. Razi, *Al-Tafsir al-Kabir,* 2:452.

ability to give life to clay birds. He had no power within himself to give life. Razi criticizes Christians for arguing that Jesus' life giving actions prove his divine status. On the contrary, God appointed Jesus to perform them as he chose Moses to perform miracles.[8] Ibn Kathir believes that God enabled prophets to perform miracles suited to the circumstances of their time. God sent Moses to outwit the Egyptian magicians who were so highly regarded in that culture. He sent Jesus to people who highly regarded science to demonstrate that God had the power to give life to the dead.[9]

The Miracles of Jesus in the Gospels

Paul: Several stories of Jesus healing the blind and lepers are found in the four Gospels. They provide much more detail than that given in the summary in the Qurʾan. For example, Mark 8:22–26 records people bringing a blind man to Jesus for healing. After Jesus spat into the man's eyes, he placed his hands on him and asked if he could see anything. When he replied that he could see people who looked like trees, Jesus placed his hands on the man's eyes and he could see clearly. In Mark 10:46–52, a blind man called out in the crowd for Jesus to have mercy on him. When Jesus asked him what he wanted, the blind man said he wanted to see. Jesus told him that he could now see because of his faith. So this blind man received his sight, not by touch, but by word of command.

Lepers were required to live separate from the community for fear of contaminating others. Jesus, however, was prepared to touch them for healing. Mark 1:40–45 recounts a leper kneeling before Jesus and declaring that Jesus had the power to heal him if he wished to. Jesus put his hand on the man, said that he wanted to heal him, and pronounced him well. Jesus told him to show himself to the priest, and to take a gift to God's house, so that everyone would know he had been healed, but that he should not talk about it to other people. But because of him talking so openly, Jesus was no longer able to enter towns, but had to receive people out in the country. Luke 17:11–19 records ten lepers asking for mercy from Jesus. He told them to go and show themselves to the priest and as they went they were healed. Only one of them came back to thank Jesus, who asked why only that man, a foreigner to the Jewish nation, was

---

8. Ibid., 2:434.
9. Ibn Kathir, *Tafsir al-Qurʾan*, 2:41.

grateful to God. Hadn't the other nine Jewish men received healing? He told the man that his faith had cleansed him from leprosy.

There are accounts of Jesus raising the dead. Luke 7:11–17 tells of Jesus encountering a funeral procession of a widow's only son. Jesus told her not to weep and went up to the dead boy and commanded him to get up. He immediately sat up and spoke. The crowd were amazed that such a prophet had come from God. John 11:1–44 gives an account of Jesus raising Lazarus from his tomb. Having asked that the stone be rolled back from the entrance to the cave, he called out to Lazarus to come out of the tomb. Lazarus emerged still wrapped in cloth, and Jesus told the people to untie him. John 11:45 records that because of this many believed in Jesus, but later the chief priests attempted to have Lazarus killed because of the numbers who were following Jesus instead of them (John 12:10–11). The two stories recorded by Razi appear to be recollections of these two accounts of Jesus raising the dead in the Gospels. According to Neal Robinson, "'Adhar is the Arabic form of Lazarus. . . . The dead son of the old woman sounds like the widow of Nain's son."[10]

The Gospels contain many more stories of Jesus healing people. These include those with evil spirits (Mark 1:21–28), the crippled (Mark 2:1–12), and the deaf and dumb (Mark 7:31–37). The purpose of the healing miracles is to show the power of God. Those who receive healing are sometimes told that their faith is central to the result. But on other occasions healing is granted by Jesus' own decision. This is obviously true of those he raised from the dead. It also applies to a crippled man in John 5:1–18, who was told by Jesus to pick up his bed and walk. When people asked the healed man who his healer was, he said that he did not know the identity of the one who had healed him.

One story of Jesus healing a crippled man shows that Jesus had more than one intention behind healing people. Mark 2:1–12 tells of four friends bringing a paralysed man on his bed to Jesus. They made a hole in the roof of the house where Jesus was teaching. Jesus was so impressed with their faith that he told the crippled man that his sins were now forgiven. At the protest of the teachers of the Law that only God can forgive sins, Jesus asked them whether it was easier to forgive sins or heal. He then said to them that to demonstrate that he had authority to forgive sins, he would tell the man to get up and take his bed home. The cripple did so and people in the crowd said they had never seen anything like it.

---

10. Robinson, *Christ*, 147.

Jesus linked healing with the authority of God. Healing the body and healing the mind were linked together. He was not a conventional doctor, but rather the bringer of God's renewal to humans. Restoring the weakness of the body included restoring the weakness of the spirit. If only God can forgive sins committed against him then Jesus was claiming to represent God to those of his day. Unlike the priests, who could pronounce lepers cleansed, Jesus had the power to cleanse. Unlike the priests, who could accept a sacrifice from the people and offer it to God to take away sin, Jesus could offer forgiveness directly.

Jesus also provided food and drink in ways that were unexpected. Mark 6:30–44 tells of Jesus multiplying bread and fish for 5,000 men in a remote place just from five loaves and two fish. "They all ate and were filled; and they took up twelve baskets full of broken pieces and of the fish" (v. 42–43). John 2:1–11 records Jesus being a guest at a wedding and turning water into wine after the host had run out of wine. John mentions that this was the first of Jesus' signs which "revealed his glory and his disciples believed in him" (v. 11). Jesus' ability to generate wine from water and surprising quantities of bread and fish demonstrate his unusual capacity to speed up and expand the processes of nature.

Then Jesus had power to alter the normal patterns of nature. Mark 5:35–41 tells how Jesus and his disciples were on a boat when a storm arose threatening to sink them. Jesus was asleep, but the terrified disciples woke him and said, "Teacher, do you not care that we are perishing?" Jesus "rebuked the wind, and said to the sea, 'Peace! Be still!'" There was complete calm and Jesus said to his disciples, "Why are you afraid? Have you still no faith?" Mark 6:45–52 records a story of the disciples in a boat at night, but Jesus was not with them. He came to them walking on the water, but they thought he was a ghost. He spoke up, "Take heart, it is I; do not be afraid" (v. 50). In these two stories Jesus challenged his disciples to avoid fear of drowning and of ghosts and to put their confidence in him as one who could change the way people expect nature to be, by calming a storm and walking on water.

Christian Interpretation of the Miracles of Jesus

Paul: The story of the child Jesus giving life to clay birds is found in *The Infancy Gospel of Thomas*. The earliest extant version is in a Syriac manuscript from the fifth century, but Elliott believes that the story arose in Greek before this time:[11]

> When this boy Jesus was five years old he was playing at the crossing of a stream. . . . Having made soft clay he moulded from it twelve sparrows. And it was the sabbath when he did these things. . . . When a certain Jew saw what Jesus was doing while playing on the sabbath, he at once went and told his father, Joseph, "See, your child is at the stream, and he took clay and moulded twelve birds and has profaned the sabbath." And when Joseph came to the place and looked, he cried out to him, saying, "Why do you do on the sabbath things which it is not lawful to do?" But Jesus clapped his hands and cried out to the sparrows and said to them, "Be gone!" And the sparrows took flight and went away chirping. The Jews were amazed when they saw this, and went away and told their leaders what they had seen Jesus do.[12]

This story is one of several describing Jesus' miraculous powers as a child. They seem to have developed to fill a gap in the four Gospels relating to the childhood of Jesus. However, these stories do not show Jesus performing miracles to help others. They are merely demonstrations of power, sometimes causing harm to others. It was for this reason that the mainstream church rejected the authenticity of these childhood miracle stories.[13]

The earliest Christian interpretation of the miraculous work of Jesus in the canonical Gospels can be seen in Peter's speech to fellow Jews in Jerusalem after the departure of Jesus into heaven (Acts 2:14–36). The leader of the disciples referred to, "Jesus of Nazareth, a man attested to you by God with deeds of power, wonders, and signs that God did through him among you, as you yourselves know" (v. 22). He went on to argue that God had appointed Jesus as "both Lord and Messiah" (v. 36).

This connection between the powerful miracles performed by Jesus and his status in God's eyes was furthered by the activities of the followers of Jesus in that period. They healed in the name of Jesus. Acts 3:1–10 tells the story of Peter and John being asked for money from a beggar outside the temple in Jerusalem. Peter said, "I have no silver or gold, but what I have I give you: in the name of Jesus Christ of Nazareth, stand up

---

11. *The Infancy Gospel of Thomas*, 69.
12. Ibid., 75–76.
13. Ibid., 70.

and walk" (v. 6). When the lame man began "walking and leaping and praising God" the news spread and people were "filled with wonder and amazement" (vv. 9–10). Peter also healed a paralyzed man called Aeneas by commanding him, "Aeneas, Jesus Christ heals you; get up and make your bed!" (Acts 9:34).

Evidence from later Christian writing shows that Jesus' miracles were regarded as signs of his divine power. Origen (d. 255) argued against Celsus—a Roman critic of Christianity, who had alleged that Jesus deceived people with magic tricks—that Jesus' miracles and teaching were designed to change people's characters for the better, and to bring humans into a relationship with God the Creator, through faith in Jesus the incarnate Son of God.[14] Gregory of Nyssa (d. c. 395) believed that the miracles Jesus performed were evidence for his divine nature.[15] This would be a common argument in subsequent generations.

It was only in the modern era that some Christians doubted that Jesus performed miracles, on the basis that God had created the world in a uniform way that did not allow for his interventions from time to time to change the normal causes of things. Rudolf Bultmann thought that the early church invented the miracle stories of Jesus to prove his divine nature.[16] However, Craig Keener reports that:

> Most scholars today working on the subject . . . accept the claim that Jesus was a healer and exorcist. The evidence is stronger for this claim than for most other specific historical claims that we could make about Jesus or earliest Christianity. Scholars often note that miracles characterized Jesus' historical activity no less than his teaching and prophetic activities did.[17]

Interaction of Islamic and Christian Accounts of the Miracles of Jesus

Paul: The Qur'an received the testimony that Jesus healed the sick and raised the dead from the Gospel accounts without elaborating any specific stories. The only detailed miracle of Jesus recounted in the Qur'an is of the boy Jesus giving life to clay birds. This interest in alternative accounts

14. Origen, *Against Celsus*, 1:68, and 3:26–28.
15. Gregory of Nyssa, *Catechetical Oration*, 34.
16. Bultmann, *History*, 219.
17. Keener, *Miracles*, 23.

of Jesus' childhood beyond the canonical Gospels is a continuation of the theme from chapter one on the birth of Jesus, where the Qur'an cites traditions from non-canonical Gospels to describe the events of Jesus' coming into the world.

However, there may also be a reference to the multiplication of the loaves and fish in the story of Jesus asking God to supply a feast for his followers in Q5:112–15, when Jesus prayed, "God our Lord, send down a table of food to us from heaven so that we can have a festival, (the first and last of us), and a sign from You. Provide for us for You are the best provider" (v. 114). Jesus looked to heaven and gave thanks for the bread and fish, according to Mark 6:41, so both the Qur'an and Mark recall that Jesus prayed to God for the feast to happen, because Jesus did not have the quantity of food needed. Some Christians have seen the Eucharist reflected in the request of Jesus for a feast sent from heaven in Q5:112. The word for "feast" in Q5:112, is *ma'ida*, a word that is borrowed from Ethiopic *ma'edde*, which means "table, dishes, or banquet."[18] Samir Khalil Samir believes that because it was the word used for the Eucharist in Ethiopic Christianity before the advent of the Qur'an, the use of the word *ma'ida* in Q5:112 reflects this origin.[19] He adds that the term *'Id* in verse 114, for "festival," derives from Syriac *'Ida*, and means "feast" or "liturgical festival." Samir argues, "Is this not the most appropriate definition of the Eucharist of Christians, which is a festive celebration and a sacramental sign?"[20]

Jesus the Miracle Worker in Muslim-Christian Conversation

Ibrahim: There is a great deal in common between the Christian accounts and the revelation of the Qur'an concerning Jesus as one who brings powerful signs from God of his creative work in this world. The great prophets, Moses and Jesus, were given miraculous signs to enable the people of their time to turn to the Creator after going astray. Moses was given the signs that confronted the godless Pharaoh, and confounded the magicians who had spiritual power over the Egyptian nation. The exodus of the children of Israel because of Moses' intervention demonstrated the reality of God, the Lord of all worlds, especially through the parting of

---

18. Kropp, "Beyond Single Words," 206.
19. Samir, "The Theological Christian Influence on the Qur'an," 149.
20. Ibid.

the red sea through which the children of Israel escaped and in which the Egyptian army drowned. Moses stretched out his rod to part the water, but there can be no doubt that it was the action of the Creator that raised the water to provide a path for the believers. Moses had no power in himself to divide the sea in this way.

The same reality applies to Jesus' miracles. He healed by God's permission, he raised the dead by the permission of God. It was the will of God to enable Jesus to do works of healing and raising the dead as signs that God had sent him to the children of Israel to turn them back to faith in God after going astray. Clearly, the children of Israel had deviated from the true path. They had killed some of the prophets sent to them by God, and at the time of the coming of Jesus, they were obviously entrenched in rebellion and unbelief. This would explain why God gave powerful signs to Jesus. The children of Israel needed something spectacular to get them to take God seriously again, and God in his great mercy and kindness sent Jesus to show them his creative power. So, the unbelieving Egyptians and the unbelieving children of Israel received messengers from God who not only brought the message of truth but demonstrated that message with powerful signs of the presence of God.

Now it is also clear that the power of God shown in the signs through Moses and Jesus was of the same origin. God performed the signs through these men. Perhaps the most helpful way to understand this is to distinguish between direct and indirect action. God is the direct actor and Moses and Jesus are the indirect actors. I think this is probably the main contention between Muslims and Christians about the miracles of Jesus. We agree that Moses was not the direct actor, but Christians seem to want to hold that Jesus was the direct actor and God the indirect actor. This comes out especially in the argument that Jesus performed miracles from his divine nature rather than his human nature. Christians have defended this view for centuries. But it seems to be questioned among more liberal Christian circles in the West in more recent times. Don't you think that this more liberal point of view would bring Christians much closer to the Muslim appreciation of Jesus and avoid the traditional tensions between our communities?

Paul: I think that the signs of Jesus are also very important in the Fourth Gospel and in subsequent Christian reflection. John said that the changing of the water into wine by Jesus at the wedding was the first of his signs. John tells us that many people believed in Jesus "because they saw the signs that he was doing" (John 2:23). These signs are defined as miracles in John 4:54, where Jesus healed a child. Not everyone believed that the miracles were signs of Jesus' true identity. John records Jews who saw the work of God but not the identity of Jesus in 10:30-39. After Jesus declared, "The Father and I are one," Jews took up stones to stone him. Jesus said to them, "I have shown you many good works from the Father. For which of these are you going to stone me?" They replied that it was not for the good works but "for blasphemy, because you, though only a human being, are making yourself God." Jesus challenged their acceptance of his works as "good." He said, "If I am not doing the works of my Father, then do not believe me. But if I do them, even though you do not believe me, believe the works, so that you may know and understand that the Father is in me and I am in the Father."

For John, the author of the Fourth Gospel, the testimony of Jesus to the miraculous works as signs of the relationship between himself and his Father was central to Jesus' teaching. John goes on to record the story of Jesus raising Lazarus from the dead and refers to it as one of his signs in 12:47-48, where the Jewish chief priests and the Pharisees called together the ruling council of the Jews and said, "What are we to do? This man is performing many signs. If we let him go on like this, everyone will believe in him, and the Romans will come and destroy both our holy place and our nation." But they were not able to prevent crowds going to Jesus because they had heard that he had raised Lazarus from his tomb (John 12:18), and the Pharisees said to one another, "You see, you can do nothing. Look, the world has gone after him!" (v. 19). You can see that the connection of the miraculous power of Jesus to his divine status is at the heart of John's Gospel, written during the first century, long before Gregory of Nyssa argued that Jesus' miracles were a product of his divine nature.

Ibrahim: But surely there is another way to interpret these accounts in the Fourth Gospel. Was Jesus not really talking about a spiritual identity with God expressed in him calling God his father? The unity he felt with God was the result of his ability to connect with the will of God that produced these spectacular signs. Other believers had not penetrated to the presence of God the way Jesus had. Is that not what Jesus talked about when he taught his disciples to pray, "Our father in heaven." He was wanting them to share in his closeness to God, to lead them into the presence of the Almighty. Did he not send out his disciples to heal the sick and cast out demons without him being there? Jesus trusted in them to perform miracles when they were only human beings. Having read the Gospels myself I have never understood how Christians think that Jesus' miracles make him divine but that the disciples' miracles are only the work of humans. Because Mark 6:12 says that the disciples "cast out many demons and anointed with oil many who were sick and cured them." Why don't Christians elevate the disciples to the same divine status that they give to Jesus? But I have not come across any Christian theologian who can explain this. One Christian theologian I admire is John Hick, who agrees with my point that Jesus had a very close relationship to God that enabled him to understand the will of God. This does not mean that Jesus came from heaven at Christmas as the second member of a trinity. In his *The Rainbow of Faiths,* Hick argues that Jesus did not teach his divinity. When Jesus pronounced forgiveness of sins to a paralyzed man in Mark 2:5 he was declaring God's forgiveness, not "presuming himself to be God."[21] Hick says that he is only following many other Christian scholars of the Gospels in believing that Paul and John gave divine status to Jesus. Do you agree with these scholars?

Paul: It is true that several Christian theologians have made a distinction between the way Jesus is presented in the first three Gospels and in the Fourth Gospel. It has been common among them to point out that the incarnation is taught only in the Fourth Gospel, which is an indication that this gospel is later than the others, and shows a development toward the belief that the eternal Word of God became human (John 1:14). For example, James D. G. Dunn argues that the doctrine of the incarnation of the Son of God is only really found in the later writings of the New Testament. According to Dunn, Matthew speaks about Jesus being "God with us" in 1:23. This is an idea of "divine presence, . . . a concept of incarnation that does not come to explicit expression." However, in the Fourth Gospel, John says that "the Word became flesh," meaning that "the concept of incarnation, as distinct from indwelling or inspiration, has come to explicit expression. Jesus is being presented as the incarnation of the divine Word."[22]

My own view is that the disciples of Jesus only slowly came to perceive his true identity. It was only after the greatest miracle of all, the raising of Jesus from death to appear alive in their company, that his disciples understood his divine identity. The evidence of the stories from all four Gospels shows that the disciples failed to see the divine nature of Jesus

---

21. Hick, *The Rainbow of Faiths,* 96.
22. Dunn, *The Christ and the Spirit,* 1:44–45.

in the signs that he showed them. When Jesus calmed a storm on lake Galilee, he challenged his disciples' lack of faith. They said to one another, "Who then is this, that even the wind and the sea obey him?" (Mark 4:41). After Jesus multiplied bread for 5,000 people and then spoke of being the bread of life, and that those who ate this bread would live forever in John 6:35 and 58, many of his disciples said, "This teaching is difficult; who can accept it? . . . and they no longer went about with him" (John 6:60 and 66). However, Simon Peter said, "Lord, to whom can we go? You have the words of eternal life. We have come to believe that you are the Holy One of God" (6:68–69). Therefore, the stories of Jesus' miraculous work contain a test of faith for the disciples. Such acts of creative power provoked different responses. Some stopped following Jesus because they could not accept the implications of his actions. Others continued to follow him as a result of realizing that in Jesus existed the very power of God to transform the natural world in ways that nobody had witnessed before. Given that they were monotheistic Jews, it was very hard for them to recognize that God had come to them in a fashion that they had not expected.

Even when the eleven disciples met the risen Jesus on a mountain in Galilee, Matthew tells us that "They worshipped him, but some doubted" (Matt 28:17). More than one of the eleven had difficulty believing that Jesus was standing there on the mountain after having been put to death and buried. Like many human beings in every generation they could not reconcile their usual experience of life with this extraordinary event of meeting a man whom they knew had been executed in Jerusalem and committed to a tomb sealed by a very large stone. The greatest sign of the presence and power of God did not activate faith in all of the disciples. That faith arrived finally when ten of the disciples were together in Jerusalem and Jesus appeared to them (John 20:25). Even then Thomas found it impossible to believe his brothers. Only after Jesus appeared to him did Thomas declare, "My Lord and my God" (John 20:28).

Now I have a question for you, Ibrahim, about the way the Qur'an presents the miracles of Jesus. In Q3:49, Jesus says, "I will make the shape of a bird for you out of clay. Then I will breathe on it and it will become a bird by the permission of God." The Arabic verb used for "make" is *khalaqa*, "to create," normally found in the Qur'an for the work of God himself. In Q5:110 after God has gathered all the messengers that he has sent, he will say to Jesus,

Remember My kindness to you and your mother. I supported you with the holy spirit, so that you spoke to people as a young child and as an adult. I taught you the Book and wisdom, the Torah and the Gospel. You made the shape of a bird out of clay by my permission, breathed on it, and it became a bird by my permission.

Only in these two contexts, Q3:49 and Q5:110, is the verb *khalaqa*, "to create," applied to a human being. Does this recognition of the power of Jesus to share in the very work of the Creator not make Jesus stand out among those who the Qur'an testifies performed miracles, like Moses?

Ibrahim: Let me say that there has been much discussion of the significance of the miraculous activity of Jesus and Moses. Many Muslims have concluded that they are both equally endowed by God with power to perform signs from God, so Jesus is no more empowered than Moses. They have often pointed out that the phrase, "with God's permission," should be understood to mean that God has caused the miracle. He worked through Jesus, who was the instrument of God's creative energy. The Qur'an commentator Fakhr al-Din al-Razi notes that in the Qur'an the subject of the verb *khalaqa* is God alone, with the exception of the references to Jesus in Q3:49 and 5:110. He interprets this to indicate that the breath of life does not belong to Jesus but to the Creator himself who works life through Jesus.[23] Those Muslims who follow this interpretation deny that Jesus had a special ability from God. They do not wish to make any differences between him and other prophets. After all, since God is the direct cause of all human actions then all the actions of prophets are caused by him. To pick out Jesus for praise is to take away from God the honor and praise that is due to him.

However, some Muslims have seen in Jesus a closeness to God that made him a person of real spiritual dynamic. I am inclined to this interpretation myself. For example, Ibn al-ʿArabi thought that Jesus was given a special spiritual nature by God to perform work that only God can do. He said in *The Bezels of Wisdom* that "Jesus came forth raising the dead because he was a divine spirit. In this the quickening was of God, while the blowing itself came from Jesus."[24] Those who follow this tradition see Jesus as "the seal of the saints," just as the Prophet Muhammad is "the seal of the prophets." That is why Muslims from my background seek the

---

23. Razi, *al-Tafsir al-Kabir*, 2:451–52.
24. Ibn al-ʿArabi, *The Bezels of Wisdom*, 176.

power God grants to the saints who, like Jesus, desire to be close to him. He permits miraculous signs to be performed through them just as he permitted signs through Jesus.

Paul: This is fascinating. In your cultural situation there are saints who are especially close to God who have been granted the ability to perform miraculous work. I myself have been impressed by the sight of pilgrims arriving at the memorial buildings erected to honor a particular saint in the hope of obtaining *baraka*, or "blessing," to solve their difficulties. That saint may have lived centuries ago, but thousands come especially on the anniversary of the saint's death to seek the mediation of the revered one. It is well known that Christians and Muslims in Egypt have visited the graves of each other's saints for the very same purpose of receiving healing for illness or success in exams. So, we return to the theme of some Christians seeking miraculous spiritual help from saints, especially Mary. While I was critical of the veneration of Mary expressed in the Orthodox and Catholic traditions, I am open to the possibility that God answers the cry for help through believers who are dedicated to being channels of his love and kindness. For me, this ministry can be performed by the simplest believer, even a child. Part of the value of the more Evangelical, Charismatic, and Pentecostal wings of the church is to open up this possibility beyond ordained and recognized leaders. In many of these churches the offer of prayer for healing has provided a space for needy people to find solace in God's presence, taken there by those who are already comfortable residing in God's court. The phenomenal growth of these churches in the world today is partly explained by this openness to serving as mediators between the Creator and humanity, and making a way for people to connect with him.

One example of an unlikely person being the means of the healing of many is the English woman Jackie Pullinger, who felt led by God to serve drug addicts in Hong Kong. Jackie arrived in Hong Kong from London in 1966 as a music teacher. She gradually became involved in teaching part-time in a school in the deprived Walled City. Exposure to drug addicts and prostitutes who lived there led her to minister to them. Jackie records her sense of God's call to the Walled City:

> The second time I went into the Walled City I had this wonderful feeling inside. This was not reasonable—of all the revolting places in the world. And yet nearly every time I was in the

underground city over the next dozen years, I was to feel the same joy.[25]

In 1967 she opened a one-room club for teenagers. Employment for Walled City kids was either as sweated labor in factories making plastic components or in crime with a Triad gang. Gangs paid better. The young people had a low view of Christianity as being for the privileged Chinese and Westerners. Ah Ping who became the first Triad gang member to open his life to Christ had told her:

> You Westerners, you come here and tell us about Jesus. You can stay for a year or two and your conscience will feel good and then you can go away. It's true some of you can raise a lot of money on behalf of us underprivileged people, but you'll still be living in your nice houses and we'll still be living here.[26]

After his conversion, he would bring other gang members to Christian meetings. When he was severely beaten by his gang he was prayed for by the little Christian group and recovered amazingly quickly. Jackie tried to get them accepted by Chinese churches outside the Walled City, but she failed. Reluctantly she developed the group into a church. She now had the help of Dora Lee, who had fluent Chinese.

Many teenagers were heroin addicts. Jackie felt irresistibly drawn to them. They came to the club to play table-tennis. She told them Jesus could set them free from addiction. This meant staying with them through withdrawal constantly praying. She had now teamed up with an American couple, Jean and Rick Williams, for prayer for addicts. They had encouraged Jackie to pray in tongues over the boys who wanted release. Jackie found that the boys who opened their lives to Christ were filled with the Spirit and instantly taken out of a craving for heroin. That was until Ah Kei. He was released from addition only for a time. Ah Kei had been boss of a Triad gang in another part of Hong Kong. When he returned to heroin, Jackie was shattered. She poured out her feelings in prayer. "Lord, I really believed you were the answer."[27] Jean Williams challenged Ah Kei to repent and offered her home for him to go through withdrawal. Eventually he came off drugs through concentrated prayer lasting several days. The problem was how to keep former addicts away from pressure to go back to heroin. They needed to live outside the

25. Pullinger, *Chasing the Dragon*, 39.
26. Ibid., 55.
27. Ibid., 147.

Walled City in neutral territory. They needed regular work. Jackie and the Williams opened an apartment for seventeen boys. Within two years they had four apartments housing seventy-five ex-heroin addicts, all of whom had come off heroin through the power of the Holy Spirit. Jackie's greatest moment was an interview with a Triad gang leader in the Walled City. Goko was in his mid-thirties. He told her he wanted to give her his addicts:

> "You have a power which I don't have. If my brothers get hooked on drugs I have them beaten up. I don't want them on heroin and I've found I can't make them quit. But I've watched you and I believe Jesus can. I'll give you all my rotten brothers and I'll keep all the good ones for myself." She said to him: "Fine. Jesus came for the rotten ones anyway."[28]

Some boys left the apartments and she lost touch with them. Some went back to crime and drugs. "Those of the boys who continued to walk in the Spirit became fine and trustworthy men. Those who had known Christ but left to follow their own desires got into trouble."[29] Jackie is a fine example of an ordinary Christian enabling faith in others through her devotion to God and her expectation that Jesus has the power to heal even the most hopeless people through the outpouring of the Spirit of God on them.

Ibrahim: This is a very moving story of dedication to the neediest people in society. This is exactly what I was getting at when I referred to the saints who are channels for the blessing of God. There are countless similar accounts of Muslims receiving healing through the mediation of a saint. That is why pilgrimages to the graves of saints are profoundly popular in many Muslim societies. The *baraka* found there has enormous consequences for the well-being of the pilgrims. I know that some Muslims are opposed to visits to the graves of saints because seeking their power is a form of *shirk*, of associating human beings with God in an unacceptable way, by diverting worship way from God to humans. We have recently all been aware of the demolition in Syria of a shrine dedicated to a saint by Muslims who take this view. But this attitude is very much a minority one and obviously exceedingly unwelcome to the clear majority of Muslims globally.

---

28. Ibid., 113.
29. Ibid., 236.

Yet there is another side to the miraculous apart from prayer for a miracle to occur. There are those who help the needy by practical means in such a way that a larger miracle happens in society. In this context, one individual empowers a community by using skill and commitment to bring about transformation of the economic situation so that large numbers of people can live more healthy lives and therefore do not need the intervention of prayer for healing. One such Muslim was the founder of the Grameen bank in Bangladesh, Muhammad Yunus:

> In 1976, as Head of the Rural Economics Program at the University of Chittagong, Yunus initiated a project to provide banking services for poor village people. He founded the Grameen Bank, a bank for rural villagers, since *"grameen"* is Bengali for "village." He wanted to help poor women especially to receive small loans so that they could invest in their small farms and become more productive. The only way these village women had been able to get loans was through money lenders who charged extortionate interest. As a result of his success he reversed the long standing tradition of "low income, low saving and low investment," into a new social pattern of "low income, injection of credit, investment, more income, more savings, more investment, more income."[30]

The bank's services were extended to other districts of Bangladesh, and it was recognized as an independent bank by the Bangladeshi government in 1983. Twenty years later, there were over 2,000 branches across Bangladesh. There are now similar banks operating in more than forty countries. The World Bank has developed a plan to finance banks that follow the Grameen method.[31]

So here is a fine example of a Muslim who put his mind to doing something radical for the poor to transform their poverty into wealth by helping them improve their own lives by their own initiatives. He undercut the ruthless selfishness of the traditional moneylenders, who kept the villagers in dire poverty and indebtedness, and set these women free to live healthier lives. The huge numbers of poor involved here are staggering. One man changed the course of history in Bangladesh and in other nations too. That is just as much a miracle as the result of praying for these women to have better lives. Here is a part of the letter he wrote

---

30. The History of the Grameen Bank, www.grameen-info.org.
31. Ibid.

to the village women of Bangladesh who were members of the Grameen Bank at his retirement in 2011:

> You increased the amount of savings that you hold, many times over. You have educated your children. Through Educational Loans, many of them are today studying to be doctors and engineers. Many of your children have completed their education and are now doctors, engineers and professors. Today, you know how to provide leadership in society. In 2006, one of the biggest news of your lifetime arrived. Grameen Bank, in other words you, won the Nobel Peace Prize. You brought the nation a very big honour. Representing you, your Board Members travelled to Norway and brought back the Nobel Peace Prize. One of you, Mossammat Taslima Begum, from Pirghachi village in Chapainawabganj district, received the Nobel Peace Prize on your behalf. And she gave her acceptance speech on your behalf to the global television. The entire world watched and listened to her words. Those who had earlier been chased out of their villages now had brought back this great honour for the nation.[32]

Paul: I agree with you. We need to demonstrate the reality of God in everyday life through serving others who need our help. These stories from Hong Kong and Bangladesh show how important it is for us to follow God's will for us as believers. He calls us to depend on him to change the world through bringing the needs of others to him in prayer. But he also calls us to answer these prayers in our actions. This connection between believing in God and serving others is central to the teaching of Jesus found in the Gospels. He taught that loving God and our neighbor are interconnected. Let us turn to that theme in out next chapter.

---

32. M. Yunus, *Letter to Grameen Bank Members*, 15 May 2011. www.grameen.com.

three

Teacher of Love for God and Neighbor

IBRAHIM INTRODUCES THE THEME of the love of God and neighbor as central to the teaching of Jesus, according to the *Common Word* document signed by 158 Muslim scholars in 2007. They called on Christians to agree with Muslims over these themes. Paul is grateful that so many modern Muslim scholars are happy to quote from the Gospels since the Qur'an does not represent Jesus teaching this. Ibrahim believes that the Qur'an does have the spirit of this teaching, but Paul replies that only love for God is commanded in the Qur'an. He points out that the Muslim scholars had to turn to the sayings of Muhammad for teaching about love for neighbors and in any case love for enemies is totally absent from both the Qur'an and the sayings of Muhammad. Ibrahim argues that God is willing to forgive those who oppose him, and that Muhammad forgave his tribe, the Quraysh, after they gave up fighting against him and accepted his leadership.

Paul insists that love for enemies is at the heart of Jesus' teaching. Even the most skeptical Christian scholars hold that Jesus really did proclaim this. The story of the lost son who returns to his father is a perfect illustration of what Jesus meant by loving one's enemies. Ibrahim agrees that God desires the wayward ones to turn back to him. He refers to the story of Abraham in the Qur'an; when Abraham challenged his family's idolatry, he prayed that his father might be forgiven. Ibrahim also recalls, according to the Qur'an, that when Moses came down from the mountain after his encounter with God he witnessed the people of God worshipping a calf. Despite his anger with the people, Moses sought the forgiveness of God for their rebellion.

They turn to the theme of love for God. Ibrahim affirms that the Sufi attitude to devotion to God was the practice of the Prophet Muhammad by referring to a saying of Muhammad that emphasizes the need to remain close to God so that his presence will motivate everything that the Muslim does. He gives the example of an early female Sufi who wrote poetry showing the centrality of disinterested love for God, loving God just for himself and not for any reward he might give to the believer. Paul brings forward examples of Christian prayer, spoken and sung, that demonstrate the crucial importance of love for God in the history of Christian worship. Ibrahim hopes that Muslims and Christians can be united over the need for love for God. He refers to the *Common Word* document being written in the light of Pope Benedict's allegation in 2006 that Islam is inherently violent. Paul seeks to defend the Pope from this misunderstanding by referring to the Pope's statement that he had not intended this. They agree that the use of violence to defend the truth against evil should be part of the next discussion on Jesus' teaching about the kingdom of God.

Love for Neighbor

Ibrahim: I'm pleased that we are now discussing the teaching of Jesus. In recent years Muslims have reminded Christians that Jesus' message is essentially the same as that of all the prophets. He was sent as a messenger to the Jews, as many other prophets had been, proclaiming that they should obey the commands of God that had been given, particularly in the Torah revealed to Moses. Thus, Jesus was re-affirming that the Jews must be dedicated to God, who had spoken to their ancestors. The problem was that rebellion was never far from the hearts and minds of the children of Israel, and Jesus was commissioned with the task of bringing wayward Jews to the true path of obedience.

While the Qurʾan does not enlarge on Jesus' teaching in the fashion of the Gospels, which contain numerous stories and sayings attributed to him, the basic thrust of the qurʾanic presentation of Jesus' teaching is like that in the Gospels. This was made clear by the 158 Muslim scholars who signed the *Common Word* document in 2007, addressing Christians worldwide after Pope Benedict had suggested in a speech in 2006 that Muslims have a problem with violence. These scholars from all schools of Islam, including Sunni and Shiʿa, joined together in harmony over the fact that Islam teaches the love of God and neighbor, the very message of Jesus Christ according to the Gospels.

Paul: I must say how impressed I have been with the way that disparate Muslim experts could reach agreement on a common document about the teaching of Jesus. I think this is an unprecedented event in the Islamic world. We are so used to Sunni and Shiʿa being in contention over how Islam should be practiced, particularly with respect to political arrangements, that many of us Christians have been pleasantly surprised by the unity among Muslims concerning the teaching of Jesus. The decision to focus on the key sayings of Jesus was a wise choice, such as his summary of the law expressed in Mark 12:28–31:

> One of the scribes came near and heard them disputing with one another, and seeing that he answered them well, he asked him, "Which commandment is the first of all?" 29 Jesus answered, "The first is, 'Hear, O Israel: the Lord our God, the Lord is one; 30 you shall love the Lord your God with all your heart, and with all your soul, and with all your mind, and with all your strength.' 31 The second is this, 'You shall love your neighbor as yourself.' There is no other commandment greater than these."

Jesus commends the summary of the law found in the Torah at Deuteronomy 6:4–5, "Hear, O Israel: The Lord is our God, the Lord alone. You shall love the Lord your God with all your heart, and with all your soul, and with all your might." Jesus adds from Leviticus 19:18, "You shall not take vengeance or bear a grudge against any of your people, but you shall love your neighbor as yourself: I am the Lord." The *Common Word* document quotes these words of Jesus and shows that he was joining together key summaries of the law from the Torah. This acknowledgement of the historical reality of Jesus' impact on the people of his time demonstrates that these leading Muslim scholars are willing to accept the testimony of the Gospels to the teaching of Jesus. After all, ʿIsa does not speak these words in the Qurʾan.

Ibrahim: That is so. Yet the spirit of these words is found within the Qurʾan as the *Common Word* document points out:

> Muslims and Christians together make up well over half of the world's population. Without peace and justice between these two religious communities, there can be no meaningful peace in the world. The future of the world depends on peace between Muslims and Christians. The basis for this peace and understanding already exists. It is part of the very foundational principles of both faiths: love of the One God, and love of the neighbour. These principles are found over and over again in

the sacred texts of Islam and Christianity. The Unity of God, the necessity of love for Him, and the necessity of love of the neighbour is thus the common ground between Islam and Christianity. The following are only a few examples: Of God's Unity, God says in the Holy Qur'an: *Say: He is God, the One! / God, the Self-Sufficient Besought of all!* (Al-Ikhlas, 112:1-2). Of the necessity of love for God, God says in the Holy Qur'an: *So invoke the Name of thy Lord and devote thyself to Him with a complete devotion* (Al-Muzzammil, 73:8). Of the necessity of love for the neighbour, the Prophet Muhammad said: *"None of you has faith until you love for your neighbour what you love for yourself."*[1]

Paul: But the Qur'an only refers to love for God not love for neighbor. The authors had to go to a saying of the Prophet Muhammad for that teaching. This means that the teaching concerning love for neighbor is not explicit in the Qur'an. In other words, the Qur'an does not represent Jesus teaching love for neighbor. Indeed, the Qur'an does not mention that the Torah requires love for neighbor. And this is strange, given that the Qur'an insists that Jesus had come to remind the Jews to follow the Torah already revealed to them through Moses in Q5:44-47:

> We revealed the Torah in which is guidance and light. The Jews were judged according to it by the prophets who submitted to God, and by the rabbis and the scribes who were entrusted with the books of God. . . . 45 We prescribed for them in it a life for a life, an eye for an eye, a nose for a nose, an ear for an ear, a tooth for a tooth, an equal wound for a wound. If anyone forgoes this out of charity, it will be an atonement for him. Those who do not judge by what God has revealed are wrongdoers. 46 We sent Jesus, son of Mary, in their footsteps, to confirm the Torah that had been sent before him. We gave him the Gospel in which is guidance and light, (a confirmation of the Torah that had been sent before him), guidance and counsel for those who fear God. 47 Let the Gospel people judge by what God has revealed in it. Those who do not judge by what God has revealed are lawbreakers.

The Qur'an mentions that recompense for harm done should be according to the type of harm. This is a true reflection of the Torah in Deuteronomy 19:21, "Show no pity: life for life, eye for eye, tooth for tooth, hand for hand, foot for foot."

---

1. *A Common Word between Us and You.*

Ibrahim: But you have overlooked the concession in Q5:45, where God commends the person who has been wronged when he forgoes the recompense that he is entitled to. If that is not sheer love and grace offered by the wronged party, then I don't know what your definition of love for neighbor is! You must see the whole context of the verse here and not just a part of it. The Qur'an shows clearly that the Torah allows for justice in disputes between people, but that the Torah also makes room for compassion, mercy, and forgiveness if that is desired by the wronged person in a dispute. There is a perfect balance between achieving justice and mercy. Therefore, the Qur'an is saying that the teaching of Jesus follows exactly what the Torah taught, have your just deserts in a dispute, but remember that God rewards those who forego justice and forgive the one who has wronged them. This is precisely the same as Jesus saying in the Gospels, love your neighbor.

Love for Enemies

Paul: I think you have made a good case about the Qur'an encouraging forgiveness in a dispute between neighbors, even though Jesus himself is not quoted to be saying this. However, in the Gospels, Jesus does not only teach that his disciples should love their neighbors, but he also insists that they love *their enemies*. In Matthew 5:43–48, Jesus shows how his disciples must be distinct from others who naturally look out for their own group:

> You have heard that it was said, "You shall love your neighbor and hate your enemy." 44 But I say to you, Love your enemies and pray for those who persecute you, 45 so that you may be children of your Father in heaven; for he makes his sun rise on the evil and on the good, and sends rain on the righteous and on the unrighteous. 46 For if you love those who love you, what reward do you have? Do not even the tax collectors do the same? 47 And if you greet only your brothers and sisters, what more are you doing than others? Do not even the gentiles do the same? 48 Be perfect, therefore, as your heavenly Father is perfect.

Here Jesus probably shocks his listeners by comparing them to tax collectors and pagans. Tax collectors were Jews who worked for the Roman government by collecting a tax on each Jew living, a head tax. This meant people were taxed just for being alive, rather than according to whether they could pay. These Jewish tax collectors were despised, not only because they worked for the hated Romans, who were not believers in the One God and who worshipped many gods, but because they took extra money from their own Jewish people to become wealthy at their expense. So, Jesus is saying that his disciples must behave differently from tax collectors who look after each other and from pagan Romans who care for each other. His disciples should love those who do not belong to their group.

Ibrahim: It seems that Jesus is emphasizing that judgment belongs to God, who is merciful and compassionate toward all human beings, the children of Israel as well as the polytheists. God, who is perfect, will reward humans, who are not perfect, at the Day of Judgment. Jesus is warning his hearers not to take the judgment of God for granted, but to take care to perform righteous acts that can be rewarded. Is Jesus not calling his disciples to join him in warning the children of Israel and the polytheists that they must get themselves prepared for the Day of Judgment?

Paul: I agree that Jesus was most probably trying to get his listeners to prepare for the judgment of God. But the nature of that judgment is not what many of his hearers were expecting. Jesus is disagreeing with those teachers of the Torah who had been saying that love for neighbor means hatred for enemies. These other teachers had argued that love for neighbor was limited to the children of Israel who were consciously following God's law. That is why he mentions Jews who collected taxes for the Romans. They were clearly going against their own people by flouting the Torah quite deliberately, and so were equivalent to traitors who had changed sides and worked for the enemy. Jesus was famous for spending time with tax collectors, receiving hospitality from them, eating meals at their invitation, and even calling some to join his intimate disciple group.

Ibrahim: The last point is quite profound. Jesus called tax collectors to join his band of disciples. He demonstrates the love of God for those who systematically defy God's law. This is the task of prophets, who have been sent to challenge the wrongdoers of their time. Moses was sent to confront Pharaoh, who was crushing God's people. The Prophet Muhammad was sent to challenge his own tribe, the Quraysh, who had been exalting many idols in the Kaʿba at Mecca. Muhammad called them join him in the worship of the One true God, and while some did, many were consistently hostile to the truth to the extent that Muhammad and his small band of disciples had to emigrate to Medina. Yet Muhammad demonstrated the love of God for the Quraysh when he finally returned to Mecca and forgave every Quraysh who had opposed him. He practiced love for his enemies on a scale that is hard to imagine nowadays when vengeance is often meted out on enemies.

Paul: it would be good to reflect on the words of Jesus, "Pray for those who persecute you." He is encouraging his followers not to flee from persecution but to bring their persecutors before God, asking him to deal with them, not merely to judge them, but to convert them to himself. They are not to pray for the judgment simply to fall as condemnation but for the judgment to be the opportunity for repentance and change of character of the persecutors. He demonstrated this when he prayed that those who had put him on the cross would be forgiven by God in Luke 23:34, "Father, forgive them; for they do not know what they are doing."

Ibrahim: Well, this comes from the story about the crucifixion of Jesus in the Gospels. I note that this prayer is only mentioned by Luke, who does not record another prayer of Jesus found in Mark and Matthew. In Mark 15:34 and Matthew 27:46, Jesus prays, "My God, my God, why have you forsaken me?" The way Jesus is portrayed by Mark and Matthew is very different from Luke. The usual Christian scholarly interpretation of this variety is to say that Mark and Matthew have the earlier account, which is modified by the later version of Luke. This means that Luke may well have put these forgiving words on Jesus' lips because Luke wanted to promote that view of Jesus as a man of forgiveness in the most extreme circumstances. However, the original story of Jesus on the cross shows how Jesus was completely broken in his spirit, not even being confident in God at the point of death. So how could a broken man, who does not know what God is doing, seek forgiveness for those who are killing him?

Paul: You have raised the issue of the perspectives of the different Gospels. In Christian scholarship, there has been an ongoing debate about the editing of the four Gospels. The Jesus Seminar would represent the more skeptical approach. But the interesting outcome of their very rigorous handling of the teaching of Jesus is that they believe that among the core sayings of Jesus is the one about forgiving enemies. One of the members of the Jesus Seminar who has written extensively on the teaching of Jesus is Dominic Crossan, who argues that we can be certain that there are some basic sayings that go back to Jesus himself. He outlines six sayings that are connected by the notion of love for others. That love extends beyond the in-group and embraces those who are enemies:

1. *The Golden Rule:* Do (not do) to others as you would (not) have them do to you.
2. *Love Your Enemies:* Love your enemies, do good to those who hate you, bless those who curse you, pray for those who abuse you.
3. *Better Than sinners:* If you love those who love you, what credit is that to you? For even sinners love those who love them.
4. *The Other Cheek:* If anyone strikes you on the right cheek, turn the other also; if anyone wants to sue you and take your coat, give your cloak as well; and if anyone forces you to go one mile, go also the second mile.
5. *Give Without Return:* Give to everyone who begs from you; and if anyone takes away your goods, do not ask for them again.
6. *As Your Father:* So that you may be children of your Father in heaven; for he makes his sun rise on the evil and on the good, and sends rain on the righteous and on the unrighteous. Be perfect, therefore, as your heavenly Father is perfect.[2]

You can see that even the most skeptical Christian scholars accept that the teaching of love for enemies who persecute the disciples is key to Jesus' instructions.

Ibrahim: Yes, I am familiar with the work of the Jesus Seminar. They are following the footsteps of the German tradition of David Strauss from the nineteenth century[3] and Rudolf Bultmann from the twentieth century, who regarded much of the four Gospels as the dramatic creation of Jesus' followers. As Bultmann said, they were created after the life of Jesus, and tell us more about the faith of the followers than about the faith of Jesus himself. As far as the words of Jesus on the cross are concerned, Bultmann thought that Jesus was defeated by the cross, not that he was strong enough to forgive his enemies:

> The greatest embarrassment to the attempt to reconstruct a portrait of Jesus is the fact that we cannot know how Jesus understood his end, his death. It is symptomatic that it is practically universally assumed that he understood this as the organic or necessary conclusion to his activity. But how do we know this, when prophecies of the passion must be understood by critical research as *vaticinia ex eventu*? . . . We cannot tell whether or

2. Crossan and Reed, *Excavating Jesus*, 176.
3. See David Strauss, *The Life of Jesus*.

how Jesus found meaning in it. We may not veil from ourselves the possibility that he suffered a collapse.[4]

The most honest Christian scholars are not sure that the four Gospels provide an accurate account of the teaching of Jesus. Therefore, you must be cautious about affirming that Jesus prayed for his enemies to be forgiven when he was hanging on the cross. The more likely scenario of crucifixion is a sad ending to a worthy life. The inability of Christians who have spent their careers studying the Gospels to agree on the basic teaching of Jesus is testimony to the fact that the Gospels do not give a simple and straightforward biography of Jesus. They are theological documents designed to instruct the church in the way that Christians ought to regard Jesus.

Paul: Perhaps we can return to the cross in a later discussion. For now, I want to remind you that Crossan and the Jesus Seminar affirm that Jesus taught his disciples to love their enemies and pray for those who persecute them. This means that even those Christian scholars who are skeptical about much of the material in the Gospels are content that the historical Jesus taught his followers to love their enemies. This is the *heart* of his teaching. It surely arises out of his understanding of the forgiveness of God for those who are manifestly opposed to him. Some of his most memorable stories are about the way that God accepts those who rebel against him.

For example, there is the story of a father who has two sons. The younger one treats his father with disloyalty and disdain, but eventually is reconciled with his father after returning home from losing his father's money and being received with warmth by his rejected father. The story is found in Luke 15:11–32 in the context of Jesus talking to tax collectors. The leading Jewish legal scholars were commenting in Jesus' hearing, "This fellow welcomes sinners and eats with them." Jesus told this story to illustrate why he was willing to spend time with rebels:

> Then Jesus said, "There was a man who had two sons. 12 The younger of them said to his father, 'Father, give me the share of the property that will belong to me.' So he divided his property between them. 13 A few days later the younger son gathered all he had and traveled to a distant country, and there he squandered his property in dissolute living. 14 When he had spent everything, a severe famine took place throughout that country,

---

4. Bultmann, "The Primitive Christian Kerygma," 22–23.

and he began to be in need. **15** So he went and hired himself out to one of the citizens of that country, who sent him to his fields to feed the pigs. **16** He would gladly have filled himself with the pods that the pigs were eating; and no one gave him anything. **17** But when he came to himself he said, 'How many of my father's hired hands have bread enough and to spare, but here I am dying of hunger! **18** I will get up and go to my father, and I will say to him, "Father, I have sinned against heaven and before you; **19** I am no longer worthy to be called your son; treat me like one of your hired hands."' **20** So he set off and went to his father. But while he was still far off, his father saw him and was filled with compassion; he ran and put his arms around him and kissed him. **21** Then the son said to him, 'Father, I have sinned against heaven and before you; I am no longer worthy to be called your son.' **22** But the father said to his slaves, 'Quickly, bring out a robe—the best one—and put it on him; put a ring on his finger and sandals on his feet. **23** And get the fatted calf and kill it, and let us eat and celebrate; **24** for this son of mine was dead and is alive again; he was lost and is found!' And they began to celebrate. **25** Now his elder son was in the field; and when he came and approached the house, he heard music and dancing. **26** He called one of the slaves and asked what was going on. **27** He replied, 'Your brother has come, and your father has killed the fatted calf, because he has got him back safe and sound.' **28** Then he became angry and refused to go in. His father came out and began to plead with him. **29** But he answered his father, 'Listen! For all these years I have been working like a slave for you, and I have never disobeyed your command; yet you have never given me even a young goat so that I might celebrate with my friends. **30** But when this son of yours came back, who has devoured your property with prostitutes, you killed the fatted calf for him!' **31** Then the father said to him, 'Son, you are always with me, and all that is mine is yours. **32** But we had to celebrate and rejoice, because this brother of yours was dead and has come to life; he was lost and has been found.'"

Notice how the father loves both of his sons, even when the younger one tests his father's love by rejecting him. The elder son appears at first to be loyal to his father, but when his younger brother is accepted back in the home after trashing his family's reputation, he refused to celebrate along with his father. Jesus is aiming this story at the legal experts who do not believe that rebels can turn into obedient servants of God. The willingness of God to forgive sinners and reinstate them is clearly implied by Jesus. As David Wenham points out in his study of Jesus' parables:

> Jesus makes it clear that the way back to God and into the kingdom is to come empty-handed and seeking God's mercy. On the other hand, there is the picture of the father who had been so insulted looking out for his son, running to meet him and overwhelming him with generous love and undeserved forgiveness. This is how Jesus understood his ministry: God was opening his arms of love to welcome the lost home.[5]

Therefore, even when a son becomes an enemy of his father, a man born a Jew who becomes an outlaw, a man who was raised in the law but chooses to rebel against it, God is looking to forgive the one who has chosen to oppose him.

Jesus told another story to make the same case about tax collectors repenting and being accepted by God in Luke 18:9–14:

> He also told this parable to some who trusted in themselves that they were righteous and regarded others with contempt: **10** "Two men went up to the temple to pray, one a Pharisee and the other a tax collector. **11** The Pharisee, standing by himself, was praying thus, 'God, I thank you that I am not like other people: thieves, rogues, adulterers, or even like this tax collector. **12** I fast twice a week; I give a tenth of all my income.' **13** But the tax collector, standing far off, would not even look up to heaven, but was beating his breast and saying, 'God, be merciful to me, a sinner!' **14** I tell you, this man went down to his home justified rather than the other; for all who exalt themselves will be humbled, but all who humble themselves will be exalted."

The final comment of Jesus confirms his view of the forgiveness of God for wrongdoers. According to Kenneth Bailey, "Sin for Jesus is not primarily a broken law but a broken relationship. The tax collector yearns to accept the gift of God's justification, while the Pharisee feels he has already earned it."[6] In summary, Jesus taught his disciples to love their enemies because God loves them.

Ibrahim: These two stories are very moving accounts of rebels having a change of heart and the message of the merciful and compassionate God who welcomes wayward ones who return to the straight path is very

---

5. Wenham, *The Parables of Jesus*, 110.
6. Bailey, *Jesus through Middle Eastern Eyes*, 350.

much the proclamation of the messengers sent by God to sinful humanity. Abraham was called to challenge his father's idolatry and because of his devotion to the One true God he was nearly stoned to death by his own family. Q26:69–90 shows how Abraham's heart was devoted to his Lord:

> Tell them the story of Abraham. 70 He said to his father and his people, "What do you worship?" 71 They said, "We worship images and we maintain our devotion to them." 72 He asked, "Do they hear you when you call? 73 Do they do you good or harm?" 74 They replied, "No. We found our fathers doing this." 75 He said, "You have invented what you worship, 76 you and your forefathers. 77 They are enemies to me, unlike the Lord of the universe 78 who created me. He guides me, 79 and He is the One who gives me food and drink. 80 When I am ill He heals me. 81 He is the One who will cause me to die and then raise me to life again, 82 and who will, I hope, forgive my faults on the Day of Judgment. 83 My Lord, give me wisdom and include me with the righteous. 84 Give me a good name among the later generations. 85 Make me one of those who inherit the Garden of Grace. 86 Forgive my father, for he is one of those who have gone astray. 87 Do not disgrace me on the Day of Resurrection, 88 the Day when neither wealth nor children will help. 89 Only to the one who comes to God with a healthy heart, 90 to the righteous, will the Garden be brought close."

Notice how Abraham has become a believer in the Lord despite being raised in a polytheistic family, and in response to God's call summons his family to give up idolatry and commit themselves unreservedly to the worship of the One God of creation. He prays that his father will be forgiven by God because he loves him. This is like the father in the story from Luke who is earnestly seeking for his lost boy to come back to his bosom. We pray for the wayward ones we love, who have become enemies of God, that they might become his devoted servants.

Moses had a similar experience with the children of Israel that God had called him to lead. When they made a golden calf to worship he was so angry with them, because his heart was totally devoted to God, but he also wanted them to turn back to the One who had called them out of slavery in Egypt. Moses did not wish for the destruction of the people under the just judgment of God. Q7:142–7 relates how God called Moses to come up a mountain to spend time with him. There the Lord gave Moses tablets with the Torah for the people he had rescued from slavery in Egypt. Verses 148–53 tell the story of the turn to idolatry by these very people set free by God's grace:

> Moses' people, in his absence, made from their jewelry the image of a calf which lowed. Did they not see that it did not speak to them or guide them on their path? Yet they took it for worship and they were wrongdoers. **149** When they became horrified after seeing that they had done wrong, they said, "If our Lord does not show mercy to us and forgive us, we will be among the lost." **150** When Moses returned to his people, angry and aggrieved, he said, "Such evil you have done in my absence. Did you want to hasten the judgment of your Lord?" He threw the Tablets down and grasping his brother's head, pulled him towards him. He [Aaron] said, "Son of my mother, the people thought I was weak and almost killed me. Do not let my enemies rejoice over my misfortune. Do not include me with these evil people." **151** Moses said, "My Lord, forgive me and my brother. Be merciful to us. You are the Most Merciful of those who show mercy." **152** Those who took the calf for worship will be afflicted by their Lord's wrath, and by disgrace in this life. This is how We repay those who invent such falsehoods. **153** As for those who do wrong then repent afterwards and believe, truly your Lord is most forgiving and most merciful towards them.

God is constantly looking for his people to turn away from wrongdoing and seek him in the knowledge that he is the Most Merciful of all. He gave this essential message to the prophets to proclaim to the people to whom they were sent. Jesus' message to the children of Israel was similar. Q57:26–28 reminds us that God sent the prophets to guide humanity to the right path:

> We sent Noah and Abraham, and gave prophethood and Scripture to their descendants. There were some among them who were rightly guided, but many of them became lawbreakers. **27** We sent more of Our messengers after them. Following them We sent Jesus, son of Mary. We gave him the Gospel and turned the hearts of those who followed him to kindness and mercy.... To those among them who believed We gave them their reward, but many of them were lawbreakers. **28** Believers, fear God and trust His Messenger. He will give you a double portion of His mercy; He will provide a light so you can walk. He will forgive you, for God is most forgiving, most merciful.

Noah preached to his people, but most of them ignored him and were drowned in the flood. Abraham was followed by some but rejected by others. Jesus brought the Gospel and had followers who were marked by devotion to God, yet among them were lawbreakers who failed to maintain their loyalty to God. Finally, God sent Muhammad, as verse 28 indicates, and offered a double portion of his mercy and forgiveness to the people of Muhammad's time and to all who have responded to Muhammad's message since then.

Love for God

Paul: The *Common Word* document also mentioned that Jesus emphasized that his followers should love God with all their heart, soul, mind, and strength. There is no doubt that this is a correct representation of Jesus' teaching according to the Gospels, and that Jesus was repeating the teaching of the Torah. His whole mission can be summed up in this idea that humans should return the love that their Creator and Sustainer has shown them. In Mark 5, Jesus healed a man who was so controlled by violent tendencies that he had to live away from his community in the graveyard. The man wanted to join Jesus' disciple band and travel around with them, but Jesus told him in verse 19, "Go home to your friends, and tell them how much the Lord has done for you, and what mercy he has shown you." The man accepted this calling and the whole neighborhood was amazed at his transformation. Jesus wanted people to live out love for God who grants life and health and turns darkness into light for those addicted to evil.

Another example of Jesus' teaching his disciples to love God comes in Mark 12:43–44, when he was sitting in the temple in Jerusalem watching people put money into the temple collection box. Many wealthy Jews put in considerable sums of money to support the work of the temple. Then a poor widow came and gave two small coins. He said to his disciples, "Truly I tell you, this poor widow has put in more than all those who are contributing to the treasury. For all of them have contributed out of their abundance; but she out of her poverty has put in everything she had, all she had to live on." Clearly Jesus believed that love for God must be expressed in the realities of everyday life.

Ibrahim: These are very good examples of true devotion to God. We have already discussed in chapter two how Jesus came to heal the sick and to restore their hope in God. It is often those who have very little of this world's goods that show love for their Lord and put the better off to shame for the poverty of their religion. The poor widow is mirrored in the famous poet Rabiʿa al-ʿAdawiyya (d. 801). She was a slave set free by her master, but she never married, preferring to concentrate on serving God. Here is an example of her devotion to God:

> O Beloved of hearts, I have none like unto Thee,
> therefore have pity this day on the sinner who comes to Thee.
> O my Hope and my Rest and my Delight,
> the heart can love none other but Thee.[7]

When she was asked why she was carrying a torch in one hand and a ewer in the other around Basra, she replied, "I want to throw fire into Paradise and pour water into Hell so that these two veils disappear, and it becomes clear who worships God out of love, not out of fear of Hell or hope for Paradise."[8]

Rabiʿa is part of the Sufi tradition in Islam that seeks to point Muslims to their duty to love God with all of their being. This was the teaching and practice of Muhammad himself, reflected in the following prophetic saying recorded by the Sufi ibn Adham (d. c. 780):

> Whoever wants to come close to me will come closest by performing what I have prescribed for him. Then the worshipping servant will continue to come close to me by performing more than I have prescribed, and so I will love him. When I love him I will be the ear with which he hears, the eye with which he sees, the tongue with which he speaks, and the hand with which he strikes.[9]

The Prophet teaches that the love of God sustains the believer in the circumstances of life, so that the very senses are attuned to God.

Paul: There is no doubt that love for God is at the core of Jesus' life and teaching. Christians have done best when they have recognized this. Augustine (d. 430) introduced his *Confessions* with this prayer:

> "You are great, Lord, and highly to be praised" (Ps. 47:2): "great is your power and your wisdom is immeasurable" (Ps. 146:5). Man, a little piece of your creation, desires to praise you, a

---

7. Smith, *Rabiʿa the Mystic*, 55.
8. Ibid., 98.
9. See Anawati and Gardet, *Mystique Musulmane*, 30–31.

human being "bearing his mortality with him" (2 Cor. 4:10), carrying with him the witness of his sin and the witness that you "resist the proud" (1 Pet 5:5). Nevertheless, to praise you is the desire of man, a little piece of your creation. You stir man to take pleasure in praising you, because you have made us for yourself, and our heart is restless until it rests in you.[10]

He had come to this realization as an adult who had followed the religion of his father, a polytheist, but who turned to his mother's Christian faith to become an outstanding theologian. This belief that humans are made to love God has been profoundly influential in the development of Christianity since his time.

Another example of the centrality of love for God comes from a song written by Charles Wesley (d. 1788) to be sung when Christians met together to worship God. It is still being sung today. Here is the opening verse:

> Love divine, all loves excelling,
> joy of heaven, to earth come down,
> fix in us thy humble dwelling,
> all thy faithful mercies crown.
> Jesus, thou art all compassion,
> pure, unbounded love thou art;
> visit us with thy salvation;
> enter every trembling heart.[11]

Charles Wesley and his brother John led a movement for deepening the love for God among English people in the eighteenth century. They were ordained ministers in the Church of England who encouraged the "Methodists" to gather for worship. Charles wrote many songs for these groups.

Ibrahim: I think that Augustine's prayer could be prayed by a sincere Muslim. Many Muslims have sought to unite with God in a spiritual sense. I count myself as one of them. You could say that there is a unity between Christians and Muslims here that overrides all the other differences between them. However, the words used by Wesley point up some of these differences in the way that Augustine's prayer does not. Wesley seems to begin by addressing God as Love, dwelling in heaven,

---

10. Augustine, *Confessions*, 3.
11. www.hymnary.org.

and coming down to the earth to meet with the believers. This would not be so controversial, but the second half of the verse addresses Jesus, and asks him to visit the believers who are eagerly waiting for him to enter their hearts. Here is the evidence for the Christian devotion to Jesus as equivalent to devotion to God. The notion that Jesus could enter the heart of a believer in some spiritual bond is clearly beyond the bounds of true religion. Q4:171 warns Christians that God will not regard such extravagance lightly. "People of the Book, do not go to excess in your religion, and do not say anything about God except the truth: the Messiah, Jesus, son of Mary, was nothing more than a messenger of God." Then in Q5:116–17, God asks Jesus, after he has taken him to heaven:

> "Jesus, son of Mary, did you say to people, 'Take me and my mother as two gods alongside God'?" he will say, "May You be exalted! I would never say what I had no right to say. . . . 117 I told them only what You commanded me to: "Worship God, my Lord and your Lord."

While Augustine's prayer is respectful of God, Wesley's song goes beyond the bounds of acceptable prayer. It was the clear purpose of the Qur'an to summon Christians to stay within the confines of the revelation that to God alone is worship due. We discussed the offering of worship to Mary in chapter one, and this was expressly forbidden by God in his revelation to the Prophet Muhammad. You agreed with this prohibition despite there being many Christians worshipping Mary.

Paul: I wouldn't want to misrepresent Augustine. Let me quote from a later prayer in his *Confessions*:

> I make my prayer through our Lord Jesus Christ your Son, "the man of your right hand, the Son of Man whom you have strengthened" (Ps. 79:18) to be mediator between yourself and us. By him you sought us when we were not seeking you (Rom. 10:20). But you sought us that we should seek you, your Word by whom you made all things including myself, your only Son by whom you have called to adoption the people who believe (Gal. 4:5), myself among them. I make my prayer to you through him "who sits at your right hand and intercedes to you for us" (Rom. 8:34).[12]

You can see that Augustine prayed to God through Jesus his Son, who uniquely intercedes for humans before God the Father, at whose side

12. *Confessions*, 223.

he sits. He came to believe this relationship between the Father and the Son by reading Paul's letters.

In any case, I'm surprised that you have suddenly come out condemning the intercession of the saints before God since you seemed to believe in this possibility for Mary earlier. There surely is a big difference between worshipping Jesus and Mary as "gods," as the Qur'an puts it, and seeking their help as resurrected humans in the presence of God. Augustine saw Jesus as sitting at the right hand of the Father, as Paul indicated in his letter to the Romans. Certainly, the role of Jesus in interceding for us is a unique one. No other human being is given this honor according to the New Testament documents, which I regard as authoritative. This is why I don't agree with Catholic and Orthodox Christians who seek the intercession of saints such as Mary. Perhaps these are themes we can return to in a later discussion. But for now, we can summarize Jesus' teaching about love for God as the number one issue on his mind.

Ibrahim: Of course, worshipping humans as divine beings is wrong, and the Qur'an is warning Christians not to go in that direction. As long as Mary and Jesus are understood to be human rather than divine beings then Christians are heeding that warning. Ibn al-ʿArabi called Jesus "the seal of the saints" and I'm more than happy to regard Jesus that way. But to give him the place of God is a step too far. The Qur'an is calling on Christians to draw back from this.

But as you say, we are discussing Jesus' teaching about love for God and neighbor. One thing that we haven't talked about is the reason that the *Common Word* document was written. You recall that Pope Benedict stated that Islam was inherently violent and Muslims used force to convert people to Islam. He was really connecting the activities of certain people who claim to be Muslims but target innocent civilians by suicide bombing, killing women and children without due thought for what is the correct way to engage in warfare. It was a very sad thing for the leader of the Catholic Church to smear all Muslims with the actions of a small number of seriously misguided people who have committed acts of violence without any authorization from a recognized government. But this smear so incensed the clear majority of Muslims that 158 scholars signed the *Common Word* document in the hope that the Pope would be able to make a distinction between a dangerous group claiming to be Muslims and real Muslims who would never commit such acts.

Paul: Well, we can take up this issue when we consider Jesus' proclamation of the coming kingdom of God. We have been considering his teaching about love for neighbor and whether there is ever a valid reason for using violence against a neighbor is a serious question to deal with. The Gospels testify that Jesus spoke about the rule of God and that he sent his disciples out two by two without him to declare that the kingdom of God was near, and even that it was already among them. There has been a great deal of debate amongst Christian scholars over just what Jesus meant by the rule of God coming or having already arrived. How would the Jews recognize God's rule when they were actually governed by polytheistic Romans? Did Jesus give support to Jews who revolted against their godless rulers and used force to try to depose them and bring in the righteous reign of God? Some Jews were involved in violent insurrection against the Romans and the Jewish aristocracy that governed the Jewish nation on behalf of the Roman Empire. Jesus called at least one of these men to join his group of twelve followers, a man named Judas Iscariot.

Pope Benedict did explain the comments he had made in his Regensburg Speech on 12 September 2006. He had returned to the University of Regensburg, where he used to teach theology, to give a speech about his view of world affairs, in which he appeared to regard Islam as acting, not by principles of reason, but by irrationality. He referred to a dialogue between the Byzantine Emperor Manuel II Paleologus and "A Certain Persian, the Worthy Mouterizes, in Anakara of Galatia" written in 1391:

> The emperor touches on the theme of the holy war. The emperor must have known that sura 2, 256 reads: "There is no compulsion in religion." According to the experts, this is one of the suras of the early period, when Mohammed was still powerless and under threat. But naturally the emperor also knew the instructions, developed later and recorded in the Qur'an, concerning holy war. . . . He addresses his interlocutor with a startling brusqueness on the central question about the relationship between religion and violence in general, saying: *"Show me just what Mohammed brought that was new, and there you will find things only evil and inhuman, such as his command to spread by the sword the faith he preached."* The emperor, after having expressed himself so forcefully, goes on to explain in detail the reasons why spreading the faith through violence is something unreasonable. Violence is incompatible with the nature of God and the nature of the soul. "God," he says, "is not pleased by blood—and not acting reasonably is contrary to God's nature. Faith is born of the soul, not the body. Whoever would lead

someone to faith needs the ability to speak well and to reason properly, without violence and threats.... To convince a reasonable soul, one does not need a strong arm, or weapons of any kind, or any other means of threatening a person with death.... The decisive statement in this argument against violent conversion is this: not to act in accordance with reason is contrary to God's nature.[13]

The outcry from Muslims who believed that the Pope was agreeing with the Byzantine Emperor led to this clarification on 16 September 2006, by Tarcisio Bertone, the Secretary of State of the Holy See:

> The position of the Pope concerning Islam is unequivocally that expressed by the conciliar document Nostra Aetate.... The Pope's option in favour of inter-religious and inter-cultural dialogue is equally unequivocal.... As for the opinion of the Byzantine emperor Manuel II Paleologus, which he quoted during his Regensburg talk, the Holy Father did not mean, nor does he mean, to make that opinion his own in any way. He simply used it as a means to undertake—in an academic context, and as is evident from a complete and attentive reading of the text—certain reflections on the theme of the relationship between religion and violence in general, and to conclude with a **clear and radical rejection of the religious motivation for violence, from whatever side it may come.** [The Pope] sincerely regrets that certain passages of his address could have sounded offensive to the sensitivities of the Muslim faithful and should have been interpreted in a manner that in no way corresponds to his intentions.[14]

The Pope obviously did not intend to argue that Islam is inherently violent. The appropriate use of force in defending the truth will need to occupy us in the next discussion on the kingdom of God in the teaching of Jesus. I'm looking forward to getting into this subject.

Ibrahim: So am I, because the use of violence to force people to adopt a religion is such an important issue right now in our time when some people who claim to be Muslims are taking this to extremes. Forcing people to pray with a gun to the head is scandalous for a Muslim like myself who does not think that religion can be authentically practiced under coercion. But defending the truth against those who wish to

---

13. "Lecture of the Holy Father—Faith, Reason and the University Memories and Reflections," *Libreria Editrice Vaticana*, 12 September 2006.

14. "Pope Apologises to Muslims," *Reuters*, 16 September 2006.

undermine it is also a serious obligation for those who follow the true religion. It is surely correct for Muslims to prevent evil people undermining what God has willed for humanity. How this works out in terms of justifiable use of force to defend the truth that God has revealed needs careful consideration.

Paul: Let us begin with Jesus' teaching on the rule of God and we'll take it from there. Clearly, we will need to pay heed to how Christians have interpreted Jesus' teaching about love for enemies. What are the limits of tolerance for evil people who seek to destroy the good world that God has intended for humanity? The whole relationship between the church and the state has been complicated in the past and there have been different responses among Christians to the use of force to defend the freedoms of the people. Muslims seem to be more united on the appropriateness of force to defend the truth. However, Christians have often felt that Muslims are much keener than they are to promote the truth through force. It appears that Muhammad practised this in leading several military campaigns in Arabia to enforce submission to Islam, but Jesus did not take up arms to establish God's rightful rule and even told Peter to put away his sword. This difference between the founders of Christianity and Islam is a continual challenge to good relations between Christians and Muslims.

four

Proclaimer of the Kingdom of God

PAUL INTRODUCES THE TEACHING of Jesus in the Gospels concerning the kingdom of God. Ibrahim suggests that Jesus' emphasis on avoiding wealth is like the teaching of John the Baptist and the Prophet Muhammad. Jesus' challenge to the rich young man to give up his wealth is paralleled by the emphasis of the Qur'an that believers should give away their wealth to help the needy. Paul agrees that the disciples of Jesus gave up work to be with him and that they are an example to all future followers of Jesus. Paul explains that Jesus spoke much about the future rule of God, and that people outside the Jewish community might be better prepared for this than many Jews. Many of his stories contain a warning to his listeners not to miss out on the kingdom through negligence. Ibrahim argues that the Qur'an is similar in warning people to be ready for the future encounter with God on the Day of Judgment.

Ibrahim questions how Jesus could not attack the rule of the Romans, while commending the faith in God of a Roman soldier. Paul suggests that Jesus felt that Rome allowed the Jews freedom to worship and therefore he did not want to provoke rebellion. Ibrahim asks what Jesus would have done if Rome had suppressed the worship of God, and Paul replies that Jesus would probably have taught a non-violent response. Ibrahim thinks that because Jesus had no army he had no opportunity to use force, but according to Chapter 19 of the Book of Revelation, Jesus will come riding on a white horse with a killing sword in his hand. Ibrahim argues that Christians have often tried to follow that idea in practice. Paul says that this picture relates to the end of the world, but that Jesus advocated non-violence. Paul contrasts Jesus' attitude to that of the Prophet Muhammad, who used force to promote the rule of God. Paul mentions the incident when Jews who had been hostile to Muhammad surrendered, and all the men were executed in cold blood. Ibrahim calls attention to Moses in Exodus 32 doing the same to men who worshipped the golden calf. Moses congratulated the Levites for killing 3,000 rebels. Jews were usually allowed to maintain their traditions if they paid a tax, thus showing how unique this execution of Jews was. Ibrahim reminds Paul that Christians have done similar things to unarmed Muslim men in the Crusades when prisoners of war were executed in public and in 1995, when 8,000 unarmed Muslim males were slaughtered by Christian Serbs in Srebrenica. Paul refers to Muslims in Turkey participating in the death of 1.5 million Armenian Christians. Both Muslims and Christians need to act with due respect for the rights of the other.

The Kingdom of God in the Gospels

Paul: The Gospels tell us that Jesus proclaimed the kingdom of God. Mark 1:15 says that when Jesus began to speak to people he told them, "The time has come. The kingdom of God is near. Repent and believe the good news." Jesus was asking Jews to turn from going in the wrong direction and make the rule of God their priority. Isn't it interesting that he thought that his contemporaries were not focusing on God's rule but were fulfilling their own ambitions. To call them to repent of wrongdoing is such a strong message to those who believed they were the chosen people of God, given the Torah to live by, and being a distinct nation among the surrounding nations. Were they not already living under the rule of God? He asked them to believe the good news about the kingdom of God being "near."

Mark also tells us that Jesus only began to speak after John the Baptist was put in prison. According to Mark 1:4, John proclaimed the need for the Jewish people to repent and find forgiveness for their wrongdoing. Therefore, Jesus was not alone in seeking for people to turn to God. The fact that Jesus himself sought a relationship with John through being baptized in the river Jordan shows that Jesus identified with John's message. He wanted to demonstrate that he was signed up to John's prophetic ministry. Some scholars have thought that Jesus was part of John's "team" to begin with, and once John was removed from public life by being imprisoned, Jesus took up John's task of proclaiming the rule of God. James Dunn agrees with the view that Jesus began as a disciple of John, though says that "disciple" may not be the best word to use.[1] However, Mark indicates that John sensed that Jesus was bigger than a teammate when he said in 1:7, "After me will come one more powerful than I, the thongs of whose sandals I am not worthy to stoop down and untie. I baptize you with water, but he will baptize you with the Holy Spirit."

Ibrahim: The Qur'an points out that John and Jesus were born in unusual circumstances around the same time and were both called to be prophets. While the story in Luke's Gospel that they were cousins may or may not be true, the Qur'an does not mention that they were related through family ties. The creative work of God is the focus of the qur'anic account of these extraordinary men. It was God who made them what they were, and gave them their message. Q3:35–46 tells how the girl Mary had been entrusted to the charge of the temple priest Zechariah by her mother. Zechariah found that she had food that he had not provided, and when he asked how this was, she said, "God provides for whoever He wishes without limit" (v. 37). So, Zechariah prayed, "My Lord, give me a pure child from your very self, for You hear prayer" (v. 38). While he stood praying angels came to him and said, "God gives you good news of John, confirming a word from God. He will be honorable and chaste, a prophet from among the righteous" (v. 39). He protested that he was old and his wife was barren. But the angel replied, "in this way God does what He wishes" (v. 40). Immediately after this, angels came to Mary in the temple and announced that God had chosen her above all women and that God was giving her "news of a word from Him: his name is the Messiah, Jesus, the son of Mary: he will be honored in this world and in the next life, and he will be among those who are near to God" (v. 45). He will "speak to people as a young child and as an adult (v. 46)." We can see how closely connected the miraculous births of John and Jesus were. The angelic announcements were virtually simultaneous to Zechariah and Mary. It would not be surprising if the two men had a close relationship as children, and it is clear that their adult work as prophets would have overlapped.

Paul: John the Baptist called for Jews to turn toward God and this was also the message of Jesus. They both preached repentance. John lived outside the towns in the area around the Jordan river and people went to him to be baptized. John did not appear to go to the urban communities to proclaim his message. Jesus was different. He visited villages and towns

---

1. Dunn, *Jesus Remembered*, 350.

in Galilee calling on Jews to turn and submit to the rule of God. So even if Jesus was affiliated to John through being baptized by him, it is clear that Jesus took John's message to the people rather than living away from them and waiting for them to come to him.

Another difference between John and Jesus was the healing work that Jesus performed everywhere he went. The Gospels do not indicate that John healed those who approached him. Perhaps they were "healed" of their rebellion toward God through coming for baptism. Confession of sin does release people from bondage to evil—which often cripples them psychologically—and thereby enables them to live a new life. Luke 3:7–14 includes conversations between John and some of those who were baptized. These verses give a good indication of the challenge John brought, but they show that John expected people to change themselves rather than be healed by him:

> John said to the crowds that came out to be baptized by him, "You brood of vipers! Who warned you to flee from the wrath to come? 8 Bear fruits worthy of repentance. Do not begin to say to yourselves, 'We have Abraham as our ancestor'; for I tell you, God is able from these stones to raise up children to Abraham. 9 Even now the axe is lying at the root of the trees; every tree therefore that does not bear good fruit is cut down and thrown into the fire." 10 And the crowds asked him, "What then should we do?" 11 In reply he said to them, "Whoever has two coats must share with anyone who has none; and whoever has food must do likewise." 12 Even tax collectors came to be baptized, and they asked him, "Teacher, what should we do?" 13 He said to them, "Collect no more than the amount prescribed for you." 14 Soldiers also asked him, "And we, what should we do?" He said to them, "Do not extort money from anyone by threats or false accusation, and be satisfied with your wages."

We can see that John challenged Jews to live a life worthy of their calling. They might have argued that since Abraham was their ancestor they were part of the longstanding chosen people of God, the Lord who had promised to be their God for all time. This was the famous covenant that God made with Abraham in Genesis 12:2–3, when God called Abraham to leave his father's home and go to the land he would show him. God said:

> I will make of you a great nation, and I will bless you, and make your name great, so that you will be a blessing. I will bless those

who bless you, and the one who curses you I will curse; and in you all the families of the earth shall be blessed.

John could hear people saying that they were already part of the people of God and could trust in God's protection. But he replied that taking the protection for granted was a dangerous thing to do. What they really needed to do was to live lives that reflected their chosen status, lives that showed the life of God. He was warning them that God could reject them and choose others to be his people. The advice John gave was to be content with that which God had given. Tax collectors and soldiers should live within their wages and not use their position of authority to extort money as they could be tempted to do. Those who had a certain measure of wealth should be ready to share with the needy. Notice how John focused on financial issues. For him, serving God had economic implications, and he obviously believed that the Jewish people should seek to level out discrepancies in wealth among themselves.

Ibrahim: Jesus too was very concerned with economic disparity. When he proclaimed that the kingdom of God was coming was he not saying the same as John? There is the story of the rich young man who wanted to be sure that he would be part of the life to come after death. Jesus told him that if he sold everything and gave it to the poor he would secure eternal life. The young man turned and went away because he couldn't give up his wealth. In Mark 10:23–27, Jesus commented on the young man to his disciples, "How hard it will be for those who have wealth to enter the kingdom of God!" When his disciples seemed not to understand, Jesus went on to say, "Children, how hard it is to enter the kingdom of God! It is easier for a camel to go through the eye of a needle than for someone who is rich to enter the kingdom of God." And when the disciples asked, "Then who can be saved?" Jesus replied, "For mortals it is impossible, but not for God; for God all things are possible."

This is basically the same message that John brought. God demands that those who are blessed by him with wealth must make sure that they are generous to the needy. For Jesus, hoarding wealth prevented Jews from the privilege of being ruled by God. The kingdom of God is for those who love their neighbors, not for those who despise them. Love for neighbor has practical outcomes. This is the heart of the message of the prophets. The Qur'an testifies to the centrality of a generous spirit that gives to those who are in financial need. The Prophet Muhammad declared to the Meccans in Q89:17–20, one of his early messages, "You do

not honor orphans; **18** You do not encourage each other to feed the poor; **19** You devour inheritance greedily; **20** and you love wealth to excess."
Then a summary of what a Muslim should be comes in Q2:177, a late message of the Prophet to the Muslim community in Medina, where Jews had rejected the prophethood of Muhammad because they did not see his message as being in the line of the prophets in their Scriptures:

> Righteousness is not turning your face towards East or West but righteousness is believing in God and the Last Day, the angels, the Book, and the prophets; it is giving wealth out of love for relatives, orphans, poor people, travellers, beggars, and to set slaves free.

The test of true prophethood is proclaiming that those who have should share with those who do not.

Paul: The kingdom of God is characterized by love for God and neighbor. Therefore, those who claim to be under God's rule must demonstrate that they put God and neighbor before themselves. This was the essential message of Jesus. Matthew begins his account of the teaching of Jesus in 5:3 with the saying, "Blessed are the poor in spirit, for theirs is the kingdom of heaven." Only those who are aware of their own poverty before God will be able to love him and only those who are aware of their own wealth before others will be able to love them. This poverty of spirit will be shown in the way that wealth is shared. Later in the block of teaching recorded by Matthew comes Jesus' warning about not showing off when giving to the needy in Matthew 6:1–4:

> Beware of practicing your piety before others in order to be seen by them; for then you have no reward from your Father in heaven. **2** So whenever you give alms, do not sound a trumpet before you, as the hypocrites do in the synagogues and in the streets, so that they may be praised by others. Truly I tell you, they have received their reward. **3** But when you give alms, do not let your left hand know what your right hand is doing, **4** so that your alms may be done in secret; and your Father who sees in secret will reward you.

This emphasis on the reward that God gives is central to Jesus' teaching. In the same message on the mountainside, Jesus urges his disciples to store up treasure not on earth but in heaven, because love for God must be seen in the affairs of everyday life (6:19–20). It is not possible to serve God while seeking wealth, according to Matthew 6:24; "No one can serve two masters; for a slave will either hate the one and love the other, or be devoted to the one and despise the other. You cannot serve God and wealth." It is God who gives wealth, so the true believer is continually grateful for any sustenance that God has provided.

Jesus encouraged his disciples who had given up their regular means of income to go around with him. After the departure of the rich young man who could not forsake his wealth for God, Peter reminded Jesus that unlike the rich young man, the disciples had left everything to follow him. Jesus reassured his disciples in Mark 10:29–30:

> Truly I tell you, there is no one who has left house or brothers or sisters or mother or father or children or fields, for my sake and for the sake of the good news, 30 who will not receive a hundredfold now in this age—houses, brothers and sisters, mothers and children, and fields, with persecutions—and in the age to come eternal life.

Ibrahim: This too was the proclamation of the Prophet Muhammad. There were Jews and Christians in his time who claimed that eternal life was dependent on being a Jew or a Christian. According to Q2:111, they both claimed that Paradise was reserved for members of their own group. But Muhammad told them what God thought of their exclusive ideas in 2:112, "No, whoever turns his face towards God and does what is good will have his reward from his Lord." Thus, it is not membership of a religious body that is essential, but rather true love for God and neighbor. Prophets challenged religious people to focus not on themselves but on the needs of others. Building up wealth in this life might mean forfeiting the experience of the life to come.

The Future Kingdom

Paul: Jesus said a lot about the life to come. Many of his sayings about the kingdom of God relate to the future life. In Mark 9:42–48, Jesus warns his disciples to take care how they live now lest they forfeit eternal life:

> If any of you put a stumbling block before one of these little ones who believe in me, it would be better for you if a great millstone were hung around your neck and you were thrown into the sea. 43 If your hand causes you to stumble, cut it off; it is better for you to enter life maimed than to have two hands and to go to hell, to the unquenchable fire. 45 And if your foot

> causes you to stumble, cut it off; it is better for you to enter life lame than to have two feet and to be thrown into hell. **47** And if your eye causes you to stumble, tear it out; it is better for you to enter the kingdom of God with one eye than to have two eyes and to be thrown into hell, **48** where their worm never dies, and the fire is never quenched.

These are very stern words for his disciples. Self-discipline is essential for those who have set their sights on the kingdom of God. Notice how Jesus contrasts the kingdom of God with hell. He teaches that there are two possible destinations for people. He does not want anyone to think lightly about the future.

Ibrahim: This is a constant theme in the Qur'an too, especially heard in the early messages Muhammad brought to the Meccans. Q90:4–20 echoes the teaching of Jesus you have quoted:

> We have created a human being to bear hardship. **5** Does he think that nobody will be his master? **6** He says, "I have spent wealth extravagantly." **7** Does he think that nobody sees him? **8** Did We not create two eyes for him, **9** a tongue, and a pair of lips, **10** and show him the two paths? **11** But he has not boldly taken the steep path. **12** What is to realize the steep path? **13** Setting free a slave, **14** or giving food in a time of hunger **15** to an orphan who is a relation, **16** or to a poor person who is destitute. **17** Then he will be among those who believe and who encourage each other to persevere and who inspire acts of kindness. **18** These are the companions of the right hand. **19** But those who reject Our signs are the companions of the left hand, **20** and the Fire will engulf them.

The Day of Judgment will separate those who practice good deeds from those who are pre-occupied with building up their own wealth and position.

Paul: Jesus refers to the kingdom of God coming at a time when people are not prepared. In Matthew 25:1–13, he tells a story about ten young women who have been invited to a wedding. Five of them brought oil for their lamps, but five did not. Since the bridegroom took such a long time to arrive, the ten girls fell asleep. But when a voice announced his arrival at midnight, the five without oil asked the other five to share their oil. They were told to go get their own oil, and while they were looking for it, the wedding banquet started. On returning, the five "foolish" girls were denied access by the bridegroom who said he didn't know them. Jesus commented in verse 13, "Keep awake therefore, for you know neither the day nor the hour."

Here the failure to enter the future kingdom is the result of lethargy and negligence, but the foolish young women symbolize the people of God who take their family inheritance for granted. They think that being invited to the kingdom will automatically grant them a share in the good things God has in store. Another story, in Matthew 8:5–13, makes this clear:

> When he entered Capernaum, a centurion came to him, appealing to him **6** and saying, "Lord, my servant is lying at home paralyzed, in terrible distress." **7** And he said to him, "I will come and cure him." **8** The centurion answered, "Lord, I am not worthy to have you come under my roof; but only speak the word, and my servant will be healed. **9** For I also am a man under authority, with soldiers under me; and I say to one, 'Go,' and he goes, and to another, 'Come,' and he comes, and to my slave, 'Do this,' and the slave does it." **10** When Jesus heard him, he was amazed and said to those who followed him, "Truly I tell you, in no one in Israel have I found such faith. **11** I tell you, many will come from east and west and will eat with Abraham and Isaac and Jacob in the kingdom of heaven, **12** while the heirs of the kingdom will be thrown into the outer darkness, where there will be weeping and gnashing of teeth." **13** And to the centurion Jesus said, "Go; let it be done for you according to your faith." And the servant was healed in that hour.

Jesus very pointedly warns his Jewish hearers that their inheritance will not suffice for entry into the future life of the kingdom. The picture of Jews being excluded from the kingdom is stark. Clearly, he is teaching that faith is essential to membership of the kingdom. Those who come to God expecting him to act already demonstrate that they are under God's rule and desire to live under his control. While Jesus did not focus his teaching on people outside the Jewish community, he welcomed those who came to him, such as this Roman army officer.

The Romans and God's Rule

Ibrahim: This story introduces another theme that we began to discuss, the extent to which Jesus taught forgiveness of enemies. Here he overlooks the fact that this soldier represented opposition to God's rule. He is very generously accepting that the officer had faith in God to heal his child without saying anything about what this man's status means for the kingdom of God. Notice that Jesus does not call the centurion to leave the army and follow him with his other disciples. Did Jesus really think that this man could continue as an army officer and be a member of the kingdom of God? The way the story is told suggests that Jesus was thinking about the future life rather than the present. He speaks about non-Jews coming from the four corners of the world to join the great fathers of the Jewish nation—Abraham, Isaac, and Jacob—in the kingdom of heaven. That this is a clear reference to the next life rather than this present life is proved from the way he quotes from the Scriptures. He must have had Psalm 47:7–9 in mind here:

> Clap your hands, all you peoples; shout to God with loud songs of joy. 2 For the Lord, the Most High, is awesome, a great king over all the earth. 3 He subdued peoples under us, and nations under our feet. 4 He chose our heritage for us, the pride of Jacob whom he loves. (Selah) 5 God has gone up with a shout, the LORD with the sound of a trumpet. 6 Sing praises to God, sing praises; sing praises to our King, sing praises. 7 For God is the king of all the earth; sing praises with a psalm. 8 God is king over the nations; God sits on his holy throne. 9 The princes of the peoples gather as the people of the God of Abraham. For the shields of the earth belong to God; he is highly exalted.

When the song writer composed this piece he surely did not think that the hostile nations would come to Jerusalem and make peace with Israel, singing songs to the One True God and repenting of worshipping false gods. No, the contrary was the case. Israel was a tiny nation surrounded by stronger nations that despised their God. The composer holds out the hope that in the future these enemies of God would submit to him. They certainly were not doing it when he wrote! It's the same with Jesus. He clearly did not expect the Roman Emperor to come to Jerusalem and worship the One True God, just because one officer in the Roman army had faith in Israel's God! The commentator on the Psalms, John Goldingay, believes that "the nobles of the peoples were compelled to acknowledge Yahweh along with Israel" and that this submission is a "sign of Yahweh's reign."[2] So there would come a time in the future when the rebellious nations would be forced to submit to God.

---

2. Goldingay, *Psalms 42–89*, 80.

In other words, one Roman soldier has faith in God, but the rest of the Roman Imperial machine is unaffected. Jesus' attitude to the Romans in his own lifetime was ambivalent in the Gospels. He seemed to accept that Roman rule was inevitable, according to Mark 12:13–17:

> Then they sent to him some Pharisees and some Herodians to trap him in what he said. 14 And they came and said to him, "Teacher, we know that you are sincere, and show deference to no one; for you do not regard people with partiality, but teach the way of God in accordance with truth. Is it lawful to pay taxes to the emperor, or not? 15 Should we pay them, or should we not?" But knowing their hypocrisy, he said to them, "Why are you putting me to the test? Bring me a denarius and let me see it." 16 And they brought one. Then he said to them, "Whose head is this, and whose title?" They answered, "The emperor's." 17 Jesus said to them, "Give to the emperor the things that are the emperor's, and to God the things that are God's." And they were utterly amazed at him.

Jesus is not willing to publicly criticize the Romans. He even separates God's rule from that of the Romans. Is he saying that God rules the heart but Caesar controls the economy? Can he really be reported accurately when he excludes God from politics? The Gospel writers appear to portray Jesus as critical of Jews who do not properly live under the One True God who they believe in. Yet he seems to be soft on the Romans who clearly defy the One True God by worshipping many deities. This is admitted by Gospel scholars. Morna Hooker, in her commentary on this passage, says, "Jesus denies that men will come to God's Kingdom by destroying Caesar's."[3]

Paul: You have touched on a very significant aspect of Jesus' teaching. The incident about paying taxes to Caesar comes after Jesus forced traders to leave the temple in Jerusalem. Mark 11:15–18 reports how this intervention in the affairs of the temple incited the Jewish leaders to want to kill him:

> Then they came to Jerusalem. And he entered the temple and began to drive out those who were selling and those who were buying in the temple, and he overturned the tables of the money changers and the seats of those who sold doves; 16 and he would not allow anyone to carry anything through the temple. 17 He was teaching and saying, "Is it not written, 'My house shall be

---

3. Hooker, *Mark*, 281.

called a house of prayer for all the nations'? But you have made it a den of robbers." 18 And when the chief priests and the scribes heard it, they kept looking for a way to kill him; for they were afraid of him, because the whole crowd was spellbound by his teaching.

While Jesus did not teach violence against the ruling Roman authorities, he certainly acted with a measure of violence in the temple, which was under Jewish control. The sale of animals in the forecourt was probably introduced by Caiaphas around 30 CE and caused heated debate within leading Jewish circles. Presumably there would have been Jews who agreed with Jesus' action. The use of the forecourt as a market prevented the gentiles from having a place of prayer. So, the cleansing of the space for gentiles to pray is an act of judgment on the temple authorities. Richard France points out that, "The protest is directed not so much against the traders themselves but against the priestly establishment who had allowed them to operate within the sacred area."[4] Is this then what Jesus meant by giving to God what belongs to him? Dominic Crossan argues that in fact this anti-trading action shows that Jesus was opposed to the whole establishment of the Jewish nation working in collusion with the Romans. Indirectly, Jesus was attacking Roman rule by attacking Jewish rule. "But his life in and enactment of the Kingdom of God, placed him on a deliberate collision course with the Kingdom of Rome."[5]

On the other hand, Jesus denies the possibility of a theocratic state. This was the longing of many in Israel. Richard France understands Jesus to be favorable to Roman rule with respect to the granting of freedom to Jews to worship their God. "Jesus asserts that it is possible to pay one's dues both to the emperor and to God, to be both a dutiful citizen and a loyal servant of God."[6] The question remains; Is there a time when disciples must resist Caesar because he has usurped God's place? "Jesus' answer assumes that the Roman government under Tiberius was not yet, as it would become later, in opposition to God."[7]

Ibrahim: You are arguing that the day might have come when Jesus would seek to overthrow ungodly Roman rule? Was it just a matter of time before this would have happened? But of course, the story in the

---

4. France, *Matthew*, 784.
5. Crossan and Reed, *Excavating Jesus*, 222.
6. France, *Matthew*, 830.
7. Ibid., 831.

Gospels ends in the Roman governor putting Jesus to death to please the Jewish leaders. I suppose you could set up a parallel with Muhammad who lived under persecution in his home town, Mecca, before departing for Medina to the north. It was only at the point of leaving Mecca that God revealed to him that it was now time to fight against those polytheists who had rejected the message that there is only One God. Jesus, on the other hand, was not able to fight his enemies at the time of his arrest and trial. Just like the followers of Muhammad in Mecca, the disciples of Jesus were probably too few to make a rebellion. But I would say that Christians have been content to use force against their enemies in the ensuing centuries. They have found a way to love their neighbors by defending them against their enemies.

Paul: This comparison of Jesus and Muhammad concerning fighting enemies is worth pursuing because it has been a matter of contention between Christians and Muslims over the years. The earliest life of Muhammad by Ibn Ishaq says that Muhammad was still living in Mecca when he received a message from God permitting him to fight against the Quraysh, his own tribe, who dominated life in Mecca. This was Q22:39–40, "Those who have been attacked are given permission to fight back because they have been wronged, and truly God has the power to help them: 40 Those who have been thrown out of their homes without cause only for saying, 'Our Lord is God.'" Ibn Ishaq comments:

> When Quraysh became insolent towards God and rejected His gracious purpose, accused His prophet of lying, and ill-treated and exiled those who served Him and proclaimed His unity, believed in His prophet, and held fast to His religion, He gave permission to His apostle to fight and to protect himself against those who wronged them and treated them badly.[8]

Only once the Muslims emigrated from Mecca to Medina did fighting against the Quraysh begin. Ibn Ishaq paints a picture of Muhammad rallying his troops to attack a Quraysh caravan returning to Mecca:

> Then the apostle went forth to the people and incited them saying, "By God in whose hand is the soul of Muhammad, no man will be slain this day fighting against them with steadfast courage advancing not retreating but God will cause him to enter Paradise."[9]

---

8. Ibn Ishaq, *Life of Muhammad*, 212.

9. Ibid., 300.

This sharpens the message of Q2:216–18, which says that the Muslims must fight the Meccans who are obdurate in opposing the truth:

> Fighting is prescribed for you, even though it is distasteful to you.... 217 They will not stop fighting you until they force you to renounce your religion if they can. Whoever among you renounces his religion and dies as an unbeliever, their deeds will be of no avail in this life and the next life. They will be the companions of the Fire, and there they will stay. 218 But those who believed, and those who emigrated and fought on behalf of God, are the ones who hope in the mercy of God; and God is most forgiving and most merciful.

There is a ring of certainty about Muhammad's speech to the troops that emphasizes that the eternal reward for dying in battle is guaranteed. There is simply no parallel to this in Jesus' teaching. Crossan's summary of the sayings of Jesus about the kingdom of God would be generally accepted by all readers of the Gospels. "The Kingdom of God is a force for nonviolent resistance to the normalcy of both social oppression by class and colonial oppression by Rome."[10] The contrast between the advocacy of non-violent resistance by Jesus and of active violence by Muhammad could not be plainer.

Ibrahim: Yes, but Jesus did not have the opportunity to advocate violence. He was not in command of a force that could have made an impact on Roman rule. The stakes were simply far too high for an insurrection. Others had attempted this and had been executed. He most probably decided that a more passive approach was the most effective way to resist godless authority. Adela Collins mentions that, "in 6 or 7 CE Judas, a Galilean, called upon his countrymen to refuse to pay tax to the Romans and to recognize only God as their ruler."[11] He suffered the consequences at the hands of the Roman government. Jesus must have looked at Judas and said to himself that the time was not right for open rebellion against Roman rule. So he taught passive resistance until the day when a more active campaign could succeed. This is recognized in the last book of the New Testament, where Rome is depicted as being thrown down by God. What fascinates me as a Muslim is the picture of Jesus riding a white horse and striking the nations with his sword. If the Book of Revelation was written in the final decade of the first century

---

10. Crossan and Reed, *Excavating Jesus*, 179.
11. Collins, *Mark*, 552.

during a fierce persecution of the Christians by the Roman Emperor, Domitian, then Richard France's argument is sound, that the time might come when the Roman Empire became actively hostile to Jesus and his followers. In that light the teaching changes. Jesus becomes a military figure of great power. Revelation 19:11–21 is an astonishingly vivid vision of Jesus at war with Rome:

> Then I saw heaven opened, and there was a white horse! Its rider is called Faithful and True, and in righteousness he judges and makes war. **12** His eyes are like a flame of fire, and on his head are many diadems; and he has a name inscribed that no one knows but himself. **13** He is clothed in a robe dipped in blood, and his name is called The Word of God. **14** And the armies of heaven, wearing fine linen, white and pure, were following him on white horses. **15** From his mouth comes a sharp sword with which to strike down the nations, and he will rule them with a rod of iron; he will tread the wine press of the fury of the wrath of God the Almighty. **16** On his robe and on his thigh he has a name inscribed, "King of kings and Lord of lords." **17** Then I saw an angel standing in the sun, and with a loud voice he called to all the birds that fly in midheaven, "Come, gather for the great supper of God, **18** to eat the flesh of kings, the flesh of captains, the flesh of the mighty, the flesh of horses and their riders—flesh of all, both free and slave, both small and great." **19** Then I saw the beast and the kings of the earth with their armies gathered to make war against the rider on the horse and against his army. **20** And the beast was captured, and with it the false prophet who had performed in its presence the signs by which he deceived those who had received the mark of the beast and those who worshiped its image. These two were thrown alive into the lake of fire that burns with sulfur. **21** And the rest were killed by the sword of the rider on the horse, the sword that came from his mouth; and all the birds were gorged with their flesh.

This is a terrifying scene! If the church accepted this passage as Scripture inspired by God's Spirit, then Christians need to acknowledge that the non-violent Jesus of the Gospels has become the violent king out to destroy those who oppose God's rule. Surely there should be no desire to excise the Book of Revelation from the New Testament without good reason.

Paul: Well, the vision in the Book of Revelation relates to the end of time when a new Jerusalem will descend to earth in which there is no war, but only peace. Furthermore, it is possible that the blood on Jesus' robes is not that of his enemies, but his own blood shed to redeem them. We should return to discuss the end times later, but for now I would like to continue the comparison of Jesus' advocacy of non-violent protest against the authorities and Muhammad's establishment of his rule in Arabia by the use of force. Ibn Ishaq says that Muhammad "took part personally in twenty-seven raids,"[12] and that "he actually fought in nine engagements."[13] These raids were generally against polytheistic Arab tribes, but some of them were attacks on Arab tribes that had embraced Judaism. According to Ibn Ishaq, the first of the Jewish tribes to "break their agreement with the apostle" were the B. Qaynuqaʿ who were part of the population in Medina. The apostle "besieged them until they surrendered unconditionally." However, he did not punish them.[14] A second Jewish tribe, the B. al-Nadir, beyond Medina, were asked to contribute to Muhammad's cause, but plotted to assassinate him. On being defeated, they asked Muhammad to let them go into exile carrying any of their property they could on camels and he agreed.[15] A third Jewish tribe, the B. Qurayza, another Jewish section of the Medinan population, were attacked for insulting the apostle. After twenty-five days of siege, Muhammad appointed Saʿd b. Muʿadh to decide what to do with them. He said, "I give judgment that the men should be killed, the property divided, and the women and children taken as captives," to which Muhammad replied, "You have given the judgment of Allah above the seven heavens."[16] After the surrender of the B. Qurayza, "the apostle went out to the market of Medina and dug trenches in it. Then he sent for them and struck off their heads in those trenches. . . . There were 600 or 700 in all, though some put the figure as high as 800 or 900."[17] Ibn Ishaq says that this story is mentioned in Q33. He is probably referring to Q33:26-27:

> Those People of the Book who gave aid to the unbelievers, God took down from their strongholds and threw terror into their hearts. Some of them you killed and some you took captive. 27 He made you inherit their land, their houses, their possessions; a land you had not set foot on. God has power over everything.

12. Ibn Ishaq, *Life of Muhammad*, 659.
13. Ibid., 660.
14. Ibid., 363.
15. Ibid., 437.
16. Ibid., 464.
17. Ibid.

It seems there is an escalation of retribution for Jewish tribes that did not fully support Muhammad's leadership, from forgiveness, to exile, and finally death for the males and captivity for their families. Jesus may have used his tongue against the religious leaders of his time and his body to prevent people trading in the temple courts, but he never executed anyone.

Ibrahim: Let me quote William Montgomery Watt, the leading Christian scholar of the life of Muhammad:

> Some European writers have criticized this sentence [the execution of the men of the B. Qurayza] for what they call its savage and inhuman character. It has to be remembered, however, that in the Arabia of that day when tribes were at war with one another or simply had no agreement, they had no obligations toward one another. . . . The behaviour of the clan during the siege of Medina was regarded as having cancelled their agreement with Muhammad.[18]

He goes on to say that the attitude of these Jews had the potential to undermine the foundation of the Islamic community by giving support to Muhammad's enemies. Those Jews who did not openly oppose him could live in Medina unmolested.[19] In any case, the B. Qurayza had reneged on their agreement to support Muhammad in time of war with men or money or both. By doing so they had become enemies within the camp.

The Muslim writer Adil Salahi believes that Muhammad treated the men of the tribe with justice, "as their own sacred books outline it."[20] He is most likely referring to the incident of the Israelites worshipping the golden calf in Exodus 32. After Moses came down from mount Sinai, he discovered the Israelites dancing around a golden calf. Verses 25 to 29 tell the story of Moses' judgment on the people:

> When Moses saw that the people were running wild (for Aaron had let them run wild, to the derision of their enemies), 26 then Moses stood in the gate of the camp, and said, "Who is on the LORD's side? Come to me!" And all the sons of Levi gathered around him. 27 He said to them, "Thus says the LORD, the God of Israel, 'Put your sword on your side, each of you! Go back and forth from gate to gate throughout the camp, and each of you

---

18. Watt, *Muhammad Prophet and Statesman*, 173.
19. Ibid., 175.
20. Salahi, *Muhammad: Man and Prophet*, 472.

kill your brother, your friend, and your neighbor.'" 28 The sons of Levi did as Moses commanded, and about three thousand of the people fell on that day. 29 Moses said, "Today you have ordained yourselves for the service of the LORD, each one at the cost of a son or a brother, and so have brought a blessing on yourselves this day."

The execution of 3,000 Israelites by the tribe of Levi is a sober reminder of the need to purify rebellion among those who have agreed together to serve the One True God. Notice that Moses congratulates the Levites for serving God without sentiment toward those who had to be punished with death. He tells them that they have been blessed by God for being obedient to this tough command.

Paul: But there is a difference between the execution of the Jewish tribe in Medina and the execution of those who worshipped the golden calf. In the former case, Jews were put to death for insulting the Prophet Muhammad and presumably not supporting him during the siege of Medina by the Meccans. In the latter case, Jews were put to death for forsaking the worship of God for an idol. There is no suggestion in Medina that the B. Qurayza had given up the worship of God. They were called the People of the Book, who were recognized as not being polytheists. Surely it is very significant that when the Arabs conquered the Middle East soon after the death of Muhammad they gave rights to the People of the Book to maintain their own community life without interference as long as they paid an annual tax. The followers of Muhammad were able to accommodate Jews and Christians as fellow worshippers of God and did not expect them to join in military campaigns. In other words, the treatment of the B. Qurayza by Muhammad was not copied because it was counter-productive to effective rule by an Arab Muslim minority over a largely Christian population dotted with Jewish groups. Morna Hooker's argument that, according to Jesus, the kingdom of God is not established by destroying Caesar's kingdom, can be applied to the followers of Muhammad, who believed that the rule of God is not established by destroying Jewish or Christian communities.

Ibrahim: It is true that the People of the Book are not regarded as polytheists. The Qur'an regularly makes this point. Muhammad observed this reality in his dealings with Jews and Christians generally. The issue of the B. Qurayza was exceptional. The followers of Muhammad understood this profoundly. That is why they left Jews and Christians free to govern their own affairs according to their own laws after they conquered Syria, Egypt, and Iraq. They didn't invent this idea, it came from the revelation of God himself to Muhammad. After the B. Qurayza affair, Muhammad was ready to attack Mecca in 631 when God told him how to deal with polytheists, hypocritical Muslims, and the People of the Book. Q9:29 outlines how he should treat the latter: "Fight those of the People of the Book who do not (truly) believe in God and the Last Day, who do not forbid what God and His Messenger have forbidden, who do not obey the rule of justice, until they pay the tax promptly and agree to submit." The tax allowed Jews and Christians to keep their traditions so long as they did not actively conspire against Muslim rule. The fact that there was no repeat of the B. Qurayza incident shows how unique that was in the life of Muhammad and in the history of Muslim rule.

Paul: I would agree that generally Muslim rulers allowed Jews and Christians to live their lives without fear of execution. Nevertheless, the payment of the *jizya* tax was a sign of second-class status and the reality that only Muslims could actually govern. Jews and Christians were simply excluded from power. The kingdom of God was administered by Muslims and the People of the Book were their servants. They were not permitted to criticize Muslim rule, or to attempt to persuade Muslims to embrace their faith. Rather there was a constant stream of Christians who became Muslims to avoid second-class status resulting in Muslims becoming a majority in Egypt, Syria, and Iraq by the time the Mongols invaded in the thirteenth century. It is interesting that Jews did not convert to Islam in the same way but maintained their distinct community life as they had done under majority Christian rule.

Ibrahim: I am glad you can acknowledge the longstanding tradition of Muslims to grant freedom to Jews and Christians to deal with the legal affairs of their communities. Christians have found it very tempting to try to enforce their rule over Muslims, and there is a tragic catalogue of violence committed against Muslims by Christians. I will give just two examples. The third crusade from 1189 to 1192 was intended to recover Jerusalem from Salah al-Din who had annihilated the crusader army and decisively ended European control in 1187 at the battle of the Horns of Hattin. Salah al-Din required all European inhabitants to leave, but he allowed native Christians to remain so long as they paid the *jizya*. Thus, the Islamic counter-offensive was targeted at the foreign invaders, rather than at Christians as such.

A Christian counter-offensive was led by two kings, Richard I of England and Philip of France. The English wore white crosses and the

French wore red ones. They failed to deliver Jerusalem, but managed to capture Acre in 1191. The killing of Muslim prisoners by the victorious crusaders is told by Baha' al-Din in his biography of Salah al-Din. Baha' al-Din reports that the Muslims had agreed to surrender Acre in return for free exit from the city. When Salah al-Din—who had come to aid them, and was outside the city—prevaricated over agreeing the terms of the surrender, Richard decided to execute the captured Muslim fighters in full view of Salah al-Din:

> They brought up the Muslim prisoners whose martyrdom God had ordained, more than three thousand men in chains. They fell on them as one man and slaughtered them in cold blood, with sword and lance. . . . From then on the Muslims did not spare enemy prisoners, except for well-known persons and strong men who could be put to work.[21]

My second example is much more recent, from the civil war in the Balkans in the 1990s. In July 1995, Orthodox Christian Serbs put to death more than 8,000 Bosnian Muslim men and boys at Srebrenica, even though a United Nations Dutch contingent was supposed to be guarding the Muslims. The Dutch soldiers watched the Serbs separate women and young children for expulsion from men and boys for killing. According to *The Observer* newspaper:

> The mass murder was later described at The Hague by Judge Fouad Riad as "written on the darkest pages of history." A sole "executioner" to turn prosecutor's evidence at the trials, Dražen Erdemovic, described how death squads asked to sit down— they were so tired, killing wave upon wave, busload after busload, of men and boys.[22]

Christian contempt for the life of Muslims unable to defend themselves is a thread running through history from the Crusades of the past and the present.

Paul: Unfortunately, both those calling themselves Christians and Muslims have committed atrocities. Just to even up the historical record, the Turks displaced the Armenian population in 1915 leading to the deaths of 1.5 million unarmed civilians. In April 1915, Armenian leaders were arrested in Istanbul and the Armenian population was ordered to be

---

21. Baha' al-Din, *Biography of Salah al-Din*, in Gabrieli, *Arab Historians*, 224.

22. Hartmann and Vulliamy, "How Britain and the US Decided to Abandon Srebrenica to Its Fate," *The Observer*, Saturday 4 July 2015.

exiled to Syria. Mehmed Reshid, governor of Diyarbakir province, oversaw the looting of property and the mass killing of Armenians. When he was asked to justify what he had done he said:

> My Turkish identity won out over my profession. I thought: we must destroy them before they destroy us. If you ask me how I as a doctor could commit murder, my answer is simple: the Armenians had become dangerous microbes in the body of this country. And surely it is a doctor's duty to kill bacteria?[23]

Then the destruction of the Twin towers in New York on 11 September, 2001 by suicide pilots with Saudi Arabian nationality resulting in the deaths of nearly 3,000 people is the most notorious recent example of Muslims attacking civilians. According to the BBC:

> Suspicion soon fell on the radical Sunni Islamist group, al-Qaeda ("The Base" in Arabic) founded in 1988 and led by Saudi-born Osama Bin Laden. There was good reason for this. Although difficult to confirm, it is thought al-Qaeda's involvement in world terrorism can be traced back to 1993, with the first World Trade Center bombing.[24]

Many other suicide bombings have taken place by Islamists since then and many civilians have lost their lives.

The rule of God is ultimately about submission to him. But Muslims disagree with Christians about what God wants us to submit to. God spoke through the prophets before the appearance of Jesus, but there is a strong testimony from the followers of Jesus that he was the definitive Word of God. Muslims too, call Jesus the word of God, a title not given to any other prophet. Let's turn our attention to this common word between Christians and Muslims in the next discussion.

---

23. See Spencer, "Armenian Massacres," *The Telegraph*, 24 April 2015.

24. BBC History website, "The 9/11 terrorist attacks," http://www.bbc.co.uk/history/events/the_september_11th_terrorist_attacks.

five

Jesus, Word and Spirit of God

PAUL BEGINS BY EXPLORING the connection between John the Baptist and Jesus, who were both messengers of God, according to both the Gospels and the Qur'an. The Fourth Gospel shows that Jesus was the Word of God, whom John the Baptist introduced to Israel. Ibrahim points out that the Qur'an calls both John the Baptist and Jesus "a word from God" and goes on to argue that all messengers of God brought his word. Jesus was not exceptional in this respect. Paul suggests that because Jesus brought the Gospel, according to the Qur'an, he did bring a distinctive message that no other prophet brought. Ibrahim suggests that the Fourth Gospel is highly dramatic and does not reflect the other three Gospels, which may be closer to the historical record. Paul believes that the Fourth Gospel comes from the Johannine community that shared a special language. Ibrahim argues that the Qur'an calls Jesus "a word from God" because Jesus is given the Gospel, just as Moses was given the Torah.

The teaching of the Johannine writings in the New Testament about Jesus as the Word of God is discussed. Paul shows how the Word became human and was experienced by the disciples. He was also experienced by Nicodemus the Jewish leader and by a Samaritan woman. While Nicodemus could not see who he was, the "heretical" woman believed. Ibrahim continues to argue that Jesus was only different from other messengers of God in degree. Moses is referred to by Muslims as the one to whom God spoke directly. Paul points out that the Word of God always existed, according to the Gospel of John, and that this makes Jesus unique among human messengers of God. Ibrahim again denies that the Synoptic Gospels make such a claim and that history is on their side.

Then Paul mentions that the Qur'an calls Jesus "a spirit from God" and expands on Jesus' relationship to God's Spirit. Ibrahim interprets this title as a reference to Jesus' miraculous conception. In any case, Jesus baptizes other people in God's Spirit, so he is not uniquely endowed with the Spirit. Paul points out that it is Jesus who has been given the authority and power to baptize with the Spirit, and surely the Qur'an reflects this authority. Ibrahim reminds Paul not to elevate Jesus to divine status, for that is the burden of the criticism of Christians in the Qur'an. Paul points out how Christian theologians in the eighth and ninth centuries tried to explain the Trinity to Muslims through these titles given to Jesus, a word from God and a spirit from him.

Jesus and John the Baptist

Paul: Let us explore the nature of prophecy and how Jesus understood his role as bringing the word of God. In Matthew 11:1–19 Jesus compares himself to John the Baptist, who has been put in prison by the Jewish ruler Herod. John sent his disciples to ask Jesus if he truly was the one who John was preparing the way for. After Jesus told them to return to John and report the healings he has performed and the good news he has proclaimed to the poor, he turned to the crowd and gave his assessment of John:

> As they went away, Jesus began to speak to the crowds about John: "What did you go out into the wilderness to look at? A reed shaken by the wind? 8 What then did you go out to see? Someone dressed in soft robes? Look, those who wear soft robes are in royal palaces. 9 What then did you go out to see? A prophet? Yes, I tell you, and more than a prophet. 10 This is the one about whom it is written, "See, I am sending my messenger ahead of you, who will prepare your way before you." 11 Truly I tell you, among those born of women no one has arisen greater than John the Baptist; yet the least in the kingdom of heaven is greater than he. 12 From the days of John the Baptist until now the kingdom of heaven has suffered violence, and the violent take it by force. 13 For all the prophets and the law prophesied until John came; 14 and if you are willing to accept it, he is Elijah who is to come. 15 Let anyone with ears listen!

Notice how Jesus includes John along with the prophets of Israel. But he intimates that John is even more significant than most of them, because he fulfills the prophecy of the last writing prophet in Israel, Malachi, who reports the word of God in Malachi 3:1, "See, I am sending my messenger to prepare the way before me, and the LORD whom you seek will suddenly come to his temple. The messenger of the covenant in whom you delight—indeed, he is coming, says the LORD of hosts." Therefore, John is the prophet who introduces the coming of *God himself* to his temple in Jerusalem. Jesus calls John a new Elijah, the famous prophet who challenged Ahab king of Israel to turn back to God after deviating toward polytheism. This too was prophesied by Malachi in Malachi 4:5–6:

> Lo, I will send you the prophet Elijah before the great and terrible day of the LORD comes. **6** He will turn the hearts of parents to their children and the hearts of children to their parents, so that I will not come and strike the land with a curse.

According to Jesus, John is the announcer of the arrival of the kingdom of God in a way that is unique among the prophets of Israel. John not only prophesied the coming of God, he actually lived to see God coming in Jesus himself.

Ibrahim: The Gospel writers tell widely different stories about John. Matthew has the account you have discussed. Mark just has the story about the baptism of Jesus by John and a long explanation as to why John was beheaded by Herod. Luke has the prophetic indictment by John of the Jewish leaders that we have looked at already. John has his own peculiar view of John the Baptist, who denies that he is the new Elijah in John 1:21, tells the crowd that Jesus is the Lamb of God who takes away the sin of the world in 1:29, and that Jesus is the Son of God in 1:34. Now it's clear that the Fourth Gospel has developed John the Baptist into a spokesperson for the theology of the writer or writers. But just how could John the Baptist proclaim that Jesus would be sacrificed as a lamb for the sins of the people? When this kind of statement is compared with everything John says in the other three Gospels there is no doubt whatsoever that the real John the Baptist never believed such a thing about Jesus. As for calling Jesus the Son of God, this is another dramatic addition to John's language in the other Gospels. What the Fourth Gospel has done is to retell the story of Jesus like a piece of theatre with characters who appear in the other Gospels becoming quite different and declaring their faith in Jesus in rather extravagant terms. In the final analysis, we don't arrive at John the Baptist by going through the Fourth Gospel.

Paul: I agree that the Gospel of John is rather different from the other three Gospels, but the Fourth Gospel is written so that readers will come to have faith in Jesus. There is a distinctive language that is seen also in the letters of John and in the Book of Revelation. In other words, the story of Jesus is written with a vocabulary and style that is unique to these documents. The Johannine community in which these pieces of writing emerged was obviously familiar with the special vocabulary, but other sections of the early church did not use some of their language. This is especially the case with the way that Jesus is called the Word of God in John 1:14, the first letter of John 1:1, and Revelation 19:13. Jesus is also called the Lamb of God in Revelation 5, where he is pictured as a wounded lamb yet fully alive in God's presence, and is hailed by an uncountable crowd of angels as "the Lamb." These titles for Jesus are not used by any other apostolic writers. There is a heightened sense of drama in the Johannine style.

Ibrahim: So you are acknowledging that there is dramatic license in the portrait of John the Baptist in the Fourth Gospel, and that if we want to get at who John the Baptist really might have been we can dispense with these extravagant statements that John was supposed to have made. The problem of claiming that the New Testament records actual events lies right here. You are left picking and choosing which stories fit with your preconception of what happened. I find it interesting that New Testament scholars say they are concerned to uncover the history of Jesus, but end up basing their history on the faith of the followers of Jesus who create alternative accounts of Jesus and those he encountered. The four different pictures of John the Baptist show just how little concern the writers of the Gospels had for the real John the Baptist. He becomes a tool in their hands for showing Jesus to be what they believe him to be, not what John believed him to be.

Paul: Perhaps we can agree that the historical record is not definitive. Historians try to get back to a basic story that is built on by the different Gospel writers. With respect to John the Baptist, it is generally agreed that he was baptizing Jews in the river Jordan, that he had a following long after his execution by Herod, and that he declared the coming judgment of God on his wayward people, Israel. They also agree that Jesus came to John to be baptized in the Jordan. James Dunn summarizes the relationship between the Baptist's teaching and that of Jesus:

> The Baptist saw the present only as opportunity to flee from the wrath to come. Jesus saw the present as already manifesting the graciousness of God. He did not denounce or abandon John's

expectation of judgment. But it was judgment prompted by grace.[1]

However, let's turn to the special language of the Fourth Gospel to explore this difference between John the Baptist and Jesus. In John 1:6–9, the Baptist is introduced as the one who announces the coming of Jesus, just as in the other Gospels:

> There was a man sent from God, whose name was John. 7 He came as a witness to testify to the light, so that all might believe through him. 8 He himself was not the light, but he came to testify to the light. 9 The true light, which enlightens everyone, was coming into the world.

In 1:15 John speaks about the one who was coming as "ranking ahead of him" and in the presence of Jesus who he has baptized, John says in 1:31, "I came baptizing with water for this reason, that he might be revealed to Israel." According to the Fourth Gospel, John the Baptist recognized that Jesus was in a different category to himself in the purposes of God. John was the one who introduced Jesus to the people, who opened up Jesus' ministry to Israel, and who would not himself be a part of Jesus' team. The Fourth Gospel makes this last point very visible by including an interrogation of the Baptist by priests from Jerusalem who had come out to the Jordan river to ask him who he was. Was he the Messiah, or Elijah? The Baptist replied in 1:23 by quoting words of Isaiah 40:3, "I am the voice of one crying out in the wilderness, 'Make straight the way of the LORD.'" When they asked him why he was baptizing people he answered in 1:26–27, "I baptize with water. Among you stands one whom you do not know, 27 the one who is coming after me; I am not worthy to untie the thong of his sandal." Therefore, the Baptist sees Jesus as having an impact way beyond anything that he himself might have because Jesus represented God in a way that the Baptist could not.

Ibrahim: According to the Qur'an 3:38, Zechariah, the father of John the Baptist was praying for a child even though his wife was advanced in years and was barren. While he was praying, angels said to him in 3:39, "God gives you good news of John, confirming a word from God." Then in 3:45, angels said to Mary, "Mary, God announces the news of a word from Him: his name is the Messiah, Jesus, the son of Mary." The connection between John the Baptist and Jesus is the expression, "a word from God." John's role is to "confirm" Jesus' status as "a word from God,"

---

1. Dunn, *Jesus Remembered*, 455.

but there is no developed story in the Qur'an about how John confirmed Jesus.

Paul: Maybe the Qur'an is reflecting the Gospel accounts of John the Baptist in this summary. I find it very interesting that the Qur'an is more concerned with the miraculous conceptions of John and Jesus than with the connection between them as adults. The role of the angels as messengers of God takes center stage while the actual preaching of John is disregarded, since their "word" is more significant than his "word." Indeed, the references to John in the Qur'an are so slight that it is not possible to get a picture of what he did as a prophet.

Ibrahim: John is not alone among the prophets in this respect. The Qur'an lists several prophets in 6:83–89; Abraham, Isaac, Jacob, Noah, David, Solomon, Job, Joseph, Moses, Aaron, Zachariah, John, Jesus, Elijah, Ishmael, Elisha, Jonah, and Lot. Like John, the work of several of these prophets is not described in any detail. Only the prophetic work of Abraham, Moses, and Jesus is narrated at any length. This is because these three prophets are held to be the most significant ones. To them Scripture was given which was not revealed to the other prophets. Q87:19 refers to "the scrolls of Abraham and Moses," which contain the message that God wants the Prophet Muhammad to proclaim. Q53:36–54 gives much greater detail about the content of these writings given to Abraham and Moses. God speaks to Muhammad about a man who turned away from the truth:

> Does he not know what is in the scrolls of Moses 37 and of Abraham who was faithful? 38 No bearer of burdens should bear the burden of another. 39 A human being will only have what he has worked for. 40 His work will be seen. 41 Then he will be rewarded with a perfect reward. 42 The ultimate goal is your Lord. 43 It is He who makes people laugh and weep. 44 It is He who causes death and gives life. 45 He created pairs of male and female 46 from ejaculated sperm. 47 From Him will come a new creation. 48 It is He who gives wealth and possessions. 49 He is the Lord of Sirius. 50 It was He who destroyed ancient ʿAd 51 and Thamud, and who did not restore them; 52 and the people of Noah before them. They were exceedingly evil and oppressive. 53 He brought cities to ruin 54 and covered them completely with the ruins.

There were written Scriptures that contained all this and the Jews were familiar with them. That is why they are repeatedly called the People of the Book in the Qur'an and are continually challenged to consult their

Scriptures to see that the message brought by Muhammad conforms to what they already have. Jesus also was given Scripture, according to Q5:46:

> We sent Jesus, son of Mary, in their footsteps, to confirm the Torah that had been sent before him. We gave him the Gospel in which is guidance and light, (a confirmation of the Torah that had been sent before him), guidance and counsel for those who fear God.

Jesus himself testified to being given Scripture as an infant, according to Q19:30, "He said, 'I am a servant of God. He has given me the Book and made me a prophet.'" Thus, the Qur'an distinguishes the three prophets, Abraham, Moses, and Jesus as recipients of Scripture from God. This implies that all the other prophets, mentioned by name or not, were not granted written Scriptures, but depended on the knowledge of the Scriptures given to Abraham, Moses, and Jesus when proclaiming the message of God. John the Baptist is in this latter category.

Jesus and Moses Given Scripture, according to the Qur'an

Paul: I would like to reflect on this distinction between prophets who proclaimed the word of God and those exceptional men who were given Scripture that was written down and not just proclaimed orally. The Qur'an refers to the People of the Book as having written Scripture in their possession. Q5:65–66 calls on the People of the Book to pay attention to the Scriptures they have been given:

> If only the People of the Book had been faithful and loyal then We would have forgiven them their evildoing and admitted them into the peaceful Garden. **66** If only they had put into practice the Torah and the Gospel and what was revealed to them from their Lord, they would have enjoyed provision from above them and from beneath their feet. A group of them are careful, but most of them commit evil.

It is interesting to observe that the books are called the Torah and the Gospel. These books were given to Moses and Jesus, but the book given to Abraham is hardly mentioned. Q42:13 is one example where Abraham is included along with Moses and Jesus as bringing Scripture:

He has prescribed laws for you in your religion that He had enjoined on Noah, (and which We have revealed to you Muhammad). We had instructed Abraham, Moses and Jesus: 'Hold firm to the religion and do not become divided over it.'

Later in verse 15, Muhammad is instructed to speak to the People of the Book, "I believe in the Book that God has sent down, and I am commanded to maintain justice between you. God is our Lord and your Lord." However, the book of Moses appears to be more prominent than that of Abraham. The two books of Moses and Jesus are mentioned together several times. Q48:29 speaks of the way believers are described in these two books:

> This is their likeness in the Torah and their likeness in the Gospel—like a seed that puts out its shoot, becomes strong, thickens, and stands straight on its stem, bringing joy to the sowers. This makes the unbelievers angry with them. To those who believe and do righteous deeds God has promised forgiveness and a great reward.

The Torah is noted as being studied by the Jews in Q5:44–45:

> We revealed the Torah in which is guidance and light. The prophets who had submitted, and the rabbis and the scribes judged the Jews by it, by the Book of God they were entrusted to keep, and to which they were witnesses. Do not be afraid of people—Fear Me. Do not sell My signs for a small price. Those who do not judge by what God has sent down—those people are unbelievers. 45 In it We prescribed for them a life for a life, an eye for an eye, a nose for a nose, an ear for an ear, a tooth for a tooth, an equal wound for a wound. Whoever forgoes this it will serve as an atonement for himself. Those who do not judge by what God has sent down—those people are evildoers.

Perhaps the book of Abraham is included in the Torah, but this is not made clear. However, the connection between the Torah and the Gospel of Jesus is certainly very clear in Q5:46–47:

> We sent Jesus, son of Mary, in their footsteps, to confirm the Torah that had been sent before him. We gave him the Gospel in which is guidance and light, (a confirmation of the Torah that had been sent before him), guidance and counsel for those who fear God. 47 Let the Gospel people judge by what God has revealed in it. Those who do not judge by what God has revealed are lawbreakers.

The impression given in the Qur'an is that Moses and Jesus were the principle bringers of Scripture among the prophets, and that the Jews especially recognized the book of Moses and the Christians the book of Jesus.

Ibrahim: Yes, this is a fair summary of the teaching of the Qur'an concerning the previous Scriptures to the Qur'an itself. This is seen in Q5:48 where God addresses Muhammad:

> We sent the Book to you with truth, confirming and safeguarding the Book in your possession. Judge between them [the People of the Book] by what God has sent down and do not follow their desires, which deviate from the truth that has come to you. We have prescribed a law and a path to each of you. If God had willed it, he would have made you one people, but He wanted to test you through that which He has given you, so out-do one another in good deeds. You will all return to God and He will make clear to you what you disagreed about.

While the Qur'an is the final authority, it confirms what God has already given to Moses and Jesus, so a proper understanding of the Qur'an will be in accord with a proper understanding of the Torah and the Gospel.

I would like to return to the name given to Jesus by the angels, "a word from God." I believe that this name refers to the Gospel that God gave to Jesus. So just as Moses received God's word to be passed on in written form as the Torah, so Jesus received God's word to be passed on to his followers in written form. From my perspective, this written Gospel is probably reflected in the sayings of Jesus found in the Four Gospels, but it is not in the original state that Jesus received. The Qur'an confirms the message of Gospel of Jesus as originally given, but there is a huge amount of interpretation in the four Gospels that often obscures the clarity of the Gospel. The way that the Fourth Gospel calls Jesus "the Word of God" is a perfect example of this re-interpretation of the original message.

Jesus as the Word of God in the Fourth Gospel

Paul: The Fourth Gospel opens with a reflection on the creation story from Genesis 1:1–3, which announces that:

> In the beginning when God created the heavens and the earth, ² the earth was a formless void and darkness covered the

face of the deep, while a wind from God swept over the face of the waters. 3 Then God said, "Let there be light"; and there was light.

The author of this gospel, traditionally thought to be the "beloved disciple" of Jesus (John 13:21–30; 18:15–18; 19:26–27; 21:7, 20), sees the Word of God as being involved in the work of creating the world in John 1:1–5:

> In the beginning was the Word, and the Word was with God, and the Word was God. 2 He was in the beginning with God. 3 All things came into being through him, and without him not one thing came into being. What has come into being 4 in him was life, and the life was the light of all people. 5 The light shines in the darkness, and the darkness did not overcome it.

See how John repeats the themes of creation and light from Genesis. A deeper understanding of the beginning of everything is found here. While Genesis describes God speaking light into existence, John describes the Word of God as a personal reality "with" God who is, at the same time, God.

The identity of the personal reality is divulged in verses 17 and 18, where John contrasts the word of God brought by Moses and the Word embodied in Jesus. "The law indeed was given through Moses; grace and truth came through Jesus Christ. 18 No one has ever seen God. It is God the only Son, who is close to the Father's heart, who has made him known." Therefore, Jesus brings something different from Moses. While God spoke through Moses in giving the Torah, He speaks in a different voice through Jesus, who is in such a close relationship with God that he can reveal God in a way that Moses could not.

Ibrahim: This contrast between Moses and Jesus has some worth in that the Torah was essentially the law. Jesus came to apply the law, rather than bring it for the first time. His mission was to bring the Jews back to the heart of the law, as we have already discussed. They should love God and neighbor rather than serve their own selfish interests. Perhaps John's emphasis on Jesus bringing "grace" reflects Jesus' concentration on the compassion of God toward those who have rebelled and who now turn back to him in loyalty. This theme is mentioned by John in 1:10–13:

> He was in the world, and the world came into being through him; yet the world did not know him. 11 He came to what was his own, and his own people did not accept him. 12 But to all

who received him, who believed in his name, he gave power to become children of God, 13 who were born, not of blood or of the will of the flesh or of the will of man, but of God.

This is like a commentary on the story that Jesus told about the rebellious son who was welcomed home by his grieving father. The son had renounced his father, but when he turned back he was accepted and given the power to be the child of his father once again. There was nothing the bad son could do to reinstate himself. He had to depend on the will of his father, because by law the father had the right to disown him. John is saying that the work of Jesus was to encourage wayward Jewish sons to return home to their father. They were relying on their birth right, but they were not behaving as true sons of God.

Paul: I like your perceptive comparison between Jesus' story and John's text. But look at what John says immediately after the piece you quoted. John 1:14 connects Jesus and the Word of God in a quite remarkable way. *"And the Word became flesh and lived among us, and we have seen his glory, the glory as of a father's only son, full of grace and truth."* The personal reality involved in the creation of the world became human, as the unique son of his father. He brought "grace," but he also brought "glory." However, this glory was not obvious to everyone who encountered him. John 1:18 states that, "No one has ever seen God. It is God the only Son, who is close to the Father's heart, who has made him known." Yet many saw nothing of the glory of God in him. The paradox of Jesus is that the glory was hidden from view from those who were in a state of rebellion against God. Only when their hearts were softened and their desire for God awakened could their eyes be opened to see the light of God shining on them through Jesus.

John tells two stories to illustrate this fact. The first one is about a leading Jewish religious scholar who comes to Jesus at night so that others might not know where he was. Nicodemus was a member of the Jewish ruling council that governed on behalf of the Romans, so he had a lot to lose by being too close to Jesus. When Nicodemus confesses that God is with Jesus because of the miracles he has performed, Jesus tells him in John 3:3, "Very truly, I tell you, no one can see the kingdom of God without being born from above." Nicodemus interprets "being born" in a physical way, but in 3:7 Jesus says that Nicodemus must have a spiritual birth even at this point in his life and experience: "You must be born from above." Nicodemus protests, "How can these things be?" (3:9). Jesus challenges him in 3:10-12:

> Are you a teacher of Israel, and yet you do not understand these things? 11 Very truly, I tell you, we speak of what we know and testify to what we have seen; yet you do not receive our testimony. 12 If I have told you about earthly things and you do not believe, how can you believe if I tell you about heavenly things?

John does not indicate whether Nicodemus responds positively to Jesus, but the impression is given that he is left bemused by Jesus. George Beasley-Murray sees the ending of the dialogue as the tragedy of Jewish rejection of Jesus:

> Nicodemus is manifestly addressed as representative of his people by the Redeemer, who represents all who bear witness to the authentic word of God. . . . Tragically the refusal of the witness by Niocodemus is also representative of its rejection by his generation.[2]

This encounter is immediately followed by another conversation between Jesus and a woman drawing water at a well in Samaria as Jesus was passing through. He offers her the water of eternal life, but she thinks that he is talking about a supply of water that will never run out. When he finally reveals that he is the Messiah, she responds with faith in him in 4:28-29. "Then the woman left her water jar and went back to the city. She said to the people, 29 'Come and see a man who told me everything I have ever done! He cannot be the Messiah, can he?'" John then indicates in verses 39-40 that many people from her town believed in Jesus as their Messiah and welcomed him to stay with them for a few days. Samaritans believed in the Torah of Moses but were rejected by Jews for not following the Torah correctly. What a contrast John paints in these chapters between a leading Jew who is impressed by Jesus' miracles but who is blind to the spiritual life that Jesus offers and a Samaritan woman who Jesus knows is living with a man she is not married to (3:18), yet who responds in faith to Jesus and introduces him to her community. The wayward daughter returns home with a new heart to love God, but the theologian is left cold by the challenge to open himself to the Spirit of God. Beasley-Murray points out how powerful the testimony of this woman was in her own community. "Many of the Samaritans believed through the

---

2. Beasley-Murray, *John*, 49.

testimony that the woman bore." Jesus only stayed with her community for two days, "But they were sufficient for the people of Sychar to grasp for themselves that the testimony of the woman was right."[3]

Ibrahim: These two stories are very powerful illustrations of the passage I quoted earlier about Jews not receiving Jesus. The heretical Samaritans are pictured as more ready to welcome Jesus than the Jews. However, the controversial aspect of John's introduction to his Gospel is the identification of Jesus with God. The language can be understood to equate Jesus with the Word of God, as if Jesus actually existed before the world was made. This has surely been the mainstream Christian interpretation of 1:14, "the word became flesh."

Paul: Perhaps it would be more correct to say that the Word existed before the world was made and that the Word became human as Jesus. The equation of the Word with Jesus is the other way around to what you have stated. It is a very bold claim for John to use the term "became" because the Greek term *egeneto* means "becoming different from what was before." Urban von Wahlde, in his commentary on this gospel, points out that the use of this term "was to affirm that not only did the Word take up existence in the world but that this existence was a truly fleshly existence."[4] In other words, John is claiming that the Word of God developed in a way that had not been the case before. God was in the habit of speaking as the Word but now God the Word *became* a human being, Jesus of Nazareth, born of Mary. It is as if the Word of God was concentrated in this one person in a fashion that was unique among the prophets who delivered God's word.

Ibrahim: Maybe it is a matter of degree between Jesus and the previous prophets. When the Qurʾan calls Jesus "a word from God" this is a title reserved only for him among the prophets, but he is still only a messenger. There is no indication in the title that God has come to the world to talk to people as a man. Rather, the title shows how faithful Jesus was to his calling, so faithful that he was entrusted with revealing Scripture that would be studied by his followers. Moses was likewise especially blessed by God because he too was given Scripture for the people of his time. In recognition of this great honor, Moses has been known as the one who bore the word of God. Q4:164 indicates that God spoke directly with Moses on the mountain and gave him the Torah, and Muslims have

---

3. Ibid., 64.
4. von Wahlde, *John*, 30.

given Moses the title of "He to whom God spoke directly" (*kalim Allah*). The titles of Moses and Jesus are quite similar in recognition of the special relationship they had with God, hearing directly from him, and receiving Scripture directly from him.

Paul: I think John intends to communicate that the Word became embodied in one physical human being to the exclusion of any other person. The impression Jesus made on John is repeated in the first letter he wrote to fellow Christians in which he begins, in 1 John 1:1–2, by emphasizing that the Word of God was not simply speech to be heard, but a human person to touch:

> We declare to you what was from the beginning, what we have heard, what we have seen with our eyes, what we have looked at and touched with our hands, concerning the word of life ² this life was revealed, and we have seen it and testify to it, and declare to you the eternal life that was with the Father and was revealed to us.

Notice how similar this opening is to the opening of the Gospel of John. The Word of God was there in the beginning, but he and others who were with him experienced the Word of God *in Jesus*, who is named in verse 3. Here the emphasis falls on the "life" of the Word of God, because John is writing to Christian communities probably in the area around Ephesus, where he was a church leader, to encourage them to see Jesus like he did, even though they had never been in Palestine or encountered Jesus in the flesh. Stephen Smalley understands John to be saying that the Word that always existed from the beginning entered history in the person of Jesus. "What was true from eternity was gradually and actually disclosed, and personally experienced, in history."[5] Jesus not only declared the word of God, but he also lived the word of God in such a way that his disciples came to realize that God's Word, which cannot be separated from God himself, had become human.

Ibrahim: But the Fourth Gospel and the first letter of John represent one kind of Christian writing gathered in the New Testament. The first three Gospels do not show the disciples talking this language. Perhaps they are closer to the historical situation than the writings attached to John's name. Many scholars do not believe that these writings came from John the disciple, and they think that the Fourth Gospel does not contain much eyewitness testimony. The first three Gospels are surely a

---

5. Smalley, *1, 2, 3 John*, 7.

more faithful reflection of how Jesus' followers reacted to him. Nowhere do these three Gospels talk about God becoming human in Jesus. We have discussed the birth stories in Matthew and Luke, but neither speak of God becoming human. The closest they get to this idea is Matthew 1:23, where Matthew interprets the birth of Jesus by means of a message from the prophet Micah 5:2, "Look, the virgin shall conceive and bear a son, and they shall name him Emmanuel," which means, "God is with us." Matthew thinks of Jesus as the presence of God with Israel, but that does not include God arriving in person as Jesus. No, Jesus is God with them as God's messenger who brings the good news of the rule of God as Matthew goes on to describe in the rest of his Gospel.

Paul: The theme of Jesus as the Word of God become human in the Johannine writings is a very significant testimony within the New Testament documents. It was a theme that became very important in the developing life of the churches after the first century. One of the earliest theologians, Irenaeus of Lyons (b. c. 130), interprets the Word of God as firstly heard but unseen and then in Jesus as both heard and seen:

> Through the creation the Word reveals God the creator. . . . By Law and Prophets the Word proclaimed himself and the Father: and the whole people alike heard; but all did not believe. And through this same Word, made visible and tangible, the Father was displayed, although all did not believe in him.[6]

Therefore, the witness of John to the Word becoming human had a deep impact on the future of Christianity. Christians have remained convinced that the prophets *proclaimed* God's Word so that people could hear it, but Jesus *embodied* the Word of God so that people could both hear and see it.

Jesus "A Spirit from God" in the Qur'an

Paul: I believe that the Qur'an refers to the Johannine witness when Jesus is called "a word from God." This is largely the result of Christians in Arabia using the title "Word of God" for Jesus. The Qur'an is reflecting their language and offering a comment about it. This is also true, I think, about another title for Jesus used in the Qur'an, "a spirit from God." This title also shows that there is a qualitative difference between Moses and Jesus. Q4:171 calls Jesus both God's word and "a spirit from Him." Jesus

---

6. Irenaeus, "Against Heresies," IV.6.5, *The Early Christian Fathers*, 76.

is a "spirit" from God. He is obviously not an angelic spirit from God because he is a human being. There are many references to angelic "spirits" in the Qur'an, but that meaning is out of the question here. In this context, the spirit is *the very life of God himself*, not a created angelic spirit with no physical reality. This title is unique to Jesus among the prophets and shows that he was imbued with the spirit of God, the breath of God, in a way that was not the case with any of the other prophets. Despite your claim that Moses and Jesus were equally honored, the Qur'an fails to give Moses such a title. Moses brought the Torah, but Jesus was the spirit of God. Moses brought the law, but Jesus bore the very life of God himself. This is not so far from the contrast made by John in 1:17–18, that God gave the law through Moses but he gave grace and truth through Jesus Christ. Since no human being has seen God himself, God decided to reveal himself in Jesus. If the Qur'an says that Jesus was God's Spirit, then this must surely imply that God's very presence was in him.

Ibrahim: It is true that the Qur'an names Jesus as "a spirit from God," but this probably is a reference to his miraculous conception told in Q19:17–22, when the angel Gabriel appeared to Mary:

> We sent Our spirit to her and he appeared to her as a typical human being. **18** She said, "I ask the Most Merciful to protect me from you, if you fear Him." **19** He said, "I am only a Messenger from your Lord, with a gift to you of a pure son." **20** She said, "How can I have a son when no man has touched me, and I have not been unchaste?" **21** He said, "This is how it will be. Your Lord said: 'It is easy for Me. We will make him a sign to humanity, and mercy from Us. The matter has been decreed.'" **22** So she conceived him.

Notice that the angel Gabriel is called "Our spirit," the same term, *ruh*, used for Jesus. Gabriel was a spirit without physicality, but he appeared to Mary as if he were a man. Jesus was a physical human being, but he was conceived by spiritual means. There was no joining of male semen with the egg within Mary. That process was bypassed. There was therefore something quite unique about Jesus. The statement that Jesus would be a "pure" son is also an indication both of his spiritual quality as a boy conceived outside the usual method, and of his special calling to bring the Gospel to the people of Israel in which he was absolutely faithful.

Paul: The four Gospels all testify to the relationship between Jesus and God's Spirit. This is something that John reports along with Matthew,

Mark, and Luke. The earliest record, in Mark 1:10, says that when Jesus was coming out of the Jordan river after John baptized him, Jesus "saw the heavens torn apart and the Spirit descending like a dove on him." Then in verse 12 "the Spirit sent him out into the desert" where he was tempted by Satan. Luke 4:14 adds to this story his account of Jesus returning from the desert, having resisted Satan, "filled with the power of the Spirit," and in 4:18–21 announcing to the men from his home town who had gathered to worship God that, "The Spirit of the Lord is upon me, because he has anointed me to bring good news to the poor. He has sent me to proclaim release to the captives and recovery of sight to the blind, to let the oppressed go free, to proclaim the year of the Lord's favor." John's Gospel tells the story of Jesus' being filled with the Spirit through the witness of John the Baptist in John 1:32–33:

> And John testified, "I saw the Spirit descending from heaven like a dove, and it remained on him. 33 I myself did not know him, but the one who sent me to baptize with water said to me, "He on whom you see the Spirit descend and remain is the one who baptizes with the Holy Spirit."

The Fourth Gospel includes the story of the descent of the Spirit on Jesus after his baptism because this event was central to Jesus' work as a proclaimer of the good news of the kingdom. Without the power of God's Spirit, Jesus could not have performed miracles, or enable other people to be filled with God's Spirit.

Ibrahim: It is interesting that the Gospels portray not only Jesus as being filled with God's Spirit, but also those who respond to the message of Jesus. The story of Nicodemus is a fine example of this. In John 3:5–8 Jesus tells Nicodemus that he must be filled with God's Spirit:

> Jesus answered him, "Very truly, I tell you, no one can see the kingdom of God without being born from above." 4 Nicodemus said to him, "How can anyone be born after having grown old? Can one enter a second time into the mother's womb and be born?" 5 Jesus answered, "Very truly, I tell you, no one can enter the kingdom of God without being born of water and Spirit. 6 What is born of the flesh is flesh, and what is born of the Spirit is spirit. 7 Do not be astonished that I said to you, 'You must be born from above.' 8 The wind blows where it chooses, and you hear the sound of it, but you do not know where it comes from or where it goes. So it is with everyone who is born of the Spirit."

Jesus' experience of the Spirit of God is to be shared with others. Is that not what happened in Acts 2:4 when the disciples were in a room in Jerusalem and "All of them were filled with the Holy Spirit"? In other words, the relationship between Jesus and God's Spirit is not an indication of a special relationship that no other human being can share. The opposite is the case. Jesus wishes to baptize his followers with the Spirit and God provides his Spirit for them.

Paul: But the fact that Jesus can baptize others with the Spirit of God is an indication of a privileged relationship with God, who fills believers with his Spirit. I think that the Qur'an reflects this Christian conviction that Jesus had a fullness of God's Spirit that he could pass on to those who were open to being filled with God's Spirit. Christian readers of the Qur'an have noticed how the titles, "a word from God" and "a spirit from God" given to Jesus in Q4:171 echo the language of John's Gospel, as I have outlined. One of the earliest Christian writings addressed to Muslims in Arabic interprets these titles for Jesus as upholding Christian convictions. Although the document is anonymous, it was most likely written by a monk living near Jerusalem around the middle of the eighth century. The anonymous writer addresses a Muslim audience by declaring, "We do not distinguish God from His Word and His Spirit. We do not worship another god alongside God in His Word and His Spirit."[7] The first sentence reflects his reading of Q4:171, where Jesus is Word and Spirit from God. The second sentence alludes to Q5:72-73, which alleges that Christians worship gods alongside the One True God, and it redefines the understanding of the One God to include Jesus the Word and Spirit of God. The writer denies that Christians worship three gods, as the Qur'an says they do. "We do not say three gods. . . . But we do say that God and His Word and His Spirit is One God and One Creator."[8] Here he rejects Q5:73, "Those who say that God is a third of three are unbelievers," and Q4:171, "Believe in God and His messengers and do not say 'three.'" He then quotes from Q4:171 and 16:102 to challenge his Muslim reader to accept this truth:

> Believe in God and His Word; and also in His Holy Spirit; surely the Holy Spirit has brought down from your Lord mercy and guidance. . . . You find in the Qur'an that God and His Word and His Spirit is One God and One Lord. You have said that

---

7. *A Treatise on the Triune Nature of God*, 75.
8. Ibid., 76.

you believe in God and His Word and His Spirit, so do not reproach us, you people, for believing in God and His Word and His Spirit.[9]

Ibrahim: The writer has certainly tried hard to read the Qur'an with some understanding. He has noticed that the Qur'an warns the Christians not to speak of God unadvisedly by claiming that he is more than One. But his attempt to argue that the Qur'an itself describes God as threefold is absolutely mistaken. He might have taken the trouble to read Q4:171 properly. There Jesus is described as a word from God and a spirit from him. Jesus is being given titles that emphasize different aspects of his mission to the Israelites. The titles cannot imply that God himself is divided into different aspects, the word and the spirit. He has both speaking and life within himself. Q4:171 points out that the Christian belief in the Trinity is a false way of thinking and speaking about God:

> People of the Book, do not exceed the bounds of your religion, and do not say anything about God except the truth. The Messiah, Jesus, son of Mary, was only a messenger of God, and His word delivered to Mary, and a spirit from Him. Therefore, believe in God and His messengers and do not say, "three." Give it up! It will be better for you! God is only one God. Glory be to Him! He is far above having a son. Everything in the heavens and on the earth belongs to Him. God is the best Protector.

Notice that the criticism of the Christians is that they have done to Jesus precisely what this eighth-century writer has done. They have taken Jesus the man and elevated him to the same level as God himself. The fact that this eighth-century writer can twist this text to come up with the Trinity is a shocking indictment of the way Christians reacted to Islam. Instead of reading the Qur'an with integrity they sought to undermine its teaching.

Paul: Well, he was probably attempting to demonstrate that the Qur'an recognizes that the status of Jesus is very different from any other messenger of God and that this is exactly what Christians think about him. He was also trying to communicate just what the Trinity means to Christians. Another Christian theologian, from the early ninth century, ʿAmmar al-Basri (d. c. 860), also used these titles for Jesus to explain the Trinity to a Muslim reader. He answered nine questions on the Trinity posed by a Muslim. The first question is "Since the Creator is one,

---

9. Ibid., 77–78.

how can one be three and three one?"[10] The answer is that there is one eternal essence in three essential properties that are not differentiated or separated. The Creator lives and speaks so "life" and "speech" can be attributed to him. "The principal essence has the attributions of His life and His speech; His speech is the source of His wisdom and His life is the source of His spirit."[11] If the opponents suggest that God's attributes, such as "hearing," "seeing," "almighty," "merciful," "generous," and "kind," mean that Christians cannot limit God to threeness, then they need to distinguish between God's names and his attributes. The names refer to actions of God whereas the attributes refer to properties essential to him. Only "life" and "speech" are essential properties in God. "Life and speech are properties in the structure of the essence, and in the quality of the essence, and the nature."[12]

Ibrahim: This is a very convoluted way of thinking about God that only shows how Christians tie themselves up in knots trying to defend the Trinity! They have decided that God is three-in-one so they have to find a way to convince Muslims that the Trinity is not a betrayal of the One True God. So here is a separation of the attributes of speaking and life from other attributes of God to uphold threeness in God. And notice that this theologian does not even mention the idea that the Trinity is Father, Son, and Holy Spirit!

Paul: I think we will need to return to the Trinity when we discuss Jesus as the Son of God. However, Christian theologians have often thought of Jesus as the Word of God in their description of the Trinity. A recent example is Thomas Torrance, who connects Jesus as God's Word in human form with the Word of God from all eternity:

> If Jesus Christ is the Word of God to us, he is the Word of God antecedently and eternally in the Godhead. Not only is he the Word of God uttered by God in the incarnation, but the Word eternally spoken by the Father in the communion of the Holy Spirit within the holy Trinity.[13]

Torrance is not addressing Muslims particularly here, but simply expressing the consequences of Jesus being called the Word of God. As you say, the Trinity is Father, Son, and Holy Spirit, and we should look

---

10. 'Ammar al-Basri, "Book of Questions and Answers," 148.
11. Ibid., 149.
12. Ibid., 156–57.
13. Torrance, *Incarnation*, 176.

at this later. But before we do that, I suggest we attend to the way Jesus speaks about himself in the Gospels. Typically, he calls himself the "Son of Man."

Ibrahim: Yes, that's a good idea. This humble attitude of Jesus regarding his own status is reflected in the title, son of Mary, in the Qur'an. Perhaps we will get to the bottom of Jesus' identity as he understood it.

six

Jesus Son of Mary, Son of Man

IBRAHIM INTRODUCES THE TITLE for Jesus common in the Qur'an, son of Mary. He shows that Jesus is called son of Mary to remind the Christians that he shared the same human nature of Mary and that there was no divine nature in him. He argues that the Prophet Muhammad was sent to make this clear to the Christians of his time. Jesus had proclaimed the Lordship of God, but some of his followers had elevated him to the same place as God by calling Jesus their Lord. Paul points out that Jesus is only called son of Mary once in the four Gospels, which indicates that his relationship to Mary was not emphasized by the early Christians. The fact that the title is found in the Syriac and Arabic infancy gospels means that it is probable that the Qur'an is echoing this style of referring to Jesus. They discuss the way Muslims have referred to Jesus as son of Mary, particularly in the Sufi tradition. They find parallels between the spirituality of Jesus and Sufi Muslims, especially in the Sufi title for Jesus, Spirit of God.

Ibrahim summarizes Christian scholarship on the title Son of Man in the Gospels. Paul acknowledges the variety of views concerning Jesus' predictions of the suffering, death, resurrection, and coming again of the Son of Man. Ibrahim prefers the view that Mark turned Jesus from a prophet of the kingdom of God into a prophet of his own death and resurrection. He expounds liberation theology as the best interpretation of Jesus' message. Paul brings up the use of Daniel 7 by Jesus as central to his approach to his work. He has been granted authority by God to judge in his lifetime and after his future coming again. He also claimed to be seated at God's right hand, following Psalm 110:1. Paul refers to Muslim liberation theology as proof that Christians and Muslims can agree on the centrality of God's concern for the oppressed. Ibrahim still wonders how much the Gospels really present the historical Jesus. Paul argues that there are very good grounds for believing that Jesus did call himself Son of Man and thought in terms of Daniel 7. Ibrahim expounds the different use of Son of Man in the Fourth Gospel and suggests there is dramatic presentation rather than history. Paul accepts that John believes that the Son of Man is also the Son of God and narrates his version of Jesus in that light.

Son of Mary in the Qur'an

Ibrahim: One of the most common names for Jesus in the Qur'an is son of Mary. The first mention of Jesus comes in Q2:87, "We gave Jesus, son of Mary, clear signs and strengthened him with the holy spirit." However, this is in a late Medinan sura and the story of Jesus' conception, birth, and miraculous work has probably already been revealed. This text summarizes the significance of the miraculous quality of his life. There was an exceptional outpouring of the spirit of God on him so that he could deliver the clear signs to the children of Israel and turn them back to their Creator and Lord after going astray. The announcement of Jesus' conception to Mary in Q3:45 is cast in terms of him carrying her name. "The angels said, 'Mary, God announces the news of a word from Him: his name is the Messiah, Jesus, the son of Mary: he will be honored in this world and in the next life, and he will be among those who are near to God.'" This text emphasizes that the conception of Jesus is an honorable thing and that any criticism of Mary for becoming pregnant without a husband is misplaced. Rather, Jesus will carry the name of Mary as a reminder of God's special favor on his mother that is heightened by the sign of God's unprecedented action in creating Jesus without a human father. This is confirmed by Q4:171, where the Christians are warned not to exaggerate Jesus' status by giving him the wrong titles:

> People of the Book, do not exceed the bounds of your religion, and do not say anything about God except the truth. The Messiah, Jesus, son of Mary, was only a messenger of God, and His word delivered to Mary, and a spirit from Him. Therefore, believe in God and His messengers and do not say, "three." Give it up! It will be better for you! God is only one God. Glory be to Him! He is far above having a son.

In this context, the name son of Mary is contrasted with the name son of God given to Jesus by the Christians. God reveals to them that their language is excessive and out of place for those who worship God. They need to return to speaking more accurately of Jesus as a *human* messenger, whose miraculous conception should not lead Christians to regard him as God in human form.

The fifth sura is particularly engaged with the status of Jesus. The warning to the Christians is now intensified so that they will be in no doubt about what God has revealed about Jesus. The first mention of the son of Mary comes in Q5:17, "Those who say that God is the Messiah, the son of Mary, are unbelievers." It is the conviction of Christians that God has come to earth in Jesus that is rejected very explicitly here. Q5:46 indicates that Jesus, son of Mary, was sent to confirm the Torah already given to the children of Israel by the Gospel that he received by revelation from God. In other words, the Gospel is not a new message but a renewal of the old one that came through Moses. The Christians are advised in Q5:47 to judge according to what God sent them and not to interpret the Gospel in a misguided way. Once again, the son of Mary is to be believed in appropriately as a specially appointed messenger whose signs were miraculous, just as Moses' signs were miraculous. The Torah and the Gospel were revealed with miraculous signs, but the Christians had made the mistake of attributing divinity to Jesus because of the miracles. At least the Jews had not done this to Moses. Q5:72 repeats the criticism of the Christians made in Q5:17: "Those who say that God is the Messiah, the son of Mary, are unbelievers. The Messiah himself said, 'Children of Israel, worship God, my Lord and your Lord.'" Here the witness of Jesus is added to help Christians to realize just how far they have gone astray. Jesus never asked his followers to worship him as divine. If they ended up calling Jesus their Lord, they were very much out of tune with him. He taught without ambiguity that God was Lord and that he was His servant. Q5:75–76 continues the challenge to the wayward Christians:

> The Messiah, son of Mary, was only a messenger among messengers who had been before him. His mother was righteous. They both ate food. See how We make these signs clear for them. See what liars they are! [76] Say to them, "Will you worship something other than God, that has no power to do you harm or good?"

The miraculous conception is a clear sign of the action of God. It should not be understood to point to a divine Jesus who has power within himself to act as God. He is called son of Mary to remind the Christians that he shared the same human nature of Mary and that there was no divine nature in him.

Q5:109–11 introduces a scene from the Day of Judgment when God gathers all his messengers together and speaks to them about their work. Interestingly, only Jesus is specified among the messengers:

> 110 Then God will say, "Jesus, son of Mary, remember my kindness to you and to your mother. I strengthened you with the holy spirit to speak to people as a young child and as an adult. I taught you the Book and wisdom, the Torah and the Gospel. By my permission, you made the shape of a bird out of clay, then you breathed on it, and it became a bird by my permission. You healed the blind and the lepers by my permission. You brought the dead to life by my permission."

Notice how God picks out Mary in his address to Jesus. The name, son of Mary, is given by God to continue the strong connection between Mary and Jesus in his revelation. This relationship between Mary and Jesus is picked up in 5:116–17, as the interrogation of Jesus continues at the Day of Judgment:

> God will say, "Jesus, son of Mary, did you say to people, 'Take me and my mother as two gods alongside God'?" He will say, "May You be glorified! I would never have said what I had no right to say. If I had said that, You would have known it. You know what is within me, though I do not know what is within You. You know the hidden things. 117 I only said to them what You commanded me to say: 'Worship God, my Lord and your Lord.'"

Here, God makes explicit his judgment of Christians who approach Jesus and Mary as divine. Mary was only a human being and those who kept pictures of her with the baby Jesus were in danger of thinking of her and her baby as two gods.

Sura 61:6 mentions Jesus son of Mary speaking to the children of Israel, "I am a messenger of God to you, confirming the Torah that came before me and announcing good news of a messenger to come after me whose name will be Ahmad." Verse 14 indicates that many rejected Jesus, but some followed him and said, "We are God's helpers." The son of Mary knew that he was one of a series of messengers going back to Abraham and forward to Muhammad. Part of his mission was to proclaim God's plan in the past and in the future. That plan meant that he was human like all the other messengers. The Prophet Muhammad was sent to make this abundantly clear to the Christians of his time. Jesus had proclaimed the Lordship of God over the children of Israel, but some who followed Jesus had elevated him to the same place as God by calling Jesus their Lord.

Paul: One of the major differences between the description of Jesus in the Qurʾan and the New Testament is this title, son of Mary, which is used only once in the Gospel of Mark and nowhere else in the Gospels or apostolic writings. And when he is called "son of Mary" in Mark 6:3, he is not being honored by the speakers. On the contrary, the people of Jesus' hometown, Nazareth, listen to him speak, and then reject his ministry by asking the following questions in Mark 6:2–3:

> "Where did this man get all this? What is this wisdom that has been given to him? What deeds of power are being done by his hands! 3 Is not this the carpenter, the son of Mary and brother of James and Joses and Judas and Simon, and are not his sisters here with us?" And they took offense at him. 4 Then Jesus said to them, "Prophets are not without honor, except in their hometown, and among their own kin, and in their own house."

However, the title is found in the Syriac and Arabic infancy gospels. Since the Syriac version probably comes from at least the fifth century, the probability that the Qurʾan is echoing this style of referring to Jesus is quite strong given the use of several alternative accounts of Jesus in the Qurʾan, as we saw in chapter one. For example, Jesus is at a dyer's house and puts all the cloth in the indigo tub. The dyer protests, "What have you done to me, son of Mary?" Jesus solves the problem by taking out the pieces of cloth one by one in the colors the dyer originally intended.[1] Then Jesus turns a group of boys into goats. Their mothers plead with him, "O our Lord Jesus, son of Mary, you are truly that good shepherd of Israel; have mercy on your handmaidens who stand before you, and who have never doubted. . . . Now we beseech you to restore these boys to their former condition." Jesus granted their request and changed the goats back into boys.[2]

---

1. See Elliot, *The Apocryphal New Testament*, 106.
2. Ibid., 106–7.

Whatever the relationship between the apocryphal gospels and the Qur'an, the problem with the use of the title son of Mary in the Qur'an is simply that it takes the portrait of Jesus further from historical reality. It is not just a question of alternative terminology but it also implies an alternative Jesus to the one described in the four Gospels. Take, for example, the question that he is asked on the Day of Judgement in 5:116, "Jesus, son of Mary, did you say to people, 'Take me and my mother as two gods alongside God'?" However, there is nothing in the four Gospels to support this accusation. If anything, the reality is the exact opposite since Jesus is portrayed as distancing himself from Mary in Mark 3:31–35:

> Then his mother and his brothers came; and standing outside, they sent to him and called him. 32 A crowd was sitting around him; and they said to him, "Your mother and your brothers and sisters are outside, asking for you." 33 And he replied, "Who are my mother and my brothers?" 34 And looking at those who sat around him, he said, "Here are my mother and my brothers! 35 Whoever does the will of God is my brother and sister and mother."

One of reasons why Jesus is not called "son of Mary," in the Gospels lies in this story. He had begun to gather followers and they were for him a new "family" of faith. Clearly, at this point in his life the rest of Jesus' family were not among those followers. We discover that his mother Mary was at his crucifixion in John 19:25 and that Jesus entrusted her care to one of his disciples, but John does not tell us whether Mary was a member of the larger group of followers. In other words, Mary is merely in the background of Jesus' life. He did not stay with her during his ministry and she saw little of him. Any elevation of Mary by Jesus as a "god alongside God" is totally out of the question. We saw in chapter one that there were sections within the Christian community that have approached Mary as an intercessor for them before God, but they have not ever thought of her as a divine being.

Another departure from historical reality in the Qur'an is the foretelling of the Prophet Muhammad by Jesus the son of Mary in 61:6. The earliest life of Muhammad found Jesus prophesying him in John 15:26, where Jesus is speaking to his disciples about his departure. "When the Advocate comes, whom I will send to you from the Father, the Spirit of truth who comes from the Father, he will testify on my behalf." Ibn Ishaq says that the "Advocate" is the Prophet Muhammad. "The Munahhemana (God bless and preserve him!) in Syriac is Muhammad; in Greek he is the paraclete."³ This interpretation has become very popular even until today among Muslims. However, Jesus is obviously promising the coming of God's Holy Spirit to the disciples.

Ibrahim: You complain that the Qur'an departs from historical reality, but you have plenty of problems with the historical reality of the four Gospels! We are going to discuss the way Matthew, Mark, and Luke portray Jesus calling himself, Son of Man, but John seldom has him say this. Then the apostolic writings call Jesus by different titles than the Son of Man. Why do they not represent Jesus the way he appeared to speak of himself? In the end, there are a variety of portraits of Jesus in the New Testament, so the fact that the Qur'an has another portrait should not raise the question of "historical reality" as if only the Qur'an is implicated in "creating" a version of Jesus. We are discussing different conceptions of Jesus and how they relate to each other.

Returning to the son of Mary title, we can notice how Muslim tradition continued to refer to Jesus as son of Mary. One example comes from the eighth-century writer 'Abdallah ibn al-Mubarak (d. 797), who included the following saying of Jesus, son of Mary in his book on asceticism. "Whenever the hour was mentioned in the presence of Jesus, he would cry out and say, 'It is not fitting that the son of Mary should remain silent when the Hour is mentioned in his presence.'"⁴ The son of Mary is mentioned here as warning people of the Day of Judgment. Jesus was often seen as an ascetic who spent much time in meditation, and who encouraged others to do the same. Abu Bakr ibn Abi al-Dunya (d. 894) records a story about Jesus and John the Baptist:

> John the son of Zechariah met Jesus the son of Mary, John smiling of face and welcoming while Jesus was frowning and gloomy. Jesus said to John, "You smile as if you feel secure." John said to Jesus, "You frown as if you are in despair." God revealed, "What John does is dearer to Us."⁵

Here the son of Mary is reprimanded by God for being too negative and not getting his life in balance through confidence in God. Jesus could have learned from John how to have appropriate faith. This story attempts to challenge the virtue of extreme asceticism put forward by ibn al-Mubarak.

3. Ibn Ishaq, *Life of Muhammad*, 103.
4. Ibn al-Mubarak, *al-Zuhd*, 77–78, translated by Khalidi, *The Muslim Jesus*, 54.
5. al-Dunya, *Kitab al-Ikhwan*, 190, translated by Khalidi, *The Muslim Jesus*, 120.

Paul: This contrast between John the Baptist and Jesus is rather ironic, given that the Gospels tell the story the other way around. John lives in the desert on locusts and wild honey and does not get involved in normal life, but Jesus is accused of being a glutton for food and drink because he attends parties hosted by well-to-do leaders in the towns he visits. I'm not sure how the story got turned around like this in Muslim tradition. I'm aware that the picture of Jesus as a type of Sufi is widespread among Muslims. Certainly, in Sunni Islam with a tolerance for Sufism, stories of Jesus as a Sufi are well known, and this is probably largely due to the influence of Ghazali, who passed on several such stories. Here is his version of Jesus fasting for a prolonged time, but instead of the devil talking to him, he is interrupted by an old man:

> It is told that Jesus spent sixty days in intimate conversation with his Lord without eating. Then the thought of bread occurred to him and his intimacy was interrupted. At once a loaf of bread appeared in his hands, so he sat down and wept for the loss of intimacy. At that moment, an old man cast his shadow upon him and Jesus said to him, "God bless you, friend of God. Pray to God for me, for I was in a trance and the thought of bread occurred to me, and so my trance was interrupted." The old man prayed, "O God! If you know that the thought of bread has occurred to me since I have known You, do not forgive me. On the contrary, if anything was brought before me, I would eat it without any thought of it."[6]

Tarif Khalidi, the compiler and translator of these Muslim accounts of Jesus, comments, "Jesus is seen as manifesting a human weakness when compared to the total godly communion of the 'old man,' who may perhaps be a model Sufi master."[7] Another story from Ghazali's *Revival of the Religious Sciences* is a conversation between Jesus and his disciples about how they can imitate him:

> The disciples asked Jesus, "Spirit of God, is there anyone on earth now who is like you?" Jesus answered, "Yes, he whose speech is a mention [of God], whose silence is contemplation [of God], and whose every glance derives a lesson—such a man is like me."[8]

---

6. al-Ghazali, *Ihya' 'ulum al-din,* 3:81, translated by Khalidi, *The Muslim Jesus,* 169–70.

7. Ibid., 170.

8. al-Ghazali, *Ihya' 'ulum al-din,* 4:411, translated by Khalidi, *The Muslim Jesus,* 180.

It is interesting that the disciples call Jesus, "Spirit of God," reflecting the title given to him in Q4:171. This also indicates the Sufi preference for heightened spiritual awareness expressed in Jesus' lifestyle. At least in this second story, Jesus is highly regarded for his spirituality, though the possibility of achieving the same degree of communion with God is held out for others.

There are parallels in these accounts with Jesus' experience of the Spirit of God in the Gospels. Luke is particularly concerned with this theme. In Luke 4:1, he narrates that after the Spirit descended on Jesus at his baptism by John the same Spirit that empowered Jesus led him into the desert to be tested by the devil. He did not eat for forty days. Having rejected the suggestions of the devil to turn stones into bread, to bow down and worship him, and to throw himself from a high place, Luke says that Jesus returned to his home territory in the power of the Spirit and proceeded to teach with power (4:32) and expel evil spirits from those possessed by them (4:35). Because of this spiritual authority,

> They were all amazed and kept saying to one another, "What kind of utterance is this? For with authority and power he commands the unclean spirits, and out they come!" 37 And a report about him began to reach every place in the region.

However, Luke 5:15–16 mentions that Jesus needed to maintain his relationship with God through withdrawal from activity. "But now more than ever the word about Jesus spread abroad; many crowds would gather to hear him and to be cured of their diseases. 16 But he would withdraw to deserted places and pray." Luke is keen to point out that Jesus sought harmony between his work of releasing people from bondage and receiving the power from God to do so. Then, according to Luke 9:1–2, "Jesus called the twelve together and gave them power and authority over all demons and to cure diseases, 2 and he sent them out to proclaim the kingdom of God and to heal." Jesus invested in his disciples the same power of God's Spirit that he had received. He could pass on the Spirit to them. Luke 9:6 tells us that the disciples went from village to village without Jesus and healed people wherever they went. You can see the way these accounts are reflected in Ghazali's stories, where Jesus is called "Spirit of God" by his disciples; he sets them an example of being alone with God for extended periods; and he believes they can match his spiritual power.

Ibrahim: It is very pleasing to see you drawing parallels between the spirituality of Jesus and his disciples in terms of Sufi tradition. As someone who has been a member of a Sufi order since teenage years I am glad that a Christian can find common ground with Muslims here. If only we could sustain this cordial relationship around the example of Jesus, then there would be much less argument between Muslims and Christians. Perhaps I can suggest to you that attending to the way Jesus speaks about himself in the Gospels would enable Christians to walk more closely with their Muslim cousins. So let me summarize Christian scholarship concerning the language that Jesus used about himself.

Jesus, Son of Man

Ibrahim: If we look at the earliest gospel, Mark, we find that Jesus called himself "the Son of Man." In Mark 2:5, Jesus announces that the sins of a crippled man are forgiven. When he is criticized by the teachers of the Law for saying what only God can say, he replies,

> "But so that you may know that the Son of Man has authority on earth to forgive sins"—he said to the paralytic— 11 "I say to you, stand up, take your mat and go to your home."

Then in Mark 2:28, Jesus rejects a criticism by the Pharisees that he allowed his disciples to pick wheat on the Sabbath, by arguing that the Pharisees had too strict a view of Sabbath rules, by saying, "so the Son of Man is lord even of the Sabbath." These two stories show that Jesus wanted to emphasize that he was a messenger who had spiritual authority from God to interpret the Torah so that people could worship God in the way God intended and not the way that the religious leaders taught.

The title "the Son of Man" is agreed by Christian scholars to be "the nearest thing in the Jesus tradition to a self-chosen self-designation."[9] James Dunn discusses different interpretations of this title, but believes that Jesus meant "a man like me."[10] He also points out that Jesus probably saw himself in the son-of-man figure in Daniel 7:13, "one like a Son of Man," who was given authority by God. This is agreed by Darrell Bock who understands the Son of Man to be a human being "with certain

---

9. Dunn, *Jesus Remembered*, 724.
10. Ibid., 760.

rights and authority."[11] He has the right to forgive sin and has authority over the Sabbath. "In saying that the Son of Man has authority to forgive sins he is not saying that all humans have the authority to forgive sins, but rather that this particular human being, who is now speaking and acting, possesses such a capability."[12] So there is a consensus that Jesus spoke about himself as a man specially appointed by God.

Paul: Yes, this is true, and I appreciate your willingness to study contemporary Christian scholarship of the Gospels. Perhaps more controversial aspects of the Son of Man title relate to the predictions by Jesus of his suffering in the second half of Mark's Gospel. In 8:31, Jesus "began to teach them that the Son of Man must undergo great suffering, and be rejected by the elders, the chief priests, and the scribes, and be killed, and after three days rise again." This prediction is repeated in 9:31 and 10:33–34. Clearly, Mark wants his audience to take notice of the significance of this prediction by repeating it three times. This has caused some difficulties for those Christian scholars who cannot imagine Jesus predicting his crucifixion and resurrection. For example, Dominic Crossan thinks that Jesus taught about the kingdom of God, as we have seen, but he does not believe that Jesus spoke of his future suffering, death, and resurrection. "It was Mark who created the suffering and rising Son of Man and placed all those units on the lips of Jesus, where they were accepted and expanded by Matthew and Luke."[13] This is echoed by Adela Collins in her commentary on Mark 8:31, when she says, "It is likely that verse 31 and the other passion predictions are Markan compositions."[14] They take the view that Jesus would not have known such details about his future death and resurrection. For these scholars, the picture of Jesus painted by Mark does not reflect the historical Jesus.

Ibrahim: Good. You have done my job for me! This is the fascinating thing about recent Christian research into the life of Jesus. There is now a strong position that the Gospel writers invented their own picture of Jesus and grafted it onto the stories they had heard about him. This is especially the case with Jesus calling himself the Son of Man. Mark turned Jesus from a prophet of the kingdom of God into a prophet of his own death and resurrection. As a Muslim, I find this honesty among

---

11. Bock, "Son of Man," 894.
12. Ibid., 897.
13. Crossan, *The Historical Jesus*, 259.
14. Collins, *Mark*, 403.

Christian intellectuals very refreshing, because it opens the door for a more accurate assessment of Jesus by the church generally. I grant that there are a majority of Christians who still believe that Jesus predicted his death and resurrection, but given time, the leadership of the scholars will have an increasing impact on the church. When you look at the rise of the theology of liberation in Latin America and its impact elsewhere you can see that there are many Christians now who believe that Jesus came to change society, to preach the proper rule of God, and to challenge the power structures that prevent ordinary people from achieving their potential as human beings.

Gustavo Gutiérrez, the Peruvian priest who invented the term "the theology of liberation" in the late 1960s was concerned with the attitude of the Catholic Church he served toward the poor, who represented most of the population in Peru and throughout Hispanic America. His rallying cry for the church to improve the life of the poor instead of focusing on keeping them in poverty and simply offering them a better life in heaven was based on his understanding of Jesus' life and ministry. He talked about Jesus having a preferential option for the poor, and for the need for Christians to return to Jesus' example:

> Jesus called the poor "fortunate." . . . The gospel of Jesus proclaims to us the love of God for the poor for being just that—poor—and not necessarily, or even primarily, for being more believing, kinder, or better, morally speaking, than others. God loves them simply because they are poor, because they are hungry, because they are persecuted. . . . Thus, in order to know and to love God, one must know the concrete life situation of the poor today, and radically transform a society that produces them. . . . Jesus' actions are directed toward testifying to the love of God for every human being through the historical, conflictive, and preferential love for the poor (Luke 4:16-20).[15]

In a later book, he spells out the implications of following Jesus in love for the poor:

> Accepting the kingdom of God means refusing to accept a world that promotes or tolerates the premature and unjust deaths of the poor. It means rejecting the hypocrisy of a society that claims to be democratic but violates the most elementary rights of the poor. It means rejecting the cynicism of the powerful of this world. To be a disciple means proclaiming the liberation of

---

15. Gutiérrez, *The Power of the Poor*, 94-96.

captives and the evangelization of the poor (Luke 4:18–19) and lifting the hopes of a people that suffers age-old injustice.[16]

In both excerpts Gutiérrez refers to Jesus speaking in his hometown of Nazareth according to Luke 4:16–21. He read in verses 18–19 from the prophet Isaiah the following words:

> The Spirit of the Lord is upon me, because he has anointed me to bring good news to the poor. He has sent me to proclaim release to the captives and recovery of sight to the blind, to let the oppressed go free, **19** to proclaim the year of the Lord's favor.

Then he announced to the people in verse 21, "Today this scripture has been fulfilled in your hearing." While this story is recorded only by Luke it has the ring of authenticity about it, because Jesus is fulfilling a prophecy made many years before about the messenger who would come in the power of God's spirit to bring those in darkness into the light, perform marvelous acts of healing, and establish the proper rule of God.

The whole movement of the theology of liberation is also an authentic response to the historical Jesus in our time. The irony is that "traditional" Christians have oppressed their poor Christian brothers and sisters in Latin America. The same was the case in South Africa where white Christians regarded colored Christians as second-class citizens not worthy to worship with them, eat in their restaurants, or live in their neighborhoods. It took the theology of liberation to unmask this false Christianity. Desmond Tutu, the Anglican leader, who was the General Secretary of the South African Council of Churches during the Apartheid period of white rule was awarded the Nobel Peace prize in 1984. That year he summed up his approach to the mission of the church in South Africa as working for those who cannot help themselves. He describes Jesus' ministry as theirs:

> Christ's work of compassion and love; feeding the hungry, providing blankets for the aged against the bitter cold winter, providing clean water supply in the rural areas and giving health education and building crèches and day care centres and giving scholarships to enable thousands of children to get secondary and tertiary education, looking after the families of political prisoners and applying legal defence for those appearing in

---

16. Gutiérrez, *The God of Life*, 103.

political cases, as well as supporting self-help community development programmes.[17]

These are inspiring examples of Christian theologians in recent times who have returned to the pattern of Jesus' own life and work. If Christians could focus on Jesus the human being who spoke as God's messenger and set free those in bondage to ignorance or ill health, then Muslims would have little to quarrel about with Christians.

Paul: I must say how impressed I am at your willingness to study such a wide range of Christian theology. If only more Muslims were like you! But I notice that you have taken the discussion of Jesus' self-designation, "the Son of Man" into a modern application. Let me return to what Jesus said about himself in Mark's Gospel. In Mark 13:24–27, Jesus prophecies that "the Son of Man" will return in the future after a time of terrible suffering for God's people:

> But in those days, after that suffering, the sun will be darkened, and the moon will not give its light, 25 and the stars will be falling from heaven, and the powers in the heavens will be shaken. 26 Then they will see "the Son of Man coming in clouds" with great power and glory. 27 Then he will send out the angels, and gather his elect from the four winds, from the ends of the earth to the ends of heaven.

Jesus is referring in verses 24 and 25 to the prophecy of Joel who spoke of the coming of God to judge the world in Joel 3:14–15, "For the day of the LORD is near in the valley of decision. 15 The sun and the moon are darkened, and the stars withdraw their shining." Then in verse 26 he is referring to the prophecy of Daniel who spoke of one like a Son of Man, a human being, coming to rule the world on God's behalf in Daniel 7:13–14:

> As I watched in the night visions, I saw one like a Son of Man coming with the clouds of heaven. And he came to the Ancient One and was presented before him. 14 To him was given dominion and glory and kingship, that all peoples, nations, and languages should serve him. His dominion is an everlasting dominion that shall not pass away, and his kingship is one that shall never be destroyed.

---

17. Tutu, *General Secretary's Report*, 8, quoted by Maimela, "Archbishop Desmond Tutu," 48.

Jesus sees himself as the man in Daniel's vision who would come to rule the world forever on behalf of "the Ancient One," the Creator himself. Clearly, Jesus did not think that this would happen in his lifetime, but that in another time he would be sent again by God.

Ibrahim: I'm aware that Christian scholars are deeply divided about all of this. Some have thought that Jesus was referring to someone else, not to himself. Others have held that Jesus would not have spoken about the future like this, so these words have been put on his lips by his followers. Maybe they will never come to a consensus about the future coming of the Son of Man. Muslims also see Jesus coming back from heaven to earth in the future. While the Qurʾan does not speak about the return of Jesus, there is a saying of the Prophet Muhammad concerning this. For example, the Qurʾan commentator Tabari—commenting on Q4:159, "There is not one of the People of the Book who will not believe in [Jesus] before his death"—says that the death of Jesus will happen after he returns from heaven. He quotes a companion of the Prophet, Abu Hurayra, who reported that Muhammad had said:

> I am the closest among humans to Jesus, Mary's son, because there is no prophet between us. He will descend, so recognize him when you see him. . . . He will break the crosses, kill the pigs, and abolish the poll tax. . . . He will die and the Muslims will pray over him and bury him.[18]

Muslims have a lively expectation that Jesus will make a second appearance in the future to establish Islam and bring Christians into conformity with the rule of God. Notice too how Muhammad refers to Jesus as son of Mary, demonstrating the central importance of this title for Jesus in the revelation of God.

Paul: Perhaps we can postpone a discussion of the Muslim view of the return of Jesus, which certainly challenges the way Jesus speaks of his future appearing in the Gospels. Let me continue looking at how Jesus refers to himself as the Son of Man in Mark's Gospel. When he is brought to trial before the Jewish High Priest in Mark 14, Jesus answers him by declaring in verse 62, "You will see the Son of Man 'seated at the right hand of the Power,' and 'coming with the clouds of heaven.'" Here Jesus refers to Psalm 110:1, 'The LORD says to my lord, 'Sit at my right hand until I make your enemies your footstool.'" Then Jesus refers to Daniel 7:13, "I saw one like a Son of Man [i.e., a human being] coming with the clouds

---

18. al-Ṭabari, *Jamiʿ al-Bayan*, 9:375, on Q4:157–59.

of heaven," as he did before. According to Mark 14:63–64, the High Priest judged that Jesus was making a claim to be acting on God's authority and condemned him for his presumption. "Then the high priest tore his clothes and said, 'Why do we still need witnesses? 64 You have heard his blasphemy! What is your decision?' All of them condemned him as deserving death."

Jesus had already made an indirect claim to be the one who would be seated at God's right hand, when he was in the Jerusalem temple after he had disrupted the selling of animals in the temple forecourt. He was speaking to a large crowd and asked them about the meaning of Psalm 110:1. The teachers of the Law of Moses said that the Messiah would come from the family of David who wrote the psalm. In Mark 12:36–37 Jesus asked the people, "David himself, by the Holy Spirit, declared, 'The Lord said to my Lord, "Sit at my right hand, until I put your enemies under your feet."' 37 David himself calls him Lord; so how can he be his son?'" Jesus was suggesting that in the psalm God was speaking to the Messiah who David called his Lord. So, the coming of the Messiah from David's line was not as significant as the role that the Messiah would have, a far greater role than that of David, the greatest king in Israel's history.

Ibrahim: There is no doubt that Jesus had a more significant role than David in the plan of God. David may have brought the Psalms but Jesus brought the Gospel. Here I recognize that the poet who leads others to worship God is of inestimable value. There is the crying need for humans to be devoted to God with heart, mind, and strength. Yet in the revelation of God, the books sent down to Moses and Jesus were of far greater importance, because they bring the voice of God directly to the human ear. The human striving in David's poetry is a valid response to the revelation of the books. We need other humans to help us respond to revelation. The poets can guide us to God. However, Jesus himself was a clearer guide in that he challenged the children of Israel to worship God with true devotion, and to obey his commands for the well-being of the whole community.

Paul: Jesus was not just for the Jews but also for the whole of humanity, for all ethnic groups. This is where the portrait of Jesus in the Gospels differs from the Qur'an, which emphasizes that Jesus came for the children of Israel. The books brought by Moses and Jesus were not for all nations, according to the Qur'an, but the book brought by Muhammad was for the whole of humanity, though initially addressed in Arabic to his contemporaries in Mecca. This has often lead Muslims to claim that

Jews and Christians, while having had the privilege of receiving revelation from God through Moses and Jesus, need to recognize the complete revelation in the book given to Muhammad. Indeed, the final book brings needed corrections to corruptions made to the Torah and Gospel by Jews and Christians. In practice this has meant that Muslims insist that the Bible is no longer trustworthy, and that humanity simply must attend to God's word as given in the Qur'an. Where Muslims have been in power, the message of the Christian Gospels has been downplayed in favor of the portrait of Jesus in the Qur'an. However, where Christians have been in power Muslims have either resisted the Christian version or have attempted to work with it as best they can.

A good example of the latter can be seen in South Africa, where the Muslim minority had to cope with the Christian majority who held power in the era of apartheid. Some Muslims kept apart from Christians and attempted to live as a community over against the Christian majority. Others worked with Christians to change society for the better. Farid Esack is an example of the second approach. He believed that seeking justice for non-whites meant that Muslims should join forces with all those who wanted a just society where no-one would be judged based on skin color, gender, or religious views. Muslims needed to make alliances with non-Muslims to achieve that kind of nation. But that would also imply a new reading of the Qur'an, which had often been understood to prohibit alliances with non-Muslims, as Q5:51 appears to teach: "You who believe, do not take the Jews and Christians as allies. They are only allies to each other. Whoever among you takes them as allies becomes one of them. God does not guide evil people." Esack argues that the context of this prohibition was active warfare against the Muslims in Medina. But this should not be applied today to working with non-Muslims who are not at war with Islam. He was active among Muslims in South Africa in the 1980s, appealing to them to band together with non-Muslim disenfranchised people to achieve equality of opportunity which they had always been denied by the white ruling minority. The prohibition of alliances would then relate to working with the white regime that was effectively at war with non-white Muslims and non-Muslims. He was inspired by Gustavo Gutierrez's appeal to the exodus of the children of Israel from slavery in Egypt as a model for Muslims who seek the divine preference for the poor and oppressed:

> The option of solidarity with the poor and oppressed, far from being an option for the particular, is really one for inclusivism and universality. There is no contradiction in God's being the Lord of humankind and his option for the downtrodden. . . . In the Exodus paradigm, we see how this support for the solidarity with the Other, though, was not limited to the religious Other, but also embraced those among the poor and downtrodden who actively rejected the religious beliefs of *Islam*. . . . Some forms of Otherness are vehemently opposed and the Qur'an does not hesitate to encourage the several forms of opposition to them. Instead, the Qur'an roots its own pluralism in a common struggle against oppression and injustice.[19]

Perhaps we can say that Christians and Muslims can agree on the centrality of God's concern for the oppressed.

Ibrahim: I wholeheartedly agree with you. Thanks for calling attention to the Muslim liberationist Esack and the situation of South African Muslims being identical to non-white Christians under white Christian rule. However, South African Christians were obviously not able to reach agreement during the apartheid era. This reminds me of the disarray among Christian scholars concerning what Jesus really taught about himself. How on earth will Christians be able to come to an accord on the Son of Man issue?

Paul: I take your point. The interpretation of the Son of Man texts is fraught with difficulty. This is partly because Jesus says quite different things about the Son of Man. Holding them all together is challenging. Howard Marshall shows how this might be accomplished. Whatever "Son of Man" originally meant is not easy to agree on, but we can draw together what Mark has recorded for us. It is a self-reference by Jesus, who only uses it to refer to himself and not to anyone else. It is the term Jesus uses when speaking about his suffering and death. It is also the title he gives himself when speaking of his coming to judge, his being seated at God's right hand, and of his gathering the people of God together.[20] Marshall asks how the first hearers of the title might have understood it, and answers that a distinction needs to be made between those reading Mark for the first time and encountering this unusual phrase in Mark 2:10 without any kind of explanation, and those reading the Gospel on a second or subsequent occasion, when they would be able to understand the

---

19. Esack, *Qurʾan Liberation & Pluralism*, 202–3.
20. Marshall, *New Testament Theology*, 83.

earlier usages in the light of the later ones, which provide unmistakable allusions to Daniel 7.[21] In the end, a reader of Mark's Gospel may have reached the conclusion that "when Jesus speaks about the Son of Man he is identifying himself as the figure prophesied in Daniel 7."[22]

Ibrahim: But he still doesn't know whether Jesus said all these things about himself. He talks about reading Mark, but does not engage with those who say that Mark put much of this teaching on Jesus' lips.

Paul: Actually, he has a discussion in a footnote:

> There is debate over the precise sense in which [the phrase "Son of Man"] was used in the original Aramaic spoken by Jesus and to what extent it is original to him. Many scholars hold that it was a term of general application that could be used by a speaker to make statements true of people in general and therefore of himself in particular, and it was so used by Jesus; however, (they say) in those texts where it is used in statements that can refer only to the speaker, it is an addition made during the development of the gospel tradition. Others, including myself, hold that it was used by Jesus to refer to himself and that the influence of Dan 7 was present at this stage.[23]

One of the ways of determining whether Jesus spoke of himself as the Son of Man is to notice that the apostolic writings do not refer to Jesus as Son of Man. It was not a title they gave to him. Darrell Bock argues that the restriction of the title to Jesus' own words in the Gospels indicates that the followers of Jesus did not invent the title for him. "The consistency of the term's use only by Jesus and the lack of its use as a confessional term of the early church elsewhere in the New Testament makes it extremely unlikely to have been the creation of the church."[24]

Ibrahim: What about the Gospel of John, which has different sayings of Jesus about the Son of Man? Surely these must have been invented by the author of the Gospel. In John 3:13–15, Jesus says, "No one has ascended into heaven except the one who descended from heaven, the Son of Man. **14** And just as Moses lifted up the serpent in the wilderness, so must the Son of Man be lifted up, **15** that whoever believes in him may have eternal life." Nowhere in the Synoptic Gospels does Jesus talk about going up to heaven. Here he claims to have already gone up to heaven

---

21. Ibid., 84.
22. Ibid., 85.
23. Ibid., 83.
24. Bock, "Son of Man," 897.

and descended from heaven. Then he says he will go up again. People who believe in him going up to heaven will receive eternal life. This is a completely different Jesus from the one we meet in the Gospel of Mark. In 5:28-29, Jesus says that when all the dead people hear the voice of the Son of Man they will rise up out of their graves and be judged. While he claims to be given authority as the Son of Man in Mark, he does not speak about such details of the Day of Judgment.

Then he talks to the audience in a place of worship in Capernaum about eating the flesh of the Son of Man in 6:53-54. "So Jesus said to them, 'Very truly, I tell you, unless you eat the flesh of the Son of Man and drink his blood, you have no life in you. 54 Those who eat my flesh and drink my blood have eternal life, and I will raise them up on the last day.'" So being raised to eternal life now depends on people eating his flesh! I suppose this must be a reference to the Last Supper in the Synoptic Gospels, where Jesus gives bread to his disciples and tells them to eat in memory of him, since he was going to be broken in death. But in John's account, there is no Last Supper and Jesus is talking, not just to his intimate disciples, but to a gathering of Jews for Sabbath worship. This shift has all the marks of dramatic creativity on the part of John. Then his disciples complain that they don't understand this teaching about eating his flesh, and Jesus replies in 6:62, "Then what if you were to see the Son of Man ascending to where he was before?" Once again John has Jesus talk about ascending to heaven from where he originally came.

In 8:28 Jesus replies to Jewish leaders who ask who he is by saying, "When you have lifted up the Son of Man, then you will realize that I am he, and that I do nothing on my own, but I speak these things as the Father instructed me." Now the Jewish leaders will raise him up! I suppose that John means that the Jewish leaders would raise him up on the cross, but maybe he wants Jesus to also mean that, without realizing it, the Jewish leaders will witness his ascension to heaven from where he gets his authority from God. All these stories about the Son of Man are unique to the Fourth Gospel and depict Jesus making claims for himself that are completely at odds with the other Gospels. You can't defend them as original to Jesus.

Paul: John intends to tell the story of Jesus from his origin in heaven. He reports Jesus speaking of coming down from heaven and being lifted up to heaven again. He places Jesus as the Word of God who was with God before the world came into existence and who was God. So, when he gets down to narrating stories about Jesus, he wants to unveil Jesus' identity as the Word of God. Therefore, John takes up the Son of Man title that Jesus used of himself and interprets it to fit with Jesus' relationship with God. The title Son of God seems to be interchangeable with Son of Man in John's Gospel. In John 3, after Jesus speaks to Nicodemus of himself as Son of Man, he switches to Son of God. Compare verse 15, where he says that whoever has faith in the Son of Man will have eternal life, with verse 16, where he says that whoever has faith in the Son of God will have eternal life. Then in 5:25, Jesus says to the crowd that those who listen to the voice of the Son of God will live, but in verse 28, he says the dead will hear the voice of the Son of Man. George Beasley-Murray points out how these titles are interchangeable for John. "In this Gospel Son of Man and Son of God are complementary concepts; they flow into one another."[25]

Ibrahim: This demonstrates my case that the Gospel of John is a dramatic presentation of the life of Jesus written from a faith perspective. As you say, John is convinced that Jesus came from heaven as a divine being who took human flesh. He combines the humanity of Jesus with the divinity of the Word of God, and the two titles, Son of Man and Son of God represent the two aspects of Jesus. He makes them interchangeable to get his point across. However, we do not get back to the real Jesus in this scenario. Jesus does not call himself Son of God in the Synoptic Gospels. Others give him that title, but he keeps to Son of Man. Let our next discussion be about the title Son of God.

Paul: Yes, it's time to look at Jesus as Son of God.

---

25. Beasley-Murray, *John*, 30.

seven

Son of God

PAUL BEGINS WITH A survey of incidents of Jesus being called "Son of God" in the Gospel of Mark. Ibrahim responds by outlining the rejection of this title for Jesus in the Qur'an. Paul argues that only in the Medinan suras is the sonship of Jesus questioned, since the Meccan suras are concerned to denounce the female deities worshipped in Arabia. This development is agreed by Ibrahim, but he is concerned to show that the Qur'an denounces Christians as well as polytheists for giving partners to God. Elevating the human Jesus to the right hand of God is just as unacceptable as worshipping multiple deities. Paul draws attention to the prayers of Jesus in the Gospels in which he calls God "Father" to demonstrate that Jesus saw himself as in a special relationship with God, as the Son of his Father. The fact that Paul, in his letters to the Romans and Galatians written in Greek, quoted the Aramaic term *Abba* proves that Jesus must have called God by this term. Ibrahim is interested in the way Jesus includes his disciples in this relationship when he speaks to them in Matthew's Gospel of "their Father" and in John's Gospel prays that his followers will experience the same intimacy with his Father that he has. In other words, argues Ibrahim, Jesus is not *uniquely* the son of God. He reminds Paul that contemporary Christian theologians often stress that Jesus was only aware of his own humanity that he shared with others, not that he was a divine incarnation come from heaven. Paul replies by pointing out that St. Paul also records a prayer to Jesus in Aramaic in his first letter to the Corinthians, *marana tha*, "Our Lord, come!" which proves that Christians even before Paul called Jesus, Lord, a title Jews reserved for God.

Paul suggests that what the Qur'an is attacking is not what Christians believe about Jesus. They did not elevate a man to the place of God, but rather believed that God had come in human form. Ibrahim notes that the Qur'an compares Jesus with Adam to show the Christians that Jesus could not be the Word made flesh as God becoming human but simply the creative act of God in sending his word to be proclaimed by Jesus, who like Adam had no human father, but was created by the command of God. Ibrahim raises the issue of the Trinity, which is denied by the Qur'an. Paul points to the experience of the Spirit of God as the Spirit of Christ in St. Paul's letter to the Romans as an indication of how the threefold name of God, as Father, Son, and Holy Spirit developed. Paul argues that the rejection of the Trinity in the Qur'an is really concerned with a Trinity of God, Jesus, and Mary, in which Christians are accused of believing that God took Mary and produced Jesus with her. Christians would wholeheartedly agree with this denunciation, since they never would have spoken about the Trinity in that way. However, the Trinity of Father, Son, and Holy Spirit still contravenes the teaching of the Qur'an, according to Ibrahim, because God has no partners. If Jesus is divine, then Christians are guilty of associating him with God in an illegitimate way. Paul accepts that the fear of giving partners to God is at the heart of the Muslim rejection of the Trinity.

The Title "Son of God"

Paul: Jesus is called Son of God by others in the Gospel of Mark, but as we have seen already he calls himself Son of Man. Mark opens his Gospel with "the good news of Jesus Christ, the Son of God." Since "gospel" means good news, it is clear that for Mark the fact that Jesus is God's Son is the heart of the good news he wants to share. He quickly follows this affirmation by reporting the voice of God at Jesus' baptism in 1:11, "You are my Son, the Beloved; with you I am well pleased." This approval is repeated in Mark 9:7, when Jesus is on a mountain with Peter, James, and John. Jesus appears to them with a dazzling white quality, and after they were enveloped in a cloud, a voice says, "This is my Son, the Beloved; listen to him!" The first divine voice is for Jesus alone, but the second is for the three disciples. Mark is telling his readers that this title, Son of God, was given *by God himself* directly to Jesus, and then the closest three disciples were informed of Jesus' status so that they would know how God regarded him.

In Mark 3:11, evil spirits that tormented people would shout, "You are the Son of God," but Jesus told them to be quiet and not reveal his identity. In Mark 5:6–8, Jesus encountered a man with an evil spirit who shouted, "What have you to do with me, Jesus, Son of the Most High God? I adjure you by God, do not torment me." This was because Jesus had said to him, "Come out of the man, you unclean spirit!" Mark is saying that the evil spirits spoke from within these "possessed" people. In other words, human beings generally were not aware of Jesus' true status as God's Son, but paradoxically, those humans terrorized by evil spirits could testify to his relationship with God. There is one exception to this in the Gospel of Mark. When Jesus died on the cross, the Roman officer in charge of Jesus' execution says in 15:39, "Truly this man was God's Son!" Notice, however, that this was not a Jew. Although Jesus had come for the Jews, only this non-Jew understood Jesus correctly. Mark was most likely writing his account for people like the Roman officer and he wanted to convince them that Jesus was God's Son.

Ibrahim: Here we come to the most serious divide between the Gospels and the Qur'an. The Christians are warned to stop calling Jesus, Son of God, in Q9:30–31:

> The Christians say, "The Messiah is the son of God." By saying this with their mouths they imitate what unbelievers said in the past. May God fight against them for they lie! 31 They take their priests and their monks as lords alongside God, and Christ, the son of Mary. But they were only commanded to worship one God. There is no god but Him. May he be glorified above what they associate with Him!

The Revelation here calls strongly for Christians to desist naming Jesus, God's son, because God has not ordained a son to serve him. The problem with Christians is that they give the glory and honor due to God to another. This is repeated in Q4:171:

> People of the Book, do not exceed the bounds of your religion, and do not say anything about God except the truth. The Messiah, Jesus, son of Mary, was only a messenger of God, and His word delivered to Mary, and a spirit from Him. Therefore, believe in God and His messengers and do not say, "three." Give it up! It will be better for you! God is only one God. Glory be to Him! He is far above having a son.

It couldn't be clearer that granting Jesus the kind of relationship implied in being Son of God is the most grievous fault of Christians. Elevating Jesus to the same level as God himself is the basic error of the Christian tradition. The Qur'an is revealed to Arabic-speaking people, among whom Christian Arabs are addressed. They need to fundamentally change their perception of Jesus, and turn back to their Lord and Creator.

Paul: I'm glad you mentioned that Christian Arabs are being addressed. For me, the interesting point about the Qur'an is that the early recitations do not mention the Christians, but rather focus on Arabs in general. The two references you have given from suras 4 and 9 come from the period after the Muslims emigrated from Mecca to Medina. However, there are several references to the widespread belief among Arabs that the high god had offspring, particularly daughters that were worshipped at the sanctuary in Mecca. Muhammad would have witnessed this worship as a child in Mecca, so it not surprising that the early messages of Muhammad concentrate on this misguided worship. There are several references to this phenomenon in the Meccan suras. In Q37:149–58, Muhammad is instructed to ask the Meccans:

> Does your Lord have daughters, while they have sons? **150** Did We create the angels as females as they witness? **151** Are they not merely inventing this when they say, **152** "God has begotten children." Such liars they are.

Three female gods are named in Q53:19, al-Lat, al-'Uzza, and Manat. Q25:2–3 points out why the worship of these so-called "daughters of god" is wrong:

> He has sovereignty over the heavens and the earth and has not begotten a son. He has no associate in his rule. He created everything and appointed everything in its exact place. **3** But they have taken, apart from Him, gods that create nothing, and are themselves created, that have no power in themselves to harm or help, and that have no power over death, life, or resurrection.

The message of Q21:26–29 challenges the Arabs who believed that God had offspring who were worthy of worship:

> They say, "The Most Merciful has begotten children." May He be glorified! No, they are only His honored servants. **27** They do not speak before He speaks and they act by His command. **28** He knows what is before them and what is behind them. They

only intercede for those who are approved. They are those who fear Him with deep reverence. **29** If one of them were to say, "I am a god apart from Him," that one We would reward with Hell. Likewise We reward the evildoers.

The Arabs who were in the habit of calling on female deities were being challenged to forsake their misguided practices. Here such female deities are regarded as angelic beings, created by God, and not as complete fabrications in the imagination of Muhammad's contemporaries. In other words, Muhammad was initially concerned to denounce the false worship of al-Lat, al-'Uzza, and Manat in Mecca. Only after arriving in Medina did he see the need to criticize Christians for calling Jesus, Son of God. And he seems to have understood Christians to be doing precisely what the polytheistic Arabs were doing, elevating created beings to the same level as the Creator himself. This is clearly seen in the language used to challenge the Christians. They have "taken" Jesus as a god alongside the True God. And just as Arabs were wrong to call their female deities "daughters of God" so the Christians Arabs were wrong to call Jesus "the son of God."

Ibrahim: I think you have portrayed the narrative of the Qur'an fairly. There does seem to be a progression from the Meccan messages to the polytheistic Arabs to the Medinan messages to the Jews and Christians, the People of the Book. The two contexts of Mecca and Medina contained different challenges to the message of the Oneness of God. Nevertheless, the content of the criticisms is basically the same. There is only One God who should be worshipped, the Lord and Creator. People should not give what is due to him to any creature he has made, whether angels or humans. The focus of these criticisms is ascribing offspring to him, whether male or female. The Qur'an condemns those who say that God took a partner in Q17:111, "Praise be to God, who has not taken a child and has no associate in sovereignty." Here, ascribing offspring to God is equivalent to demeaning his capability of ruling the world he has made. Q23:91 takes this case further. "God has not taken a child. There is no god beside Him. If there were, each god would have destroyed what he created by contending with the others." Putting any other being on the same level as God would imply a fight for supremacy between them. That is why it is dangerous to call angels or humans "the offspring of God." There can be no struggle for supremacy. Q35:40 shows the central importance of this theme. "Have you seen your associates that you call on apart from God. Show me what they created on the earth! Or do they have a share of the heavens?" At the heart of these false beliefs is the notion that God took a female partner in order to have such offspring as Q72:3 indicates; "He has taken neither spouse nor child."

Jesus Called God "Father"

Paul: Perhaps this concern for guarding the Oneness of God blends the criticism of Arab polytheistic practices of calling on several gods with the Christian Arab naming of Jesus as Son of God. But in historical reality, Christians simply reflected the narrative in Mark and the later Gospels. Jesus was named Son of God by Mark and the divine approval of Jesus was enough for Jesus' followers to feel confident that there was a special relationship between Jesus and God. When we look at how Jesus spoke to God in the Gospels, we find that he called God his Father. There is one reference to Jesus praying in Mark 14:35–36; "Abba, Father, for you all things are possible; remove this cup from me; yet, not what I want, but what you want." Here you can see that the language of Jesus, Aramaic, is preserved in the name for God, *Abba*, even though Mark wrote in Greek for Greek speakers. Matthew 19:25–26 records another prayer of Jesus; "I thank you, Father, Lord of heaven and earth, because you have hidden these things from the wise and the intelligent and have revealed them to infants; 26 yes, Father, for such was your gracious will." Luke 23:34–5 has a prayer of Jesus on the cross; "Father, forgive them; for they do not know what they are doing."

The apostle Paul uses the Aramaic word *abba* in his letters written in Greek. He wrote his letter to the Galatians around 50 C.E., less than twenty years after Jesus' death. In Galatians 4:6 he says, "Because you are [his] children, God has sent the Spirit of his Son into our hearts, crying, "Abba! Father!"" Paul is writing to Greek speakers, but thinks it is good to use the Aramaic name for God that Jesus used. Leon Morris argues that Paul's desire to maintain the Aramaic expression indicates that "We are probably correct in seeing it as an accepted expression in the early church, not improbably being derived from Jesus' usage."[1] Paul also refers to Abba in his letter to the Romans 8:14–16:

> For all who are led by the Spirit of God are children of God. 15 For you did not receive a spirit of slavery to fall back into fear, but you have received a spirit of adoption. When we

---

1. Morris, *Galatians*, 131.

cry, "Abba! Father!" **16** it is that very Spirit bearing witness with our spirit that we are children of God.

James Dunn is sure that Paul's use of the Aramaic *Abba* reflects Jesus' prayer life:

> The reason why "Abba" had become so firmly established is presumably that it was remembered as a word given its particular resonance by Jesus himself. . . . Jesus' characteristic prayer address was unusual precisely because "Abba" was so much a family word, expressive of family familiarity and intimacy. For the typical Jewish piety of the period it was almost certainly too bold, overfamiliar, probably considered impudent and irreverent by most. But evidently it was just such familiarity and intimacy the first Christians experienced too.[2]

If Paul could reflect the original language of Jesus in describing Christians praying to God as Abba, Father, then it is highly likely that Jesus really did talk to God as his Father. This is another reason why people called him God's Son.

Ibrahim: What I find so interesting in the Gospels and Paul's letters is the insistence that the followers of Jesus are God's sons. Paul encourages the Roman Christians to think of themselves as God's children and for them to talk to God as their Father. Jesus teaches this especially in Matthew's Gospel. In Matthew 6:9, Jesus teaches his disciples to pray, "*Our* Father in heaven, hallowed be your name." Then he reminds them in Matthew 6:14 that *their* Father in heaven will forgive them if they forgive others, in 6:18 that *their* Father in heaven will reward them for fasting, in 6:26 that *their* Father in heaven takes care of them as he takes care of the birds, and in 7:11 that *their* Father in heaven will give good things to those who ask.

There is a collective sense in all of this that believers are united in calling God Father. Jesus appears to be the big brother of the believers. This is especially clear in John 17:11, where Jesus prays for his followers, "Holy Father, protect them in your name that you have given me, so that they may be one, as we are one." He prays that the unity between himself and God is shared with his followers. He doesn't want them to miss out on the relationship he has with God. Then John depicts Jesus praying for people who will come to believe in the future in much the same way in verse 21, "As you, Father, are in me and I am in you, may they also

---

2. Dunn, *Romans 1–8*, 461.

be in us." John emphasizes that all believers have potentially the same relationship with God that Jesus had. I think the spirit of these prayers of Jesus in John's Gospel is close to the kind of intimacy with God that Sufis seek. They too hold that any believer can potentially have a relationship with God of the quality Jesus had as "the seal of the saints." One way of reducing the tensions between the Qur'an and the New Testament is to interpret Jesus' relationship to God as an example of what others can experience.

There are Christian theologians who wish to interpret Jesus as spiritually in tune with God but not making claims to being divine. John Hick is well known for changing his mind on Jesus in the midst of his theological career. He talks about going through a Copernican revolution in his thinking after many years of believing that Jesus was divine. This came about partly through dialoguing with Muslims in Birmingham, UK after he became Professor of Theology at Birmingham University in 1967. He was persuaded by Gospel scholars that the historical Jesus did not claim to be divine. "Jesus thought of God in monotheistic and Unitarian terms."[3] Christians should acknowledge this reality by regarding Jesus as conscious of God's presence in an exceptional way, but not as God become human. In a later book which dealt with criticisms from Christians of his views, Hick responds to the belief that Jesus implied his divinity in forgiving sins. "In pronouncing forgiveness for sins Jesus was, out of his vivid awareness of God's mercy, declaring God's forgiveness, . . . not presuming himself to be God."[4]

Early Christians Called Jesus "Lord"

Paul: Hick is certainly in the same camp as Crossan and the members of the Jesus Seminar in holding that Jesus never claimed to be divine. They see the Gospel of John as being essentially different from the Synoptic Gospels in beginning with the divine nature of Jesus. They disregard the letters of Paul, which were written so soon after the death of Jesus by a Rabbi who went through his own "Copernican revolution" from rejecting the worship of Jesus as blasphemy to becoming an outstanding advocate of that worship. How can the skeptics explain this remarkable development in the followers of Jesus, from seeing him as a wonderful

---

3. Hick, "A Recent Development within Christian Monotheism," 6.
4. Hick, *The Rainbow of Faiths*, 96.

teacher and lover of God to the Lord who will come to judge humanity now seated at God's right hand, exercising divine power and authority? Larry Hurtado shows this quite eloquently:

> For Paul Jesus' divine sonship expressed the total opposite of what he had thought of Jesus prior to his conversion. Whereas previously the zealous Pharisee had regarded Jesus as a miserable false teacher who justly had suffered an accursed death, Paul came to see Jesus as sent by God and as having a uniquely favored status and relationship to God; and for Paul the biblical category "Son" was a profoundly expressive way of registering this radically changed view of Jesus.[5]

While this might still fit into the idea that Jesus was an exceptionally spiritual man, Paul also called Jesus "Lord," a title he accepted from the very Christians he had been persecuting. This was the name for God in the Jewish tradition, now applied to Jesus, and must have been used that way by the very first followers of Jesus after his death. Paul refers to Jesus in his first letter to the Corinthians with an Aramaic expression *marana tha*, "Our Lord, come!" The fact that he quotes this prayer in Aramaic in a letter written in Greek to Greek-speaking Christians shows that the first Christians called Jesus *Lord*, as Hurtado points out:

> The expression certainly comes from circles of Aramaic-speaking Jewish Christians, where it was a feature of their worship practice, an invocation to the glorified Jesus appealing either for his presence in the worship setting or for his eschatological appearance.... The practice of invoking Jesus as "our Lord" must already have been sufficiently routinized in Aramaic-speaking circles by the time Paul taught the phrase to the Corinthians, that it carried a certain cachet of tradition and could serve to unite believers across linguistic and cultural lines in a shared devotional practice.[6]

Paul also quotes from a song sung by Christians honoring Jesus as Lord in his letter to the Christians in Philippi, 2:5–11:

> Let the same mind be in you that was in Christ Jesus, **6** who, though he was in the form of God, did not regard equality with God as something to be exploited, **7** but emptied himself, taking the form of a slave, being born in human likeness. And being

---

5. Hurtado, *Lord Jesus Christ*, 108.
6. Ibid., 110.

found in human form, **8** he humbled himself and became obedient to the point of death—even death on a cross. **9** Therefore God also highly exalted him and gave him the name that is above every name, **10** so that at the name of Jesus every knee should bend, in heaven and on earth and under the earth, **11** and every tongue should confess that Jesus Christ is Lord, to the glory of God the Father.

Hurtado shows that the bestowal of the name above every name on Jesus at which every knee should bend is a reference to Isaiah 45:23, "By myself I [the Lord] have sworn, from my mouth has gone forth in righteousness a word that shall not return: 'To me every knee shall bow, every tongue shall swear.'" He argues that the title Lord "must be the Greek equivalent of bearing the Old Testament name of God."[7] Paul borrows this song from the worship of Greek-speaking churches and is happy to commend the Lordship of Jesus to the churches he founds.

Ibrahim: The elevation of Jesus to a place alongside God is the basic problem that the Qur'an is attacking. The early Christians seem to have taken the spiritual man Jesus and very quickly raised him into a divine being. How could they have done this? Jews were taught to have no other gods but God in Exodus 20:2-3, "I am the Lord your God, who brought you out of the land of Egypt, out of the house of slavery; 3 you shall have no other gods before me." It is astonishing that a Jewish Rabbi, like Paul, could depart so far from the revelation of God. It is no wonder that Muslims have often seen Paul as the main culprit in leading Christians astray from the worship of the One True God.

Paul: But what the Qur'an is attacking is not what Paul teaches. He does *not* raise a spiritual man into a divine being. If we look more closely at the accusations the Qur'an makes against Christians, we see that they are criticized for taking *people* as lords in Q9:31, "They take their priests and their monks as lords alongside God, and Christ, the son of Mary. But they were only commanded to worship one God. There is no god but He. May He be glorified above what they associate with Him!" Jesus is placed in the same category as church leaders in this condemnation. While it is true that Christians were in the habit of calling their leaders "father" or "lord," there was no hint at all that they regarded them as divine figures. What the Qur'an is doing here is to remind Christians that their language is misguided, because they ought not to use terms restricted to God for human beings. They were definitely not making

---

7. Ibid., 112.

their leaders into partners of God. The same is true for the Christian language about Jesus. The Qur'an is sensitive to titles being given to him that should be kept for God. However, Christians did not actually regard Jesus in the same way as their leaders. They worshipped him as Lord, but they never did this to their leaders. And they worshipped Jesus as Lord because they believed that he had come from God, as the song quoted by Paul shows. Jesus "did not regard equality with God as something to be exploited" means that these early Christians saw Jesus as equal to God. They perceived that Jesus was with God before emptying himself and "being born in human likeness." In other words, they did not elevate a man into equality with God. On the contrary, they saw that God had become human by emptying himself of his divine powers in order to be a human being. Thus, the criticism in Q9:31 does not relate to what the Christians normally believed. Could it be that there were people who claimed to be Christians in Arabia who gave the impression that they elevated humans to divine status?

The Qur'an Denies that God has Offspring

Paul: I would like to return to the way the Qur'an denies that God has a son. Once again, what the Qur'an is attacking is not what Christians believe God's Son to be. We have seen that the conception of Jesus was by means of God's Spirit. If God is the Father of Jesus then it is basically the same story in Matthew, Luke, and the Qur'an, since there was no human father. Given that the Qur'an understands Jesus to be conceived by God directly without a human father being involved, there can be no doubt that the Christians in and around Arabia would have wholeheartedly agreed with this. Their understanding of the relationship of the Father to Jesus, his Son, follows this reality. However, the Qur'an criticizes Christians for claiming that God had a son. It appears that the Christians are being blamed for holding a similar view to the polytheistic Arabs who worshipped several female deities as daughters of the high god. They may well have thought in terms of the high god taking a female partner and producing daughters with her. While the beliefs of the polytheistic Arabs are not well documented, the Qur'an seems to be alleging this. However, the Christian Arabs of Najran in the south of the Arabian Peninsula shared the same convictions about Jesus as the Ethiopian Christians across the Red Sea. They believed that the Word of God became human in Jesus, just as John states in his Gospel. There was *no question whatsoever* of these Christians thinking that God took a female partner and had Jesus with her. But this appears to be the accusation that the Qur'an makes of the Christians.

Mahmoud Ayoub has suggested that his fellow Muslims should revisit the texts in the Qur'an that deny that Jesus is God's son. He points out that "neither the Qur'an nor the Gospel nativity story implies that God had a female consort in Mary, or a physically engendered son in Christ."[8] This is reflected in the language used in the Qur'an:

> *Ibn* ("son"), which is used only once in the Qur'an in relation to Jesus, may be understood metaphorically to mean "son" through a relationship of love or adoption. The term *walad,* on the other hand, means "offspring," and thus primarily signifies physical generation and sonship. It is this latter term that is often used by Qur'an commentators to argue against the Christian concept of Christ's divine sonship. The Qur'an, however, does not use the term *walad* specifically to refer to Jesus. That is to say, the Qur'an nowhere accuses Christians of calling Jesus the *walad* offspring of God.[9]

I think this is very helpful, because Ayoub has shown that it is possible to separate the qur'anic accusation against the polytheists from that against the Christians.

Ibrahim: Even if this were to be done, the Qur'an is still warning Christians not to associate Jesus with God as an equal partner. This is precisely what the Najran Christians were doing. By holding to the Word of God becoming human in Jesus they were making a partner for God. Of course, this does not need to have anything to do with a female consort with whom God produced Jesus. The Qur'an recognizes that Jesus is a word from God, and perhaps this title arises from the Christian community. But he is not "the Word of God" with God in eternity, as Christians asserted. Rather, he *carries* God's word as his messenger. Therefore, the Qur'an insists that when God wishes to create a human being he only needs to say, "Be" and it happens. God speaks things into existence, so Jesus is a product of God's command to come into existence. I believe that this revelation was given for the Christians especially, who thought

---

8. Omar, *A Muslim View of Christianity,* 120.
9. Ibid., 118.

too highly of Jesus as God's Word as if Jesus was the only real example of the speech of God.

The Christians called Jesus God's Son as if God had a unique relationship with him. It was this claim to uniqueness that resulted in the reminder in the Qur'an that Adam was created without a human father or mother. Jesus said to his disciples in Q3:50–51, "Fear God and obey me. 51 God is my Lord and your Lord, so serve Him." Then a comparison of Jesus is made with Adam in Q3:59, "Jesus is like Adam before God. He created him from dust, then said to him, 'Be', and he came into being." The Qur'an goes on to challenge the People of the Book to give up believing in the divinity of Jesus by accepting that there is only one divine being in Q3:64, "'People of the Book, let us arrive at the same statement between us and you: that we worship God alone, we do not associate anyone with Him, and none of us takes others apart from God as lords.'"

Paul: This is the very passage used by the composers of the *Common Word* document we discussed earlier. We saw how they selectively quoted words of Jesus from the Synoptic Gospels that seemed to fit this picture of him you have outlined here. He sought to announce God's rule and bring his fellow Jews into true submission to God. The document does not stray from this narrow path into the kind of teaching that we have been examining from the Gospels, which shows how Jesus saw himself as one who was granted authority to forgive sin and who was called by God to lay down his life so that others might find forgiveness for sin. There is no discussion of his relationship with God expressed in his prayers to his Father.

Ibrahim: You would not expect 158 Muslim scholars to digress from their main concern to reach agreement with Christians on that which is common to Muslims and Christians by reminding the Christians of what separates them.

Paul: Many Christians responded to the *Common Word* document by pointing out just what I have said, because the context of Q3:64 is a call to Christians to accept that they are in the wrong about Jesus. Q3:61–63 shows how the Muslims are called to challenge the Christians to see Jesus like Adam, which is the truth from the Lord:

> If somebody argues with you about this after you have come to know it, say, "Come, let us summon our sons and your sons, our women and your women, ourselves and yourselves, and let us pray and lay a curse from God on the liars. 62 This is the true

account. There is no god but God. God is the Exalted, the Wise."
63 If they turn away then God knows the corrupt ones.

These are very strong words addressed to Christians! The allegation that they are guilty of corrupting the truth is severe. No wonder that some Christians reacted to the *Common Word* document by saying that they were being invited by the Muslim scholars to enter Islam by accepting a Muslim version of Jesus.

Ibrahim: Doubtless the differences between Muslims and Christians will continue to create tension between them, but we are doing our best to understand each other. Surely that is necessary if we are to get along in society without being in totally sealed-off communities. At least our discussions set a model for good relations within serious disagreement. Democracy is all about respecting those who we think are wrong, and this Muslim believes that democracy is much better than dictatorship of one community over another.

How did the early Christians come to believe in the Trinity?

Ibrahim: We have not so far talked about how the Christian belief in the divinity of Jesus led to the doctrine of the Trinity. I have always been puzzled about the third member of the Trinity, the Holy Spirit. I can see how early Christians like Paul and John came to believe in Jesus as God's unique Son who came from God and would return to him. There is an obvious duality here between God as the Father of his Son Jesus. But how did Christians add on the Holy Spirit to make God three-in-one?

Paul: Christians took their cue from the statement of Jesus in Matthew 28:18–19, "Jesus came and said to them, 'All authority in heaven and on earth has been given to me. 19 Go therefore and make disciples of all nations, baptizing them in the name of the Father and of the Son and of the Holy Spirit.'" Jesus himself refers to God in a threefold way. These are the final words of Jesus before he ascended to heaven, according to Matthew, though the other Gospels do not have them. Scholars have noted that Christians baptized in the name of Jesus in Acts 2:38, where Peter, the leading disciple after the departure of Jesus, calls on his audience of Jews in Jerusalem to "Repent, and be baptized every one of you in the name of Jesus Christ so that your sins may be forgiven; and you will receive the gift of the Holy Spirit." If Peter heard the final words of Jesus in Matthew's Gospel, then he interpreted them in a different way. But it seems more likely that Matthew is reflecting the developed practice of baptizing new Christians in the threefold name rather than just in the name of Jesus, which was the earliest practice. As Richard France concedes, "Matthew here expresses Jesus' instructions in terms which would be taken for granted in his own church."[10] There are some Christian churches today that baptize in the name of Jesus only, such as the Oneness Pentecostals, but all the others baptize in the name of the Father, Son, and Holy Spirit.

The threefold name arises from the actual experience of Jesus at his own baptism, where we have already noticed that The Father proclaimed that he was pleased with his Son and anointed him with his Spirit. If Matthew wrote his Gospel in the 70s of the first century, then baptism in the threefold name had become accepted practice in the churches he represented. Thomas Torrance explains how the baptism of Jesus was the crucible for the Trinity:

> When he set out upon his mission as the obedient servant Son, acknowledged by the Father in heaven as his beloved Son, for it was then that the heavens were opened and God sent down his Spirit upon his incarnate Son. It was not that he needed that Spirit, for he was already born of the Spirit. He was already the Son of God in perfect communion with the Father and the Spirit, and had been from all eternity, but now as the incarnate Son he received the anointing of the Spirit upon our humanity which he wore, so that upon him and through him the doors of heaven are opened and the divine blessings are poured out.[11]

It was the outpouring of the Spirit on Jesus that enabled Christians to perceive that the Spirit of God at work in the world needed to be acknowledged explicitly in baptism. Just as the Spirit of God had been poured out on Jesus at his baptism, so God's Spirit would be poured out on those who were being baptized.

The apostle Paul also wrestled with the relationship between God the Father, Son, and Holy Spirit. Whilst he never included the Spirit in a threefold grouping as Matthew did, nevertheless, we can see how he sees the Spirit as both the Spirit of *God* and at the same time the Spirit of *Jesus*. In his letter to the Christians at Rome he uses "Spirit of God" and "Spirit of Christ" interchangeably in 8:9–11:

---

10. France, *Matthew*, 1118.
11. Torrance, *Incarnation*, 125.

> But you are not in the flesh; you are in the Spirit, since the *Spirit of God* dwells in you. Anyone who does not have the *Spirit of Christ* does not belong to him. **10** But if Christ is in you, though the body is dead because of sin, the Spirit is life because of righteousness. **11** If the Spirit of him who raised Jesus from the dead dwells in you, he who raised Christ from the dead will give life to your mortal bodies also through his Spirit that dwells in you.

You can see that Paul believes that the Spirit of God dwells within the Christians at Rome, though he has never been there. He defines Christians as those who have the Spirit of Christ within them. This is obviously the same Spirit, not a second kind of Spirit. Then he goes on to define Christians as those who have Christ within them. Paul conceptualizes the Spirit of Christ as Christ himself or as the one who mediates the presence of Christ. He encourages them to believe that they will experience resurrection from death because God has given them his Spirit, who was involved in the resurrection of Jesus from death. Paul understands the threefold nature of God at work in the experience of faith. He goes on to argue in Romans 8:14–17 that the Christian experience of God's Spirit guarantees the same experience that Jesus had of the Spirit enabling him to call God his Father:

> For all who are led by the Spirit of God are children of God. **15** For you did not receive a spirit of slavery to fall back into fear, but you have received a spirit of adoption. When we cry, "Abba! Father!" **16** it is that very Spirit bearing witness with our spirit that we are children of God, **17** and if children, then heirs, heirs of God and joint heirs with Christ—if, in fact, we suffer with him so that we may also be glorified with him.

Just as Jesus called God his Father, so Christians are entitled to do the same because they are led to do so by God's Spirit. They are adopted sons of the Father, but they have the same privileges as the true Son of the Father, Jesus himself, who is the proper "heir" entitled to inherit everything belonging to his Father. Notice that Paul warns that Christians must not shrink from suffering with Jesus in his being rejected and executed. They too may experience similar rejection from society. James Dunn sums this interlocking of the Spirit of God with the Spirit of Christ in the thinking of Paul:

> For Paul the Spirit is the power of God which integrates emotion, thought, and conduct in a life-giving way (there is of

course an alternative, pernicious integration of flesh and sin on the way to death). But it does so precisely as the Spirit of Christ, the Spirit who brings us to share in the same intimate sonship which Jesus enjoyed on earth, and does so as the beginning of that process which ends in the final integration of the body into the wholeness of complete salvation (vv 9–11, 15–16). To possess the Spirit is to have the Spirit of Christ, is to share his sonship, is to live as a son led by the Spirit.[12]

Paul wrote this letter in the late 50s before Matthew wrote his Gospel, and his writing shows how the early Christians were wrestling with the ways God was at work in the life of the church. The threefold work of God as Father, Son, and Spirit, which was based on their actual experience of God, led to the recognition that God is three-in-one. They never doubted that God was one. But as Jews raised to uphold the oneness of God they came to see that the oneness could be expressed in three ways without disrupting the oneness.

The Qur'an Denies the Trinity as Making Partners for God

Ibrahim: Here lies a great difficulty for Muslims who have been taught in the Qur'an not to call God "three." Q4:171 connects belief in the sonship of Jesus with talking of threeness in God:

> Believe in God and His messengers and do not say, "three." Give it up! It will be better for you! God is only one God. Glory be to Him! He is far above having a son. Everything in the heavens and on the earth belongs to Him. God is the best Protector.

Therefore, the Christians have gone astray in their devotion to Jesus, which has taken them away from proper devotion to God. Q5:73–74 warns Christians that their insistence on calling God three-in-one will lead to disaster, and offers them the opportunity to turn back to God, who is ready to forgive them:

> Those who say that God is the third of three are unbelievers. There is only One God. If they do not renounce what they say then those who do not believe will be inflicted with a terrible torment. 74 Why do they not turn back to God and ask for His forgiveness? God is Most Forgiving, Most Merciful.

---

12. Dunn, *Romans 1–8*, 462.

SON OF GOD 145

Whatever happened among the early followers of Jesus they should not have gone down the road of seeing God as three-in-one. You might say that the Qur'an was revealed at a late stage in the development of Christianity to correct such inappropriate developments, all within the patience and kindness of God toward human beings who failed to honor him correctly. He waited a long time before revealing his final word, because he is a merciful and compassionate God who does not want his created beings to be led astray on a path that leads to destruction, but to walk on the right path that leads to life.

Paul: You have not referred to Q5:116–17, where the Trinity appears to be God, Jesus, and Mary:

> God said, "Jesus, son of Mary, did you say to people, 'Take me and my mother as two gods alongside God'?" He replied, "May You be exalted! I would not have said what I had no right to say. If I had said such a thing You would have known about it. You know what is in my inner being, but I do not know what is in Your inner being. You know what is hidden. ¹¹⁷ I only said to them what You commanded me to say: 'Worship God, my Lord, and your Lord.'"

If there were people in Arabia who believed that Mary was a divine being, then this criticism would be fair. However, we have no evidence that Christians regarded Mary as divine in that period, as we have discussed before. But this Trinity of God, Jesus, and Mary may well be the subject of the other verses you have cited. Naturally, Christians are going to react by stating categorically that the criticism of the Trinity in the Qur'an is not about them but about some strange group in Arabia that did not represent them! Muslims have not always been willing to accept this scenario. At least I can quote Farid Esack, who understands the implications of this verse for good relations with Christians:

> The Qur'an naturally dealt only with the behaviour and beliefs of those of the People of the Book with whom the early Muslim community were in actual social contact. To employ the qur'anic category of People of the Book in a generalized manner of simplistic identification of all Jews and Christians in contemporary society is to avoid the historical realities of Medinan society, as well as the theological diversity among both earlier and contemporary Christians and Jews. . . . I do not wish to suggest that there are no Christians who believe in the concept of a triune deity. Justice, however, requires that no one be held

captive to categories which applied to a community or individuals fourteen centuries ago, merely because they share a common descriptive term, a term that may even have been imposed on them by Muslims and rejected by them.[13]

He is aware that Christians engaged in dialogue with Muslims have often made this argument against a blanket condemnation of the Trinity by Muslims. "The qur'anic accusation of *shirk* against the Christians because of their alleged worshipping of three deities (4:171–3; 5:72–73) is a case in point; most Christians insist that the doctrine of the Trinity is not the same as Tritheism, the worship of three gods."[14]

Ibrahim: Yes, I concur with Esack here. He is not alone among contemporary Muslims who wish to listen carefully to Christians who are attempting to relate their trinitarian faith to unitarian Islam. Seyyed Hossein Nasr, one of the scholars who signed the *Common Word* document, contributed an essay to a volume discussing that document, in which he regards Christians as affirming the unity of God. He is critical of unthinking Christians who say that their God is not the same as the Muslim God, who is really an Arabian lunar deity. And this is what he says to unthinking fellow Muslims. "Nor is God simply to be identified with one member of the Christian Trinity, one part of three divinities that some Muslims believe wrongly that Christians worship."[15]

I think that Muslims need to pay heed to what Christians *actually* believe. Clearly they do not think that Jesus was the result of a union between God and Mary, so Muslims need to recognize this. Indeed, Christians can readily point out that they agree with the Qur'an when this criticism is made. However, Christians must also pay heed to what the Qur'an will not allow them to believe about Jesus. There can be no room for partners for God. Therefore, the triune nature of God will always be impossible for Muslims to accept. Why should he be divided? If Christians could see God the Father as having his representative, Jesus, then there would be no real difficulty, but so long as Christians see Jesus *as* God, Muslims will continue to oppose them. In another volume of essays on the *Common Word* document, Joseph Lumbard puts the Muslim case precisely:

---

13. Esack, *Qur'an Liberation & Pluralism*, 152–53.
14. Ibid., 177.
15. Nasr, "The Word of God: The Bridge between Him, You, and Us," 115.

> Muslims can only accept the efficacy of the Christian understanding of Father, Son, and Holy Spirit so long as the Father remains God as such, the one transpersonal and ineffable source of divinity, as in the opening apposition of the Nicene Creed: "I believe in one God, the Father Almighty, Maker of heaven and earth, and of all things visible and invisible." But Muslims cannot accept that the Father, Son, and Holy Spirit are all of the same essence (*homoousios*) and thus equally divine, such that what can be predicated of one can be predicated of the other. . . . The fact that anything is seen as sharing in any way with the Ultimate Divine Principle will appear as the ultimate sin of *shirk*—associating others with God.[16]

For Muslims, making partners for the One True God is the issue to be avoided by Christians. Therefore, the more progressive Christian theologians who have come to separate the real Jesus from the developed faith of Paul or John are more likely to be well received by Muslims, who will say to more traditional Christians, "Why can't you see the truth of your scholars?" The churches need a new reformation along these lines.

Paul: I reckon that the fear of *shirk* is at the heart of Muslim attitudes to the Trinity. Why would God choose to become human? Is not this the basic problem? If God is altogether different from his creation, how would he wish to enter it by taking on human nature? Perhaps the transcendence of God is the real stumbling block for Muslims. The Christian scholars who see Jesus as a spiritual man, but not God-in-flesh answer the Muslim question in a Muslim way. God did not need to become human, so the Johannine testimony to the Word of God becoming human in Jesus is opposite to what Jesus believed about himself. The Christian philosopher, Richard Swinburne, shows the importance of the Johannine view. He asks the question, how could God become human?

> To be human is to have a human way of thinking and acting and (at least normally) a human body through which to act. Being essentially divine, he could not cease to be divine. So a divine person could only become human by acquiring a human way of thinking and acting and a human body in addition to his divine way of thinking and acting. Although God does not need a body, he could acquire one, and this body would be uniquely his in that he was the only person to act through it.[17]

---

16. Lumbard, "What of the Word Is Common?" 104.
17. Swinburne, *Was Jesus God?* 41.

But he acknowledges that this way of seeing Jesus has been questioned in recent times by those who hold that Jesus himself did not claim to be divine:

> Jesus did not say explicitly and openly during his earthly life "I am God." But there is a reason why Jesus could not make a claim to be divine in such a direct way during his earthly life. If God was to become incarnate he needed to take a human nature (a human way of thinking and acting) and a human body in addition to his divine nature. If Jesus had announced during his earthly ministry "I am God," this would have been understood as a claim to be a pagan god, a powerful and lustful being who had temporarily occupied a human body, and not the all-good source of all being. . . . This is a message which Jesus could begin to proclaim openly only after his crucifixion had made very plain the reality of his humanity and so the kind of God he would have to have been; and after the resurrection had provided evidence of his unique status. And there is evidence that, given that Jesus rose from the dead, he proclaimed his divinity more openly after his resurrection. The command to baptize "in the name of the Father, and of the Son, and of the Holy Spirit" (Mt 28:19) . . . puts "the Son" (Jesus) on a level with God the Father.[18]

Swinburne argues that the Synoptic Gospels do contain the self-confessed belief of Jesus that he was divine. Jesus had to conceal his divine status so that people would not misunderstand him. In Mark's Gospel, he does not want his identity to be spoken about publicly. He wants to keep it a secret. This secrecy theme should be the next issue for our discussions, because it is so essential to the narrative of the earliest Gospel. The whole idea is that the time would come for Jesus to proclaim openly who he was. As Swinburne puts it, only after his death and resurrection could he speak about his true divine identity. Let us turn to a study of the Messiah who came to die as a ransom for many as Jesus said of himself in Mark 10:45.

---

18. Ibid., 102–3.

eight

Jesus Messiah and Redeemer

IBRAHIM OPENS THE DISCUSSION of the title "Messiah" given to Jesus in the Qur'an. Paul expounds the meaning of Messiah for prophets of the Old Testament, such as Micah and Isaiah. Ibrahim draws attention to the fact that, according to the Gospels, Jesus did not call himself Messiah. This was probably because he rejected the military role of the Messiah, since he had been sent to bring back the Jews to obedience to God. Paul agrees with this assessment and adds that Jesus wanted to redefine the concept of Messiah to include laying down his life as a sacrifice for the sins of others. Ibrahim regards Jesus as an example to follow by patient forbearance in the face of opposition, but it is not possible to see him as a sacrifice to take away sin. It is better to see him as a martyr to truth.

Paul points out that Jesus announced that he would lay down his life as a ransom for many, quoting words from Isaiah 53 concerning a suffering servant who would bear the sins of many. Ibrahim refers to several Christian scholars who do not think Jesus was referring to the suffering servant but to the Maccabean martyrs who laid down their lives to set Israel free from godless Greek rule. Paul argues that Jesus' words at the Last Supper indicate that he intended to die for sin, to create a new community of redeemed sinners, including both Jews and gentiles.

Paul raises a question about whether the Qur'an denies that Jesus died on the cross. He points out that most Muslims have understood that Jesus was rescued from crucifixion and that one of his disciples, usually Judas Iscariot, was crucified instead. Ibrahim places himself in a minority that believes that Jesus did die on the cross, but argues that this death is an example to others of dying for the truth and cannot be a sacrifice to take away their sin. Ibrahim points out that Jesus died as a human being who wanted to avoid death. How can Christians insist that Jesus was divine if he was not initially in accord with the will of God? Paul argues that the disciples believed that he was both divine and human. Ibrahim asks how the divine nature can die if divinity is eternal. Paul believes that the Triune God is involved in the death of Jesus. The Father hands the Son over as a sacrifice for sin, but feels the suffering of death in doing so, and then the Father raises Jesus to life through the Spirit. In this way, God goes through the experience of dying, but is not dead.

Jesus as Messiah

Ibrahim: Now we turn to the title "the Messiah" given to Jesus in the Qur'an several times. We have already seen that when Jesus is called "son of Mary" he is also called "the Messiah." The angels announce these names to Mary in Q3:45, "The angels said, 'Mary, God announces the news of a word from Him: his name is the Messiah, Jesus, the son of Mary.'" Notice that the first title is "the Messiah." Q4:157 reports Jews saying that they had killed "The Messiah, Jesus, son of Mary." Q4:171 has the same group of titles when the People of the Book are admonished, "The Messiah, Jesus, son of Mary, was only a messenger of God, and His word delivered to Mary, and a spirit from Him." Q5:72 challenges "Those who say that God is the Messiah, the son of Mary," because "The Messiah himself said, 'Children of Israel, worship God, my Lord and your Lord.'" The precise significance of this title is not made clear in these references, and there has been some debate among Qur'an commentators about the meaning of this name. Some have noted that "the Messiah" is referred to in the Bible with the meaning of "the anointed." So perhaps it would be good to see how this title was used by the People of the Book in the time of the revelation of the Qur'an.

Paul: Yes, that's a good idea since "the Messiah" is a very important name in the Bible for Jesus. Mark calls Jesus "the Messiah" in the opening statement of his Gospel, "The beginning of the good news of Jesus Christ, the Son of God." The Greek name "Christ" is retained in the English translation, but it is itself a translation of the Hebrew name "the Messiah." Mark announces that Jesus is "the Messiah" that the Jews had been waiting for. The prophets had pointed to an anointed ruler who God would establish after the exile of the Jews to Assyria and Babylon. Once the Jews returned to Jerusalem after the exile they looked for this anointed person who would lead them. A good example of the prophetic vision is in Micah 5:2–5:

> But you, O Bethlehem of Ephrathah, who are one of the little clans of Judah, from you shall come forth for me one who is to rule in Israel, whose origin is from of old, from ancient days. 3 Therefore he shall give them up until the time when she who is in labor has brought forth; then the rest of his kindred shall return to the people of Israel. 4 And he shall stand and feed his flock in the strength of the Lord, in the majesty of the name of the Lord his God. And they shall live secure, for now he shall be great to the ends of the earth; 5 and he shall be the one of peace.

Here the prophet Micah sees the Assyrians coming to defeat the children of Israel and to remove them from the promised land, but he also sees a ruler arising from Judah who will gather them back together in the land to live in security. Although some Jews had been able to return to the promised land after being taken away, they were subsequently ruled by Greeks and then Romans. The vision of Micah was cherished by Jews right up to the time of Jesus when they were ruled by the Romans, who did not believe in the One True God. The emphasis on Bethlehem relates to the anointed one coming from the line of the great king David, who was from Bethlehem. The prophet Isaiah looks forward to the arrival of a Davidic king who would bring back the rule of God instead of the rule of the godless (9:6–7):

> For a child has been born for us, a son given to us; authority rests upon his shoulders; and he is named Wonderful Counselor, Mighty God, Everlasting Father, Prince of Peace. 7 His authority shall grow continually, and there shall be endless peace for the throne of David and his kingdom. He will establish and uphold it with justice and with righteousness from this time onward and forevermore.

This is why the apostle Paul begins his letter to the Christians in Rome with a declaration that he is the servant of the Messiah, who is a descendent of David:

> Paul, a servant of Jesus Christ, called to be an apostle, set apart for the gospel of God, 2 which he promised beforehand through his prophets in the holy scriptures, 3 the gospel concerning his Son, who was descended from David according to the flesh.

Notice how Paul echoes the prophecy of Isaiah here in speaking of Jesus as the promised Son of God from the line of David. By calling Jesus "Christ" Paul is proclaiming that he is the anointed one that the Jews were longing to see. The title "Christ" is widespread in Paul's letters showing how central the idea of Jesus being the Messiah was in the early church.

Ibrahim: It is a remarkable fact that the early disciples of Jesus seemed to have agreed that he was the Messiah when Jesus himself never claimed to be the king of the Jews. Christian scholars have often pointed out that Jesus would not have wanted to be enthroned as king in the way that the prophets expected. Messianic psalms such as Psalm 2 indicate that the Messiah would defeat the enemies of God, but Jesus did not attempt to raise an army to fight the Romans:

> Why do the nations conspire, and the peoples plot in vain? 2 The kings of the earth set themselves, and the rulers take counsel together, against the LORD and his anointed, saying, 3 "Let us burst their bonds asunder, and cast their cords from us." 4 He who sits in the heavens laughs; the LORD has them in derision. 5 Then he will speak to them in his wrath, and terrify them in his fury, saying, 6 "I have set my king on Zion, my holy hill." 7 I will tell of the decree of the LORD: He said to me, "You are my son; today I have begotten you. 8 Ask of me, and I will make the nations your heritage, and the ends of the earth your possession. 9 You shall break them with a rod of iron, and dash them in pieces like a potter's vessel." 10 Now therefore, O kings, be wise; be warned, O rulers of the earth. 11 Serve the LORD with fear, with trembling 12 kiss his feet, or he will be angry, and you will perish in the way; for his wrath is quickly kindled. Happy are all who take refuge in him.

In order for peace to be established, the king in Jerusalem, the "son of God," will smash the power of the kings of the world unless they submit to him. John Goldingay interprets this to mean that:

> God made a permanent commitment to David that his line would always reign. Yahweh would have a father-son relationship with him, defeat his enemies, make him the greatest king in the world, and thus make him a witness to Yahweh's might and purpose.[1]

But according to Matthew 26:52, Jesus told his disciples, "Put your sword away. Anyone who lives by fighting will die by fighting." It is very

---

1. Goldingay, *Psalms 1-41*, 95.

clear that Jesus did not feel that he fitted the messianic role laid out in the Scriptures.

Paul: You have made a good point here. When we read Mark's Gospel we indeed find that Jesus never calls himself the Messiah, but refers to himself as the Son of Man. When Peter calls him the Messiah in Mark 8:29, Jesus warns his disciples not to tell anyone about him. This has been described as "the messianic secret." He seems to want his audience to guess who he is by his teaching and actions. But immediately after Peter's declaration, Jesus announces that he will suffer death at the hands of the authorities. Peter instantly rebukes Jesus for talking that way, but Jesus warns him that he is thinking like Satan and not like God. Mark is telling us that Jesus' view of his calling was not identical to the messianic expectations that many Jews had of a mighty king who would sweep away ungodly rulers. On the contrary, he had come to lay down his life in the will of God. This is the reason for his reluctance to be called the Messiah—he did not want people to think he would defeat the Romans by military power. Larry Hurtado sums up a widely held view of Mark 8:29-33: "Jesus forbids the disciples to speak of him as Messiah (8:30) because, in his divinely mandated sufferings which he refers to repeatedly in the following chapter, he must first (re)define and reveal what messiahship really means."[2] We have already discussed how Jesus called himself Son of Man, but in this context we can see that one of the main reasons for him doing this was to deflect attention away from the notion of fighting to establish the rule of God, which was built into the picture of the Messiah in Psalm 2.

Ibrahim: In Islamic tradition, Jesus was not sent to use military means to bring down apostate rulers. That was the mission of Muhammad. Jesus' role was to bring his own people, the Jews, back to a right obedience to God. He did this by his teaching and example. We saw how Jesus was often called son of Mary in Muslim writing, but he was also called the Messiah. For example, Ahmad Ibn Hanbal (d. 855) includes several sayings of Jesus the Messiah in his work on asceticism that show how Muslims in the eighth and ninth centuries saw Jesus as an exemplary ascetic. Here is a saying in which Jesus gives advice to those who would devote themselves to God:

> Christ said, "Make frequent mention of God the Exalted, also of His praise and glorification, and obey Him. It suffices for one of

2. Hurtado, *Lord Jesus Christ*, 289.

you when praying, and if God is truly pleased with him, to say: 'O God, forgive my sins, reform my way of life, and keep me safe from hateful things, O my God.'"[3]

Another saying shows the importance of passing on knowledge of God to others. Christ said, "Whoever has learned, acted, and imparted knowledge—he is the one who is called great in the kingdom of heaven."[4] A summary of the teaching of Jesus found in the Gospels is recorded in this saying:

> Christ said, "If you desire to devote yourselves entirely to God and to be the light of the children of Adam, forgive those who have done you evil, visit the sick who do not visit you, be kind to those who are unkind to you, and lend to those who do not repay you."[5]

As a Sufi who has followed this understanding of Jesus, I have always admired his fortitude in the face of intense opposition, his conviction that love for God is essential to true worship, and that being kind to others is key to the right order of society. This is the Messiah for me.

Jesus Dies as a Sacrifice for the Sins of Others

Paul: While this sentiment reflects much of the teaching and behavior of Jesus, there is more to be included. In Mark 10:45 he declared that, "The Son of Man came not to be served but to serve, and to give his life a ransom for many." By speaking of a ransom, he was most likely referring to the kind of payment made to release slaves. He saw his death as a means of release of others from bondage. Mark is telling his readers that the three predictions Jesus made of his death at the hands of the chief priests and teachers of the Law made in 8:31, 9:31, and 10:33–34, are not just to be understood as the leading Jews getting rid of him, but are also the way that Jesus could lay down his life for the sake of others. Jesus was probably thinking of himself in terms of the servant of God mentioned in Isaiah 53 who lays down his life to redeem his fellow Jews from their wrongdoing, disobedience, and going astray from the will of God:

3. Ibn Hanbal, *al-Zuhd*, 93 (no. 302), translated by Khalidi, *The Muslim Jesus*, 69.

4. Ibn Hanbal, *al-Zuhd*, 98–99 (no. 330), translated by Khalidi, *The Muslim Jesus*, 78.

5. Ibn Hanbal, *al-Zuhd*, 144–45 (no. 480), translated by Khalidi, *The Muslim Jesus*, 88.

> He was despised and rejected by others; a man of suffering and acquainted with infirmity; and as one from whom others hide their faces he was despised, and we held him of no account. 4 Surely he has borne our infirmities and carried our diseases; yet we accounted him stricken, struck down by God, and afflicted. 5 But he was wounded for our transgressions, crushed for our iniquities; upon him was the punishment that made us whole, and by his bruises we are healed. 6 All we like sheep have gone astray; we have all turned to our own way, and the LORD has laid on him the iniquity of us all. 7 He was oppressed, and he was afflicted, yet he did not open his mouth; like a lamb that is led to the slaughter, and like a sheep that before its shearers is silent, so he did not open his mouth. 8 By a perversion of justice he was taken away. Who could have imagined his future? For he was cut off from the land of the living, stricken for the transgression of my people. 9 They made his grave with the wicked and his tomb with the rich, although he had done no violence, and there was no deceit in his mouth. 10 Yet it was the will of the LORD to crush him with pain. When you make his life an offering for sin, he shall see his offspring, and shall prolong his days; through him the will of the LORD shall prosper. 11 Out of his anguish he shall see light; he shall find satisfaction through his knowledge. The righteous one, my servant, shall make many righteous, and he shall bear their iniquities. 12 Therefore I will allot him a portion with the great, and he shall divide the spoil with the strong; because he poured out himself to death, and was numbered with the transgressors; yet he bore the sin of many, and made intercession for the transgressors.

This vision of God's servant bearing the sins of others surely lies behind Jesus' intention to sacrifice himself in order that the wrongdoing of others could be cancelled out in God's sight. Richard France argues that Jesus saw himself as the servant of God who suffers to release others from their slavery to sin. "The whole thrust of Isaiah 53 is to present the servant as one who suffers and dies for the redemption of his people, whose life is offered as a substitute for their guilt."[6] In other words, Jesus announced to his disciples that he was going to his death to redeem them and many others as the fulfillment of the vision of the servant in Isaiah 53. It is here that we see the real meaning of "Messiah" for Jesus. This is confirmed in Luke 24:26, where Jesus tells two disciples after his resurrection, "Was it not necessary that the Messiah should suffer these things

---

6. France, *Mark*, 420–21.

and then enter into his glory?" While the two disciples were depressed that Jesus had been executed, the risen Jesus came to them to affirm that he *had* to die as the Messiah. For Jesus, the Messiah was the servant who was sent to suffer and die to redeem the people.

Ibrahim: We have already noted that not all Christian scholars believe that Jesus intended to die for sinners. Adela Collins thinks that Mark added the saying about dying as a ransom from the traditions that were shared by the early church. She mentions that Paul taught that Jesus died as a ransom for sin before Mark wrote his Gospel, but argues that, "It is unlikely that Mark is dependent on Paul in 10:45. It is more likely that they [Paul and Mark] drew independently upon similar earlier traditions."[7] Therefore, the disciples of Jesus came to believe that Jesus had intended to die for sinners, but Jesus himself did not teach this. Morna Hooker thinks that Jesus saw himself as a martyr in Mark 10:45. She points to the Maccabean martyrs who laid down their lives in a struggle against Greek dominance of the Jews described in the Books of Maccabees:

> The Maccabean martyrs, whose tortures are described in 4 Maccabees might well have been said to have given their lives for many. Mark 10:45 reminds us that suffering and victory belong to each other, and that it is only through the former that the latter is achieved.[8]

Hooker thinks that Jesus regarded himself as a representative of the people of God who would deliver his people, not as a substitute for sin. Dominic Crossan doubts whether Jesus intended to die because he did not intend any role for himself. Jesus did something to draw attention to himself in the courts of the Jerusalem temple and prophesied that the temple would be destroyed in a symbolic way. Because of "the confined and tinder-box atmosphere of the Temple at Passover, especially under Pilate," Jesus' attitude "*could* easily have led to arrest and execution."[9] So there are many Christian interpreters who do not think it is possible that Jesus intended to die as a sacrifice to redeem others from sin.

Paul: I recognize that there are scholars who find it difficult to conceive of Jesus intending to go to the cross to be a sacrifice for the sins of many. However, they must account, among other things, for the words of Jesus at the Last Supper held with his disciples before his death. If

---

7. Collins, *Mark*, 503.
8. Hooker, *Mark*, 250–51.
9. Crossan, *The Historical Jesus*, 360.

the disciples invented the idea of Jesus being a sacrifice for sin and put the words on Jesus' lips, then the motivation for this must be seriously considered. What they would have done, in effect, was to create an image of Jesus. If the story of the disciples fleeing from Jesus at the point of his arrest is historical, and if the denial of Peter that he knew Jesus is a true account of Peter, then the disciples were in no state to invent ideas that had not been suggested by Jesus himself. If the notion of Jesus being a martyr for the sake of the redemption of Israel was central to Jesus' teaching, then that would have been made clear by the apostles in their writing. Yet unanimously, the apostolic writings speak of Jesus laying down his life to redeem others from sin, not to redeem Israel from foreign rulers as the Maccabees attempted to do by dying in battle against the Greek invaders. The conclusion must be that Jesus spoke of dying to redeem others from sin.

When we look at what he said at the Last Supper, we see that he turned the traditional Passover meal into a memorial of his death. The Passover celebrated the departure of the children of Israel from slavery in Egypt. Jesus had gathered his disciples to celebrate the Passover meal, and at the end of the traditional meal he took bread and wine and said that they represented his body given for them and his blood poured out for them. Mark 14:22–24 reports what Jesus said:

> While they were eating, he took a loaf of bread, and after blessing it he broke it, gave it to them, and said, "Take; this is my body." 23 Then he took a cup, and after giving thanks he gave it to them, and all of them drank from it. 24 He said to them, "This is my blood of the covenant, which is poured out for many."

The phrase "poured out for many" repeats the language of Isaiah 53:11–12, "he poured out himself to death," and "he bore the sin of many." It was the memory of these words that filled the minds of the disciples who fled from him. They could not possibly have thought up such words after his death to exalt their defeated master. Remember that their concept of Messiah was the military hero who would defeat the enemy and live to rule. Jesus' concept of the Messiah was a suffering servant who could only come to rule after laying down his life to redeem the people. If the disciples were fixed on the powerful Messiah of Daniel 7, then Jesus was saying that he could only be served as the glorious Son of Man of Daniel 7 after he had given himself in service to others by dying to bear the sins of many. John Dennis argues that this is what Jesus was teaching.

"Jesus will fulfil the full destiny of the glorified and powerful Son of Man, but only after he has suffered and died."[10]

Ibrahim: But you must consider the fact that the earliest testimony to these words of Jesus comes from Paul in his first letter to the Corinthians. He was not present at the Last Supper, yet he reports the event. What if Paul himself invented the story to back up his own interpretation of the death of Jesus? He seems to be very keen on the idea of Jesus as a sacrifice for sin, and perhaps he is the one who first suggested it. Even a fairly conservative scholar such as James Dunn does not think that Jesus thought of himself as the suffering servant of Isaiah. "A convincing case cannot be made that Jesus saw himself as the suffering servant."[11] On the contrary, Jesus saw himself as a martyr who would "share the fate of the prophets to suffer as a man in the hands of men."[12] The obvious conclusion is that the sacrifice for sin idea originated with the early church and not Jesus himself. Paul is the best candidate for this originality, given that his letters are the earliest documents we have of what was believed about Jesus.

Paul: It is true, of course, that Paul wrote in the 50s and Mark may not have written until as late as the 70s, so the earliest record of the last supper is in Paul's first letter to the Corinthians. But note what Paul says in 1 Corinthians 11:23–26:

> For I received from the Lord what I also handed on to you, that the Lord Jesus on the night when he was betrayed took a loaf of bread, 24 and when he had given thanks, he broke it and said, "This is my body that is for you. Do this in remembrance of me." 25 In the same way he took the cup also, after supper, saying, "This cup is the new covenant in my blood. Do this, as often as you drink it, in remembrance of me." 26 For as often as you eat this bread and drink the cup, you proclaim the Lord's death until he comes.

Paul is telling the Christians in Corinth that he *received* this from the Lord. For Paul, the Lord is Jesus himself. Whether he heard the words directly from Jesus or from those who were present at the Last Supper is not clear, but scholars are united in holding that the words are not Paul's normal vocabulary and style and must come from an earlier source. Anthony Thiselton states, "There can be no doubt whatever that

---

10. Dennis, "Death of Jesus," 179.
11. Dunn, *Jesus Remembered*, 817.
12. Ibid., 805.

these verses are pre-Pauline."[13] Far from inventing these words, Paul was quoting another source that existed before he wrote the letter. Someone else spoke these words in a different style from that of Paul. Thiselton draws the conclusion that "Jesus presided at a Passover meal which proclaimed his own broken body and shed blood as the new Passover for Christian believers."[14] Mark reports these words in very similar terms to Paul, which points to him relying on a similar source. By far the most plausible interpretation of these words is that Jesus himself spoke of his death not only for Israel but for many others. Nicholas Perrin shows this double intention in Jesus' declaration at the Last Supper. "Jesus' death not only would atone for Israel's covenantal unfaithfulness but also would seal the terms of a new covenant, affording a fresh basis for a new salvific economy."[15] Therefore, there are very good grounds for believing that Jesus went to the cross to redeem both wayward Jews and gentiles, who needed his sacrifice to become part of a new community of God's people that expanded beyond the Jewish nation.

Ibrahim: For a Muslim, it is inconceivable that Jesus should think of himself as a sacrifice for the sins of others. While it is possible for the saints to intercede before God for the sins of others, they do this not by laying down their lives to death as a substitute for the sins of others, but by praying for them. Jesus, then, as the greatest of the saints might pray, but he certainly did not die for them.

Did Jesus Escape Crucifixion according to the Qur'an?

Paul: It is deeper than this surely for Muslims, because the Qur'an denies that Jesus was put to death on the cross in Q4:157:

> [The People of the Book] said, "We killed the Messiah, Jesus, son of Mary, the Messenger of God." They did not kill him, and they did not crucify him, but it seemed so to them. Those that do not agree with this are in doubt about it, do not have knowledge of it, and follow mere opinion. They certainly did not kill him.

There is no doubt that most Muslims have interpreted this passage to mean that the New Testament story of Jesus being crucified is simply fiction. Within a few decades of the coming of Islam, the idea developed

---

13. Thiselton, *First Corinthians*, 867.
14. Ibid., 874.
15. Perrin, "Last Supper," 494.

that God put the likeness of Jesus on someone else who was crucified by the authorities who thought they had got Jesus. The first mention of this was by ibn ʿAbbas (d. 687), who held that the likeness of Jesus was cast upon Natyanus, one of the friends of the Jews, so they killed him instead of Jesus.[16] This interpretation has been repeated for centuries by virtually all commentators. Usually the person chosen by God to resemble Jesus is Judas Iscariot, the disciple who betrayed Jesus to the leading Jews. The earliest known representative of this view is Wahb ibn Munabbih (d. 732), who believed that:

> One of the disciples came to the Jews and offered to lead them to Jesus for a price. At some point previous, this disciple was changed into the likeness of Jesus, so the Jews took him, sure that he was Jesus. . . . They crucified what "appeared to them."[17]

So, in the first century of Islam the idea that God protected Jesus from crucifixion became a fixed view among Muslims. Things have not changed much even today when Muslims are much more aware of historical reality. For example, Seyyed Hossein Nasr, one of the signatories of the *Common Word* document, states plainly that, "The non-crucifixion of Jesus is the one irreducible fact separating Christianity and Islam."[18] The substitution theory still commands broad support. Z. H. Assfy thinks that Judas who betrayed Jesus was "miraculously transformed to resemble Jesus in all his physical features" and was crucified.[19] Muslims fly in the face of history by continuing to refuse to accept that Jesus was crucified.

Ibrahim: I accept that most Muslims hold the substitution view, but I am in the minority that think this is not the kind of miracle that God would perform. I agree with Razi, who rejected the substitution theory because God would not have been the author of confusion in the true identification of people:

> If we saw Zayd it would be possible that it was not really Zayd, but that the likeness of Zayd had been cast upon another. This would imply the nullification of social contracts such as marriage

---

16. See al-Fīruzabadi, *Tanwir al-miqbas min tafsir ibn ʿAbbas*, 68, reported in Lawson, *The Crucifixion and the Qurʾan*, 46.
17. See Lawson, *The Crucifixion and the Qurʾan*, 51.
18. Nasr, *Islamic Life and Thought*, 210.
19. Assfy, *Islam and Christianity*, 56–57.

and ownership.... Such confusion about perceived phenomena would threaten the foundations of all religious laws.²⁰

Todd Lawson asks why few commentators on this verse have followed this view. "It is puzzling that this *tafsir* has had so little influence on later Muslim exegetes."²¹

I also am among the minority who think that Jesus was crucified. If history testifies that Jesus was executed by the Roman government, as Roman historians such as Tacitus recognize, then this fact can be aligned with the denial in Q4:157 that the People of the Book crucified Jesus. The *Jews* did not crucify Jesus, because they had no power to do so. Only the Roman governor, Pontius Pilate, could condemn a man to crucifixion. Therefore, the Jewish leaders sought Jesus' crucifixion but had to appeal to Pilate to get it done. This resolves the age-old contention between Muslims and Christians about whether Jesus was actually crucified. Muslims simply must accept historical truth in this issue. After all, a scholar such as Dominic Crossan, who is skeptical about much of the material in the Gospels, affirms the reality of the crucifixion. He states that, "There is not the slightest doubt about the *fact* of Jesus' crucifixion under Pontius Pilate."²² I note that Seyyed Hossein Nasr has come around to thinking that God may have revealed the crucifixion of Jesus to Christians while at the same time revealing the non-crucifixion of Jesus to Muslims. He struggles with the weight of history by talking about different ways of seeing the same event:

> Was Christ crucified or was he taken alive to Heaven and not crucified as asserted by Islam? Here one faces what seems to be an insurmountable obstacle. One could say that a major cosmic event at the end of the earthly life of Christ could in fact be "seen" and "known" in more than one way, and that it is God's will that Christianity should be given to "see" that end in one way and Islam in another.²³

But this twofold revelation is simply impossible to imagine. How could God confuse two huge sections of humanity in this way? We are

20. al-Razi, *Al-Tafsir al-Kabir*, 11:99, on Q4:157, translated by Lawson, *The Crucifixion and the Qur'an*, 106.

21. Lawson, *The Crucifixion and the Qur'an*, 107.

22. Crossan, *The Historical Jesus*, 375.

23. Nasr, "Comments on a Few Theological Issues in the Islamic-Christian Dialogue," 464.

back to Razi's argument about God confusing people about the identity of individuals. No, the only option is to interpret Q4:157 in the light of the historical situation at the end of Jesus' life.

Paul: Your candor is refreshing. I'm also impressed by the recent book by Mona Siddiqui, *Christians, Muslims & Jesus,* in which she attempts to understand Christian faith in the crucified Jesus. She asked her Christian colleagues in the Faculty of Divinity at Edinburgh University to share what the cross meant to them. While the reactions were diverse they all pointed to one central reality:

> All the various meanings of the cross still point to one truth, which is that at the centre of the Christian faith is the passion and death of Christ on the cross, the very focus of its sacramental *anamnesis* in "the bread and wine" of the Eucharist.[24]

She points out that "Nothing in Islam compares to this and, if anything, Muslims have either rejected or ignored the significance of the cross."[25] She writes that as she sits in church before the cross it does not draw her in. She "cannot incline towards what it says about a God in human form, a God who undergoes this inexplicable agony for an inexplicable act of mercy."[26] She does not expound Q4:157, but she hints that the very ambiguity of the text allows for different possible interpretations. Most Muslims have rejected the fact of the cross, while a few have accepted the fact of the cross but not the Christian meaning of it:

> Some Muslims like Muhammad 'Abduh and Rashid Rida rejected the view that Jesus was taken up from this world without dying. They maintained that Jesus did die on the cross but that his soul was taken to heaven. The issue is that even if Muslims came to believe that Jesus did die on the cross before he was raised, in the Qur'anic frame of references this death has no atoning significance and would not be seen as the decisive event in the redemption plan for humankind.[27]

Siddiqui appears to agree with you that it is possible to interpret Q4:157 to include the crucifixion of Jesus, but it is not possible to believe in the redemption of the sin of others through Jesus' death.

---

24. Siddiqui, *Christians, Muslims & Jesus,* 238.
25. Ibid.
26. Ibid., 242.
27. Ibid., 231.

Jesus Dies as a Martyr to Truth

Ibrahim: Yes, her approach is very similar to mine. I'm inclined to agree with the notion that Jesus died as a martyr to truth, put forward by Mahmoud Ayoub. He argues that the Qur'an should be understood to be saying that they could kill the body of Jesus but not the word of God that he represented. According to Ayoub:

> The Qur'an is not speaking here about a man, righteous and wronged though he may be, but about the Word of God who was sent to earth and who returned to God. Thus the denial of the killing of Jesus is a denial of the power of human beings to vanquish and destroy the divine Word, which is forever victorious.[28]

In other words, Ayoub interprets the outright denial that Jesus was put to death by crucifixion as a denial that human beings can put *God's word* to death. If the Qur'an can be read as referring to the *meaning* of the death of Jesus, rather than the *fact* of the cross, then it is possible to bring the teaching of the Qur'an into line with the historical reality that Jesus of Nazareth was executed by the Romans. They may have killed the man, but the word of God that he represented can never die. The Qur'an is speaking not so much about history as about God not being vanquished by human arrogance. There may have been people who rejected God's message proclaimed by Jesus to the extent that they got rid of him by means of the cross, but they did not reckon with the fact that God has the last word, and no-one can silence him.

Ayoub believes that Jesus died a martyr's death that has inherent power to influence others. In an article entitled, "The Idea of Redemption in Christianity and Islam," he points out that for Western Christians, Christ redeems them from sin on "an altar of suffering," while for Eastern Christians Christ redeems them from death "on a throne of glory."[29] He compares these beliefs with the conviction of Muslims that Jesus will redeem humanity from the anti-God *al-Dajjal* at the end of time, when Jesus returns from heaven to kill the pigs, break the crosses, and establish Islam. This is closely paralleled by the picture of Jesus in the Book of Revelation, returning to earth "not as the meek lamb of God but as the man who has a sword of fire coming out of his mouth with every word he

---

28. Ayoub, "Toward an Islamic Christology II," 176.
29. Ayoub, "The Idea of Redemption in Christianity and Islam," 92.

utters. Before the new earth and the new heaven appear, replacing the old earth and heaven, judgement must be executed on the wicked."[30]

How might the martyrdom of Jesus impact others? Perhaps like the Shiʻi martyrs such as Husayn, the grandson of the Prophet Muhammad, who through being killed in God's way by the Sunni majority, redeem those who weep for them, because they have the permission of God to intercede for others. The Shiʻa believe that, "Whoever weeps even one drop of tears for the sufferings of the imams will have the reward of paradise."[31] Thus, the notion that Jesus laid down his life for his friends is a Johannine theme that Ayoub can integrate into his Islamic worldview. He believes that "Christ redeemed and continues to redeem us, not simply and only by his divine act but by his humanity, a humanity that cared."[32] What exactly does Ayoub mean by Jesus' "divine act"? He does not elaborate this here, but by referring to his Christology article it is possible to say that Christ exemplified the divine word. His teaching was the word of God, which he acted out in compassion for the needs of others. He healed the lepers and the blind, fed his disciples with miraculous food, and even raised the dead. He was the greatest of the saints who empty themselves for the sake of others.

Paul: You can accommodate Shiʻi martyrs in your Sunni Sufism, Ibrahim. That is very broad-minded of you. Husayn died in battle, but Jesus died without putting up armed resistance to his enemies. The Maccabees died fighting the Greeks, but Jesus told Peter to put away his sword when Jesus was arrested, according to John 18:11. So it is important to distinguish Jesus' "martyrdom" from that of noble men who died fighting for the truth as they saw it. It is interesting that Peter came to understand this difference when he wrote his first letter. He addresses Christians in what is modern Turkey and advises them to submit to the governing authorities who may well have made life troublesome for Christians in some areas. In 1 Peter 2:13–14, Peter urges them to be good citizens. "For the Lord's sake accept the authority of every human institution, whether of the emperor as supreme, 14 or of governors, as sent by him to punish those who do wrong and to praise those who do right." There is no room for armed struggle here to protect the truth. He then advises slaves in

---

30. Ibid., 96.
31. Ibid.
32. Ibid., 97.

the churches, of whom there would be significant numbers, to submit to their masters in 1 Peter 2:18–21:

> Slaves, accept the authority of your masters with all deference, not only those who are kind and gentle but also those who are harsh. 19 For it is a credit to you if, being aware of God, you endure pain while suffering unjustly. 20 If you endure when you are beaten for doing wrong, what credit is that? But if you endure when you do right and suffer for it, you have God's approval. 21 For to this you have been called, because Christ also suffered for you, leaving you an example, so that you should follow in his steps.

Peter calls on the example of Jesus to help slaves who are suffering under cruel masters not to rebel but to accept unjust suffering as Jesus did. He then goes on to show in verses 22 to 25 that Jesus suffered to death for their sake by submitting to the cruelty of those in authority:

> "He committed no sin, and no deceit was found in his mouth." 23 When he was abused, he did not return abuse; when he suffered, he did not threaten; but he entrusted himself to the one who judges justly. 24 He himself bore our sins in his body on the cross, so that, free from sins, we might live for righteousness; by his wounds you have been healed. 25 For you were going astray like sheep, but now you have returned to the shepherd and guardian of your souls.

You can see how many references there are to the servant of Isaiah 53 in this passage. Peter had come to see that the Jesus he had tried to protect at the point of being arrested was the suffering servant of God who was guilty of no crime, but took the punishment for the crimes of many others, including Peter. The wounds of the suffering servant have healed those who have turned to him in faith. The wandering sheep have found security in the Good Shepherd. Notice the wonder of Peter recovering from his denial that he knew Jesus when he was outside the court where Jesus was being tried. Peter was now encouraging Christians not to resist the authorities, but to accept suffering as Jesus did. Peter had once known desperate fear of suffering and death when he vehemently denied being a disciple of Jesus, a story told in all four Gospels. Now he has a calm assurance that God will provide a new life for those who die in the faith. It is said that Peter was crucified upside down in Rome during the severe persecution of the Roman Christians by Emperor Nero in the

60s. He died as a martyr along with thousands of other Christians, having come to accept that death is not the end but the beginning of a new life.

Ibrahim: It is a remarkable story of complete recovery and transformation in the leading disciple of Jesus. The inspiration that Peter found in the martyrdom of Jesus enabled him to follow his master's path. I believe that the example of Jesus continues to inspire people today. He was sent by God not to conquer by military means but to show how we can believe in the rule of God even when humans seem all powerful. We can draw strength from his trust in God in the garden when he asked for the impending suffering to be taken away. He was a human being just like the rest of us and feared death the way all of us do. In Mark 14:34–36, Jesus pleaded with God to let him live:

> And going a little farther, he threw himself on the ground and prayed that, if it were possible, the hour might pass from him. 36 He said, "Abba, Father, for you all things are possible; remove this cup from me; yet, not what I want, but what you want."

As a normal human being he wants to avoid death, but as a submitted servant of God he wants to do the will of his Lord. This is an inspiration to all believers in God, especially to those who are near to him. Ghazali notices Jesus' fear of death and his prayer to God for strength. "Jesus said to his disciples, 'Pray God that He may make this agony—meaning death—easy for me, for I have come to fear death so much that my fear of death has made me acquainted with death.'"[33] There is a parallel in the Sufi tradition with dying to self in the presence of God, that can be a fearful experience of surrender and loss of control. Jesus is an exemplar for those who would let go of desire for permanence and who would seek to become one with the Beloved. Tarif Khalidi points out that Ghazali's inclusion of this saying of Jesus from "the agony in the Garden of Gethsemane . . . underlines the human frailty of Jesus."[34]

This story of Jesus' surrender to the will of God demonstrates that he was not on the same level as God. Whatever we make of the will of God at this juncture, we can readily understand that Jesus did not initially wish to fulfill God's will. If Jesus were truly equal to God then he would not have wanted to challenge that will. He would have gone to his death

---

33. al-Ghazali, *Ihya' 'ulum al-din*, 4:446. Translated by Khalidi, *The Muslim Jesus*, 181.

34. Khalidi, *The Muslim Jesus*, 181.

without a murmur. It is very interesting that the writer of the letter to the Hebrews does think Jesus went happily to his death in 12:2. He writes in Chapter 12 to encourage Christians to run the race of life like athletes:

> Therefore, since we are surrounded by so great a cloud of witnesses, let us also lay aside every weight and the sin that clings so closely, and let us run with perseverance the race that is set before us, 2 looking to Jesus the pioneer and perfecter of our faith, who for the sake of the joy that was set before him endured the cross, disregarding its shame, and has taken his seat at the right hand of the throne of God.

Here Jesus does not waver before his impending death on the cross because he knows that he will be seated at God's right hand. But the historical Jesus was clearly quite different from this conception. When Jesus is thought of as equal to God, sharing his throne, and ruling humanity as a divine being, then the picture given in the Gospels changes, and the struggling human Jesus gives way to a glorious, triumphant Jesus who knows that his trials will be short lived and that he will be vindicated by God in glory.

Paul: But if Jesus was both divine and human, he could respond to events in different ways. The ultimate joy of setting others free from sin by his sacrificial death would motivate him to endure the suffering. Joy within pain is not an unusual experience for human beings. Women can experience joy at the arrival of a baby despite the agony of giving birth. Soldiers can feel a sense of dying for the glory of the cause in the face of impending death. And there was another aspect of joy for Jesus in facing his death. He would set others free from the power of death and grant them access to a new life. This was something Peter mentioned at the beginning of his letter in chapter 1:3-4:

> Blessed be the God and Father of our Lord Jesus Christ! By his great mercy he has given us a new birth into a living hope through the resurrection of Jesus Christ from the dead, 4 and into an inheritance that is imperishable, undefiled, and unfading, kept in heaven for you.

The death of Jesus opened up the reality of his being raised from the dead and created the prospect of another life after death for those who trusted in him. Peter encourages his readers to live in that trust, because the impermanence of life was all too real for them. The whole theme of the resurrection of Jesus should be our next discussion.

Does the Divine Nature Die?

Ibrahim: Yes, that is the logical next step, to look at the raising up of Jesus. However, your claim that Jesus was both divine and human is sorely tested at the crucifixion. If the divine nature in Jesus died, then it follows that death affected God in such a way that he would experience death. This is not logically possible, since divinity is eternal and can never come to an end, even temporarily for three days in a rock tomb outside Jerusalem.

Paul: Perhaps it is also true that God does not govern the universe by the logic that we think we observe in what he has made. He can transcend the usual patterns of life. This is indeed what he did in the virginal conception, in which we both believe, but it is not logical for a child to be conceived without male sperm. The early Christians were convinced that Jesus was both divine and human. When we look at the song quoted by Paul in Philippians 2:6–11, we see the conviction that the Messiah was truly divine but took human nature to identify with us even to the point of death on a cross. The one who dies is divine as well as human. Even before Paul, there were Christians singing songs like this about the divine and human Messiah. Paul affirms this belief of the early church. N. T. Wright makes this clear:

> Paul insists that when Jesus dies what we are seeing is the love of God in action. If the one who died on the cross was not somehow identified with the one true God, then his death would reveal, not how much God loved, but how much God managed to escape the consequences of genuine love. The One God, who will not share his glory with another, has shared it with Jesus—precisely because he has been "obedient to death, yes, the death of the cross." For Paul in Philippians, the crucifixion of Jesus is not something which happened despite the fact that he was God incarnate, but because of it. He has done what only God can do.[35]

Some Christians have argued that only the human nature of Jesus died on the cross. In the earliest recorded debate on the crucifixion between a Muslim and a Christian in 781–82, the Caliph al-Mahdi asked the Patriarch of the East Syrian church "Is it possible that God died, supposing that he [Christ] is God?" Patriarch Timothy replied, "In so far as he was God, Christ did not die; but in so far as he was human, in his human

---

35. Wright, *Pauline Perspectives*, 315.

nature he died."[36] However, dividing Jesus up into parts like this is not the wisest approach. It is better to hold the divine and human together so that there is no separation between them. Contemporary Christian theologians have grasped this point. Jürgen Moltmann has challenged this tradition of keeping the divinity of Jesus free from suffering and death:

> What is in question in the relationship of Christ to his Father is not his divinity and humanity and their relationship to each other but the total, personal aspect of the Sonship of Jesus. . . . In the cross, Father and Son are most deeply separated in forsakenness and at the same time are most inwardly one in their surrender. What proceeds from this event between Father and Son is the Spirit which justifies the godless, fills the forsaken with love and even brings the dead alive.[37]

For many Christians now it seems impossible to regard only the human Jesus as dying on the cross. Thomas Torrance is another theologian who thinks this way:

> The whole of our salvation depends on the fact that it is God in Christ who suffers and bears the sin of the world, and reconciles the world to himself. The validity of our salvation depends on the fact that he who died on the cross under divine judgement is also God the judge, so that he who forgives is also he who judges. . . . Everything depends upon the fact that the cross is lodged in the heart of the Father. Put God in heaven, and Jesus on the cross only as a man, and you destroy all hope and trust, and preach a doctrine of the blackest and most abysmal despair. Denial of the deity of Christ destroys faith in God and in man, and turns the cross into the bottomless pit of darkness. But put God on the cross, and the cross becomes the world's salvation.[38]

What the death of Jesus reveals is the inner working of the Triune God, Father, Son, and Spirit. Michael Welker sums up this relationship. "Insofar as the cross reveals God's pain and impotence, so also does the inner communion between Creator, Spirit, and Jesus Christ become discernible over against a world that closes itself off from God."[39] God suffers death in Jesus, but is not dead, because the Eternal God has entered time

36. Timothy I, "Dialogue between the Caliph al-Mahdi and Timothy I," appendix, 44.
37. Moltmann. *The Crucified God*, 244–45.
38. Torrance, *Incarnation*, 189–90.
39. Welker, *God the Revealed: Christology*, 208.

in Jesus, but is not exhausted in him. The Father and the Spirit commune with Jesus even through death, but are not consumed by it. The Father raises Jesus from death to new life through the Spirit. This conviction takes us to a conversation on the resurrection of Jesus.

nine

Raised from Death

PAUL BEGINS THE DISCUSSION of the resurrection with the apostle Paul's experience of meeting the resurrected Jesus while still an opponent of Christians. This must have been a true encounter since Paul was transformed by it into an ardent disciple of Jesus. Ibrahim argues that Paul's experience was the basis for the stories of the encounters of Jesus with the disciples in the Gospels. Their visions were modelled on his. Paul replies that the meetings with Jesus were real, and could have been photographed. So they were not dream-state visions. Ibrahim wonders how Jesus could have gone through walls and doors if he were flesh and blood. He must have had a remarkably different kind of body. They discuss different levels of faith in the resurrected Jesus and how some of the disciples could doubt him on the mountain in Galilee when they met after the resurrection. Ibrahim suggests that some thought of Jesus as a remarkable man exalted by God while others came to regard him as divine. Paul admits that the Messiah was not thought of by Jews as divine, but that Christians did believe that he was divine. Ibrahim questions whether Stephen and Paul had different views of the divine status of Jesus.

Ibrahim expounds the teaching of the Qur'an and the sayings of the Prophet Muhammad about the ascension of Jesus. The Qur'an speaks of Jesus being raised to heaven, and most Muslims interpret the Qur'an to mean that Jesus was raised without going through death. Ibrahim explains that he is in the minority who accept that Jesus died as a martyr to truth and was vindicated by God raising him to himself. Paul asks whether the story about Muhammad being taken to heaven one night and meeting Jesus among other prophets has influenced Muslim interpretation of the Qur'an. Ibrahim argues that the night journey of Muhammad demonstrates that Jesus is not alone in being raised by God, other prophets are raised too. This means that the raising of Jesus should not be isolated and made too much of by Christians. Paul points out, on the contrary, that the resurrection of Jesus was unique. No other human being had been raised from the dead before him. Jesus is the first-fruits of the resurrection of everyone else. Without the resurrection of Jesus there is no guarantee of anyone else experiencing eternal life with God. Ibrahim asks how such a guarantee works when those who may say they believe in the resurrection of Jesus then fail to love God or their neighbor. Surely faith must be completed by right intentions and actions. Paul agrees that faith will have these results.

Paul returns to discuss the empty tomb as evidence for the resurrection. He believes that Jesus predicted his being raised on the third day. Ibrahim sides with those who doubt that Jesus said this. Ibrahim then highlights the apostle Paul's teaching that Jesus will bring everything into submission to God, and wonders how Paul conceives of the relationship between Jesus and God. Jesus appears to be a man who is not equal to God. Paul points to other writing of the apostle Paul that speak of Jesus as the image and fullness of God to balance the teaching in 1 Corinthians. Ibrahim states that the Muslim expectation is that Jesus will return from heaven to earth to bring everyone into submission to God, but that he will submit to God once this task is complete. Paul agrees that they should discuss the return of Jesus in the following chapter. However, from the Christian perspective, the resurrection of Jesus will be fully known at the end of time. In this interim period we live by faith not by sight, but the day will come when all humanity will see Jesus and come to bow the knee before him and acknowledge that he is Lord.

The Resurrection in the Experience of the Apostle Paul

Paul: I would like to begin, not with the stories of the resurrection of Jesus in the Gospels, but with the apostle Paul's statement in 1 Corinthians 15:3–9:

> For I handed on to you as of first importance what I in turn had received: that Christ died for our sins in accordance with the scriptures, **4** and that he was buried, and that he was raised on the third day in accordance with the scriptures, **5** and that he appeared to Cephas, then to the twelve. **6** Then he appeared to more than five hundred brothers and sisters at one time, most of whom are still alive, though some have died. **7** Then he appeared

to James, then to all the apostles. **8** Last of all, as to one untimely born, he appeared also to me. **9** For I am the least of the apostles, unfit to be called an apostle, because I persecuted the church of God.

Notice that Paul is reporting what he has received from others, apart from the last statement about his own experience of encountering Jesus when he was engaged in persecuting the followers of Jesus. He has a profound sense of shame and guilt for his evil behavior, which is seen in his amazement that Jesus should appear to *him* and call *him* to be his apostle, and join the group of apostles already called by Jesus. These are Cephas (Peter), the rest of the twelve disciples, James, the brother of Jesus, who we have seen was skeptical about Jesus' status at one time along with the rest of Jesus' family. Then there are other apostles not named here. Since Paul probably had this experience within a couple of years of the death of Jesus, these stories of Jesus appearing to the apostles took place before this. In other words, the numerous encounters of Jesus with his chosen disciples after his death can only mean that a very significant number of people met Jesus risen from death. It is certainly not a question of Paul inventing the resurrection of Jesus out of his encounter with him. The stories recorded in the Gospels were probably written down in the 70s (Mark), the 80s (Matthew and Luke), and 90s (John). Paul's letter to the Corinthians is from the 50s, so is the oldest testimony to the resurrection of Jesus in the writings of the early Christians.

There can be little doubt that the appearance of Jesus to Paul on the road from Jerusalem to Damascus in the early 30s dramatically turned Paul from a hater to a lover of Jesus. Paul refers to this meeting in his letter to the Christians in Galatia, in modern Turkey, in 1:13–19:

> You have heard, no doubt, of my earlier life in Judaism. I was violently persecuting the church of God and was trying to destroy it. **14** I advanced in Judaism beyond many among my people of the same age, for I was far more zealous for the traditions of my ancestors. **15** But when God, who had set me apart before I was born and called me through his grace, was pleased **16** to reveal his Son to me, so that I might proclaim him among the gentiles, I did not confer with any human being, **17** nor did I go up to Jerusalem to those who were already apostles before me, but I went away at once into Arabia, and afterwards I returned to Damascus. **18** Then after three years I did go up to Jerusalem

to visit Cephas and stayed with him fifteen days; **19** but I did not see any other apostle except James the Lord's brother.

Paul has come to be aware that God had chosen him before his birth, despite his antagonism to God's Son. The encounter on the road to Damascus led Paul eventually to return to Jerusalem to consult the leaders of the Christian community there, Peter and Jesus' brother James. It seems likely that during the fifteen-day stay with Peter, Paul received the information he relates in 1 Corinthians 15. The actual story of Jesus' meeting Paul is recorded by Luke in the Acts of the Apostles 9:1–8:

> Meanwhile Saul, still breathing threats and murder against the disciples of the Lord, went to the high priest **2** and asked him for letters to the synagogues at Damascus, so that if he found any who belonged to the Way, men or women, he might bring them bound to Jerusalem. **3** Now as he was going along and approaching Damascus, suddenly a light from heaven flashed around him. **4** He fell to the ground and heard a voice saying to him, "Saul, Saul, why do you persecute me?" **5** He asked, "Who are you, Lord?" The reply came, "I am Jesus, whom you are persecuting. **6** But get up and enter the city, and you will be told what you are to do." **7** The men who were traveling with him stood speechless because they heard the voice but saw no one. **8** Saul got up from the ground, and though his eyes were open, he could see nothing; so they led him by the hand and brought him into Damascus.

Within this blinding light, Paul, who was at that time named Saul, hears Jesus speak. The fact that Jesus would be the last person that Paul was expecting to talk to him intimates the truth of the story. There is no way that Paul would have invented it, given his hatred of everything that Jesus had done, in his opinion, to undermine the Jewish nation.

Ibrahim: This is a famous conversion story. It shows the beginning of the idea of Jesus being raised up to another realm from which he could appear. Jesus was not walking along the road greeting Paul as a fellow traveller. No, he came to Paul in a heavenly blinding light. It would have been impossible for Paul to see Jesus with his dazzled eyes. Luke reports that the people with Paul heard a voice, but did not see the one who spoke. This was no conventional meeting. There was no human being in view. Jesus seems to be a rather spiritual character, more like an angel than a human. Is this conception of Jesus raised to heaven and transformed into a spiritual rather than physical person not the origin of the other stories found in the Gospels? Christian scholars have suggested this. For example, Dominic Crossan does not believe that the stories in the Gospels are historically accurate. The story about Jesus being laid in a tomb from which he was raised to life after three days was developed after the experiences of people encountering Jesus as a heavenly being. Jesus' disciples fled so none of them could possibly have known where his body was. "By Easter Sunday morning, those who cared did not know where it was, and those who knew did not care."[1] When you look at some of the stories in the Gospels you see this phenomenon of a person who can appear in a locked room without coming through the door in John 20:19 and 26. No wonder the disciples thought he was a ghost, according to Luke 24:37.

The Relationship of Paul's Encounter with Jesus and the Resurrection Stories in the Gospels

Paul: The disciples fled when Jesus was arrested, but Peter was at the trial when he denied knowing Jesus. John was at the cross when Jesus asked him to look after his mother Mary, according to John 19:26–27. The disciples could have found out where Jesus was buried because they had not left Jerusalem. In any case, Joseph of Arimathea asked Pilate for Jesus' body so he could place it in his own rock tomb. This story is related by all four Gospel writers and is very likely to be a true account, since the early Christians would not have invented a story in which a leading Jew put his good reputation at stake by honouring someone his peers in the Jewish leadership regarded as a blasphemous imposter. William Lane Craig has published a critique of Crossan's view and makes this very point:

> We appear to have in Mark a primitive tradition recounting Joseph's begging the body of Jesus and his laying it, wrapped in linen, in a tomb, a tradition which has not been significantly overlaid with either theology or apologetics. With respect to Joseph of Arimathea in particular, even skeptical scholars agree that it is unlikely that Joseph, as a member of the Sanhedrin, was a Christian invention. Again Crossan disagrees, asserting that Mark invented Joseph of Arimathea to take Jesus' burial from his enemies to his friends.[2]

---

1. Crossan, *The Historical Jesus*, 394.
2. Craig, "John Dominic Crossan and the Resurrection," 255–56.

The four Gospels also agree that women went to the tomb to anoint Jesus' body. This was a traditional task for Jewish women. They were informed by angels that Jesus had been raised from the dead, and then Matthew 28:9–10 mentions that Jesus met them and greeted them. They prostrated themselves before him and held onto his feet. Jesus said, "Do not be afraid; go and tell my brothers to go to Galilee; there they will see me." John 20:11–18 tells of Jesus greeting Mary Magdalene and giving her the same commission to tell the disciples that he had risen from death and would be going to be with his Father.

These encounters with Jesus show that the women knew him, and their desire to hold onto his feet in reverence tells us that he was no ghost or phantom. There is no reason why the early Christians would have made up such a story if it were not true. The testimony of women was not regarded highly in Jewish society. If you wanted to invent a good story then why not have credible men meet Jesus, as Dale Allison argues:

> Surely adherents of Jesus were not helping themselves when they admitted that women were the only firsthand human witnesses to some of the events of Easter morning.... Why is it not Peter and his male companions who are at the tomb first thing Easter morning?[3]

Jesus was raised to life with a new body. He was not an apparition. I agree with the Christian philosopher Stephen Davis when he says, "Anybody who had been there beside Mary Magdalene could also have seen the risen Jesus. A camera could have taken a snapshot of the risen Jesus."[4]

Ibrahim: Hold on! You say that Jesus had a new body, but he could do things that bodies cannot do, so his new body must have been strange! In any case, Paul never held his feet as far as the story goes. You must admit that there are various accounts of people meeting Jesus after his death which don't all add up to the same kind of encounter. Luke 24:36–51 says that Jesus met his disciples and told them that ghosts do not have flesh and blood. He asked for a piece of fish and ate it. So far so good, he is keen to prove that he has a normal body. But then in verse 51 he ascended to heaven. What kind of new body can simply ascend to heaven? There is a contradiction here which is not easily resolved. According to Luke, Paul met the exalted, heavenly Jesus, but Paul himself does not describe

---

3. Allison, *Resurrecting Jesus*, 329.
4. Davis, "'Seeing' the Risen Jesus," 128.

the encounter in any detail. He just says in 1 Corinthians 9:1, "Have I not seen Jesus our Lord?" Then in 2 Corinthians 12:2–4 he speaks about being taken up to heaven in a vision:

> I know a person in Christ who fourteen years ago was caught up to the third heaven—whether in the body or out of the body I do not know; God knows. 3 And I know that such a person—whether in the body or out of the body I do not know; God knows—4 was caught up into Paradise and heard things that are not to be told, that no mortal is permitted to repeat.

So Christ invited Paul to come to heaven and be told amazing secrets. Surely this is Paul's own testimony to his encounters with Jesus. He does not talk about Jesus having a new body because that would not be relevant. What is important to Paul is that God raised Jesus up to heaven from where he comes to meet us in visions.

Paul: Yet Paul tells the Corinthian Christians that Jesus certainly had a new body after being raised from death. He insists that everyone who is raised from death receives a new body just like Jesus. He says in 1 Corinthians 15:42–44 that just as a seed becomes very different when it grows into a plant, so our bodies become rather different when they are raised to life. "What is sown is perishable, what is raised is imperishable. 43 It is sown in dishonor, it is raised in glory. It is sown in weakness, it is raised in power. 44 It is sown a physical body, it is raised a spiritual body." The spiritual body has different properties to the physical body we now possess. Presumably this is why Jesus was able to appear to his disciples and then disappear after his resurrection. His ascension to heaven took place because he had a new spiritual body that enabled him to do what his pre-resurrection body was not capable of doing.

Ibrahim: But that is exactly my point. The kind of body Jesus had after his death is not the same as the one he had before. Paul speaks about a radically different kind of body, just as a seed becomes radically different when it is the finished plant. The fact that Paul contrasts our physical bodies with our new spiritual bodies shows that the continuity between the two kinds of bodies is not simple. In any case, the Gospels include references to disciples doubting the resurrection of Jesus, so the reality of his new body was not so obvious to those who knew him well during his life. Matthew 28:16–17 tells of Jesus meeting his disciples on a mountain in Galilee after his resurrection. "When they saw him, they worshiped him; but some doubted." How could they doubt that Jesus was there? Surely it was because he was not the normal physical person they had known. Visions are not the same as meeting physical people, that is why some believed and some didn't. Paul had a vision of Jesus, but his travelling companions didn't.

Paul: There is an element of truth in what you say. However, when Jesus made himself known to Thomas in John 20:26–29, he specifically offered his hands and side for Thomas to touch. He wanted to confirm that his new body was continuous with his old one, including the nail prints in his hands and the spear mark in his side from the event of the crucifixion. The doubting Thomas then declared his faith in Jesus in verse 28, "My Lord and my God!" Then in the following verse, Jesus acknowledged that many people would come to believe in him without being able to see and touch him. "Have you believed because you have seen me? Blessed are those who have not seen and yet have come to believe." In other words, seeing the risen Jesus was a special privilege granted to a few, but faith in the risen Jesus is granted to many. Yet faith and doubt are both real possibilities for each person. Perhaps the disciples who doubted Jesus on the mountain in Galilee really did think Jesus was there in front of them, but found it hard to believe in the prospects of life without him being with them. Maybe that is why Jesus reassured them that he would be with them always in Matthew 28:20. They doubted his presence with them because he had risen and was not usually with them. Dale Allison makes the valuable point that history has to become our experience for it to become real to us. "Those who behold Jesus with their own eyes do not always know him for who he is. There is doubt among those who worship the risen Jesus in Matt 28:17. . . . We require more than history if we are to find the truth of things."[5] Stephen Davis argues the same way:

> Only the person to whom God has given the gift of faith will have the insight to be able to say: "He is here alive because God raised him from the dead." Or even: "He is Lord." A person who makes such a confession, whether that person was a member of the first generation of Christians or lives today, is a witness to the resurrection.[6]

---

5. Allison, *Resurrecting Jesus*, 351.
6. Davis, "'Seeing' the Risen Jesus," 147.

Faith in the Risen Jesus

Ibrahim: I think there are different levels of faith at work. There is the basic encounter with the resurrected Jesus that includes doubt about who he is. Then there is the belief that he is truly the same person in a different form. After that there is the conviction that he is divine in some sense. What if the disciples on the mountain who doubted Jesus were unable to believe in the latter? What if some of the disciples came to regard Jesus as divine as a result of the resurrection, while others found that a step too far? There are indications in the Acts that Stephen did not think of Jesus as divine. When he was being stoned by the crowd in Jerusalem he said in Acts 7:56, "I see the heavens opened and the Son of Man standing at the right hand of God!" He doesn't call Jesus, "Son of God," but "Son of Man." He has a vision of Jesus at God's right hand but he does not proclaim his divine status. Maybe Stephen is in a group of disciples that see Jesus as an exalted prophet, while Paul represents those who see the exalted Jesus as divine. Paul became a Christian after witnessing Stephen's stoning to death. Ruqaiyyah Waris Maqsood, who embraced Islam after being a Christian theologian, makes this case:

> To a Muslim, a "resurrection" of Jesus would not prove his divinity, or that he was God incarnate. . . . The "resurrection" of Jesus would not, therefore, make him unique: special yes, but not divine. The first Christians assumed he had been *raised by God*, and not that he *was* God.[7]

Paul: But the idea that Jesus was invited to sit at God's right hand was central to the belief in his divine status, so Stephen most probably did worship Jesus, just as Paul did, as Son of God. You must consider that the picture of the Messiah being seated at God's right hand from Psalm 110:1 was not thought of by Jews as giving divine status to the Messiah. However, Jews who followed Jesus came to see him as the Messiah exalted to heaven after his resurrection. It was the resurrection that demonstrated his divinity. Michael Licona, in his exhaustive study of the resurrection, makes this point:

> There is amazement over the devotion of the earliest Christians toward Jesus, which was to such an extent that they felt obliged to worship him. How did this devotion come about, especially when it would certainly seem blasphemous to do so? There are

---

7. Maqsood, *The Mysteries of Jesus*, 62.

no hints of any Jews who believed the Messiah was divine. Since many Jews believed in the general resurrection on the final day, neither would being resurrected require the conclusion that the one resurrected was a divine figure.[8]

So how did these early Christians come to worship Jesus? They concluded that Jesus was Son of God in a restrained way during his life, but the resurrection opened up the full nature of his power. Paul puts this succinctly in the opening verses of his letter to the Romans 1:3–4, where introduces his message as an apostle. He proclaims "the gospel concerning his Son, who was descended from David according to the flesh 4 and was declared to be Son of God with power according to the spirit of holiness by resurrection from the dead, Jesus Christ our Lord." Howard Marshall draws out the implications of the resurrection for the status of Jesus in Paul's thinking:

> Paul does justice to the Davidic sonship of Jesus, which qualifies him to be the Messiah, and to his status after the resurrection in which he exercises the function of Son of God with a power that was not evident previously. . . . The form of words implies that he was Son of God throughout his career (Gal 4:4) but became the enthroned Son of God after the resurrection. . . . There is no suggestion of two stages in the career of Jesus with messiahship during his earthly life being followed by "adoption" or "enthronement" as God's Son from the resurrection onward, or with messiahship as a preliminary but inferior status.[9]

The exaltation of Jesus meant that he was fully *recognized* as God's Son.

The Teaching of the Qur'an and the Sayings of the Prophet Muhammad about the Ascension of Jesus

Ibrahim: Both Stephen and Paul saw Jesus as exalted to God's right hand, but the evidence of the Acts does not show that Stephen had the same view as Paul. In any case, as Mona Siddiqui has argued, Muslims see Jesus exalted to heaven, but they do not regard him as divine as a result:

> In Islam, there is no paschal mystery and Jesus is simply gone, however his ascension is understood. Although he will return at the end times, neither the story of the crucifixion nor his return

---

8. Licona, *The Resurrection of Jesus*, 605.
9. Marshall, *New Testament Theology*, 426.

indicates a divine nature, redemption, or salvation for humankind; even in his second coming he remains God's messenger only, a sign of formidable events to come.[10]

In order to unpack this Muslim picture of Jesus' ascension and return we need to turn to the teaching of the Qur'an and the sayings of the Prophet Muhammad. The Qur'an refers to the raising of Jesus in 19:33, when the infant Jesus declares to Mary's family, "Peace was on me the day I was born, and will be on me the day I die and the day I am raised to life." Q3:55 shows how God promises to take Jesus to himself:

> God said, "Jesus, I will take you and raise you to Me, and purify you from those who do not believe. I will place those who follow you above those who do not believe on the Day of Resurrection. Then you will all return to Me and I will judge between you concerning what you disagree about.

This raising up of Jesus appears to be before the Day of Resurrection, and this is how the text has been understood among Qur'an commentators. Tabari records a saying of the Prophet Muhammad reported by Hasan al-Basri (d. 728), "The Messenger of God said to the Jews, 'Jesus did not die. He will return to you before the Day of Resurrection.'"[11] Muhammad taught that Jesus would only die after he returned from heaven where God raised him.

Paul: So how can you argue that Jesus died on the cross when Muhammad denied it? Surely the sayings of Muhammad are just as important to Muslims as the Qur'an. Perhaps you could argue that this saying is not reported by a companion of the Prophet.

Ibrahim: We need to distinguish between sayings of the Prophet that have authentic origins from sayings that are in fact later interpretations that cannot be assuredly traced to him. This is a well-known problem in the development of interpretation of the Qur'an. Therefore, all purported sayings of the Prophet have to be tested against the clear teaching of the Qur'an. This is one instance where the Qur'an may have the final word over the raising of Jesus. If we look at Q19:15, we find that John the Baptist is described by God in these terms; "Peace on him the day he was born, the day he dies, and the day he will be raised to life." Notice how similar this is to the language of Jesus in 19:33 that we quoted above; "Peace was on me the day I was born, and will be on me the day

---

10. Siddiqui, *Christians, Muslims, and Jesus*, 231–32.
11. Robinson, *Christ*, 119–20.

I die and the day I am raised to life." Neal Robinson, the New Testament scholar who became a leading expert in Qur'an interpretation, points out:

> It has been inferred that Jesus will be raised alive at the general resurrection. There is not the slightest hint, however, that his death also lies in the future. On the contrary, given only this sura, the assumption would be that it already lay in the past like John's.[12]

He challenges the traditional reading of the text by returning to the plain sense of the Qur'an. I agree with this assessment, and apply it to Q4:158, which states that "God raised him up to himself." Robinson makes this text agree with 19:33. "Q4:157-9 can be read as a denial of the ultimate reality of Jesus' death rather than a categorical denial that he died."[13]

Paul: Okay, but there is the tradition of Muhammad ascending to heaven and meeting Jesus, along with Moses and Abraham. Hasn't that story been very influential in Muslim interpretation of the raising of Jesus? It is first recorded in *The Life of Muhammad* by Ibn Ishaq. He mentions several versions of the story. Muhammad is reported to have said that during the night he was taken to heaven, where he met Abraham, Moses, and Jesus, who he described as follows:

> I have never seen a man more like myself than Abraham. Moses was a ruddy faced man, tall, thinly fleshed, curly haired with a hooked nose as though he were of the Sharru'a. Jesus, Son of Mary, was a reddish man of medium height with lank hair with many freckles on his face as though he had just come from a bath. One would suppose that his head was dripping with water, though there was no water on it.[14]

Another version of the story mentions other prophets that Muhammad encountered on his visit to heaven. "Then I was taken up to the second heaven and there were the two maternal cousins, Jesus, son of Mary, and John, son of Zechariah." In the third heaven he met Joseph, Idris in the fourth, Aaron in the fifth, Moses in the sixth, and in the seventh heaven he met Abraham. "Then Gabriel took me into Paradise."[15]

---

12. Robinson, "Jesus," 17.
13. Ibid., 20.
14. Ibn Ishaq, *Life of Muhammad*, 184-85.
15. Ibid., 186.

It is very interesting to read Ibn Ishaq's evaluation of these various stories. "Only God knows how revelation came and he saw what he saw. But whether he was asleep or awake, it was all true and actually happened."[16] Surely there must be some kernel of an original story told by Muhammad about his being taken up to heaven during the night as mentioned in Q17:1, "Glory to the One who made His servant travel by night from the sacred mosque to the furthest mosque." Abdel Haleem comments in his introduction to sura 17, "Towards the end of the Meccan period, God caused Muhammad, in the space of a single night, to journey from Mecca to Jerusalem and from there to heaven and back again."[17]

Ibrahim: Notice that Muhammad met several prophets in heaven. They all died before being raised there. There is no inconsistency in holding that Jesus, like them, died before being raised to join them. Indeed, it would be rather inconsistent for Jesus to be in a different category from them, and there is no suggestion in these stories that Jesus had been raised without going through the process of death. However, what these stories tell us is that the raising of Jesus is not any more significant than the raising of all the other prophets. To make the resurrection of Jesus unique in human history, as Christians have done, is to go beyond the bounds of reality, and this is the heart of the issue for Muslims. There will be a resurrection of the dead and a Day of Judgment when all humanity from all periods of history will be assessed. Q4:159 speaks of Jesus acting as a witness on the Day of Judgment against those among the People of the Book who think wrongly about him. "On the Day of Resurrection he will be a witness against them." So, it is incredibly important for Christians to think rightly about Jesus. In the end, how Jesus was raised is not the central concern. It is enough that he was raised to heaven to join the other prophets there. Maqsood puts this very well: "Muslims feel that the argument over whether or not the resurrection of Jesus' body took place has no bearing on whether or not there is life after death, or on our fate after death."[18]

---

16. Ibid., 183.
17. Abdel Haleem, *The Qur'an*, 175.
18. Maqsood, *The Mysteries of Jesus*, 63.

The Centrality of the Resurrection of Jesus' Body after Death for Christian Faith

Paul: Christians feel that our fate after death depends utterly on the resurrection of Jesus. This is Paul's argument in 1 Corinthians 15:17-19. "If Christ has not been raised, your faith is futile and you are still in your sins. 18 Then those also who have died in Christ have perished. 19 If for this life only we have hoped in Christ, we are of all people most to be pitied." Being granted new life after death depends on Jesus being raised from death. Howard Marshall sums up Paul's argument here by referring to what he says in his letter to the Romans:

> If not even Christ rose, what chance is there for anybody else? There is also no forgiveness of sins. This point also emerges in Romans 4:24-25, where justification is granted to those who believe in the God who raised Jesus from the dead; Jesus was handed over to death because of our sins and was raised from the dead so that we might be justified. For Paul the death of Christ by itself would not have had saving efficacy. There had to be the evidence that God accepted the death of his Son as an efficacious offering, and the resurrection is understood as the act of acceptance.[19]

The heart of the gospel, the good news, is that Jesus has offered himself as a sacrifice for the wrongdoing and rebellion of humanity and that God accepts this self-giving of Jesus by raising him from the dead. The death of Jesus is only one half of the good news, the other half is the resounding defeat of death and the guarantee of eternal life with God given freely to those who trust in Jesus. Arland Hultgren puts this so well. "In the crucified and risen Christ God has reconciled the world to himself—totally and unconditionally—and that the gospel, the good news, declares that that is so."[20]

Ibrahim: But you cannot be content with such "good news" because the rebellion of human beings is not so easily quashed. Each of us is responsible for our intentions and actions. Faith does not guarantee right intentions and actions, since we can come in and out of faith throughout our lives. Think of those Christians who have praised God at Easter for the resurrection of Jesus and have gone out of church to do their neighbors down, and to get an advantage over them. Remember Karl Marx,

---

19. Marshall, *New Testament Theology*, 278.
20. Hultgren, *Christ and His Benefits*, 206.

who was raised as a Christian by his Jewish father who had converted to Christianity in Germany to advance himself in society. Marx began to realize that business leaders used the hope of eternal life to oppress their workers. He famously proclaimed that religion was the opiate of the people. Telling their workers that the toil and poverty of this life would be recompensed by the joy of the next life was a palliative to keep them from rebelling against the conditions in which they were enslaved.[21] You see that focusing on the resurrection of Jesus can absolve people from being responsible for acting justly in this life. From a Muslim perspective, the light is cast on the behavior of the believer because faith in God should result in obedience to his law. The threat of meeting God at the Day of Judgement is a key component in encouraging right intentions that lead to good actions. There is no free pass just through faith. Rather, faith has to be proven by deeds.

Paul: This is an important issue that we should discuss in the light of the return of Jesus to judge humanity. There is no doubt that Paul believed that just being involved in the Christian community did not guarantee eternal life. In 1 Corinthians 15:34 he rebukes some of the members of the church for their bad behavior, "Come to a sober and right mind, and sin no more; for some people have no knowledge of God. I say this to your shame." Therefore, belonging to a church does not guarantee the presence of faith that produces good actions. We can both agree that right intentions are central to good actions, but that being a member of a community does not always bring about right outcomes. Perhaps we can look at the process of judgment in our next discussion.

For now, I want to return to the truth of the empty tomb and the fact that Jesus was raised from the dead. N. T. Wright sums up the evidence for the resurrection of Jesus in his massive treatment of Jewish attitudes to resurrection. "The best *historical* explanation is the one which inevitably raises all kinds of theological questions: the tomb was indeed empty, and Jesus was indeed seen alive, because he was truly raised from the dead."[22] Jews believed in Enoch and Elijah being raised to heaven without going through death, but they did not have a conception of a resurrection from death and a return to this life. However, this is exactly what happened to Jesus. There was no precedent for this in Jewish culture. Dale Allison unpacks this Jewish background:

21. See Karl Marx, *Early Writings*, 166–67.
22. Wright, *The Resurrection of the Son of God*, 10.

> What occasioned belief that God had brought Jesus back to life? A satisfying answer must account for at least three facts: (a) we know of no comparable claim for any other ancient Jew; (b) not all Jews embraced the Pharisaic notion of bodily resurrection; (c) those who did believe it tended to envisage the resurrection as a corporate event, with either all people or all righteous people coming back to life.... We might have expected believers in Jesus to articulate his post-mortem vindication in terms of the triumph of his soul or spirit and to imagine his resurrection, like that of everyone else dead and buried, as still belonging to the future.... Believers might also, like some later so-called heretics, have convinced themselves that Jesus had only seemed to die, that in reality he had ascended to heaven in the manner of Enoch and Elijah.[23]

The last point is just what the clear majority of Muslims have believed from earliest times in the history of Islam. Here are two very early Muslim interpretations of the raising of Jesus. The first if by Wahb ibn Munabbih (d. 732):

> One of the disciples came to the Jews and offered to lead them to Jesus for a price. At some point previous, this disciple was changed into the likeness of Jesus, so the Jews took him, sure that he was Jesus.... They crucified what "appeared to them." And he remained crucified seven hours. Then Jesus' mother, and the woman he had treated and whom God had freed from madness, came weeping before the crucified one. Jesus appeared to them and asked them why they were weeping. They said, "For you." He said: "Verily, God has raised me to himself, and nothing but good can befall me. This thing 'only appears so to them'; so, send for the disciples that they may meet me at such-and-such a place."[24]

The second is by Muqatil ibn Sulayman (d. 767):

> The substitute for Jesus was the guard whom the Jews had placed over him. Jesus was raised alive to heaven, "During the month of Ramadan, on the night of Power, and he was thirty-three years old when he was raised from the mount of Jerusalem."[25]

---

23. Allison, *Constructing Jesus*, 55–57.
24. al-Tabari, *Jamiʿal-Bayan*, 9:370, translated by Todd Lawson, 51.
25. al-Tabari, *Jamiʿal-Bayan*, 9:373, translated by Todd Lawson, 61.

Notice that Muqatil visualizes Jesus being raised to heaven, but that Wahb sees Jesus talking to his mother and Mary Magdalene after God raised him. Wahb has relied on Gospel accounts while Muqatil has not. But both believe another person was crucified, rather than Jesus, so the raising of Jesus is not from death.

Ibrahim: Yes, they represent the majority view. However, there have been alternative interpretations such as that of the tenth-century Brethren of Purity, a Sufi group who thought highly of Jesus:

> So Jesus went the next day and appeared to the people and summoned them and preached to them until he was seized and taken to the king of the *banu isra'il*. The king ordered his crucifixion, so his *nasut* (physical reality) was crucified, and his hands were nailed to the wooden cross and he stayed crucified from morning till evening. And he asked for water but was given vinegar [to drink]. Then he was pierced with a lance and buried in a place near the cross while forty troops guarded the tomb. And all of this occurred in the presence of the disciples. . . . And Jesus did appear to them and they saw that mark which was known by them. The news was spread among the *banu isra'il* that the Messiah was not killed. So the tomb was opened and the *nasut* was not found. Thus the troops DIFFERED AMONG THEMSELVES and much idle chatter ensued, and the story was complicated.[26]

Here Jesus died by crucifixion, was buried in a tomb, guarded so that no-one could tamper with the body, and was raised to life and appeared to his disciples showing the marks of crucifixion. The Jews found the tomb empty but spread the story that Jesus had not been killed. There were two different versions of the ending of Jesus' life, one from the disciples and the other from the Jews.

I prefer the disciples' story to the one told by the Jews. I agree with Dominic Crossan that Jesus did not predict his resurrection, but that the disciples experienced his presence after his martyrdom:

> Resurrection is not the same as exaltation. Within Jewish tradition, certain very holy persons were taken up to God rather than being consigned to an earthly tomb, for example, Enoch from among the patriarchs or Elijah from among the prophets. The Greco-Roman equivalent was apotheosis; for example, Augustan coins showed Julius Caesar's spirit ascending like an upward

26. *Letters of the Brethren of Purity* 4:97, translated by Todd Lawson, 86.

> shooting star to take its place among the heavenly divinities. Those were uniquely individual cases and had no general relationship to the fate of others. If one wanted to say that about Jesus, the proper terms were *exaltation, ascension, or apotheosis*, not *resurrection*. Put another way, with regard to Jesus, you could not have resurrection without exaltation, but you could have exaltation without resurrection. Jesus could be at the right hand of God without ever mentioning resurrection. . . . *To say that God raised Jesus from the dead was to assert that the general resurrection had thereby begun.*[27]

The disciples came to believe that Jesus was the first to be raised to life as a forerunner of the resurrection of all humanity. Therefore, Paul linked the resurrection of Jesus to the resurrection of everyone else. The appearances of Jesus to the disciples and to Paul were decisive in developing this belief.

Paul: We have already discussed the evidence for the death and resurrection of Jesus. It could not have simply been a case of the disciples concluding that Jesus had risen because they met him after his death. They also witnessed the empty tomb, despite Crossan doubting this. Here is Dale Allison emphasizing that Jesus preached about the resurrection:

> It is not unduly credulous to believe that the theological frame of reference for some early Christian groups was Jesus' preaching. . . . Easter faith may have been born after the crucifixion, but it was conceived before. . . . Without antecedent expectation of the imminent resurrection of the dead in general, there would have been no proclamation of the resurrection of Jesus in particular.[28]

I would like to suggest that it makes better sense of Jesus' preaching to include not just the resurrection of the dead in general, but his own expectation of being raised after three days. Richard Swinburne seeks to defend the authenticity of Jesus' predictions:

> Did Jesus predict the resurrection? Mark's Gospel tells us that he predicted both his passion and resurrection explicitly on three separate occasions, but many modern critics doubt whether Jesus really made these predictions. . . . Three important predictions which Jesus did make were fulfilled (in whole or part) by his resurrection. The first is his claim that he would provide

---

27. Crossan *Excavating Jesus*, 259–60.
28. Allison, *Constructing Jesus*, 59.

the sacrifice of his own life to make atonement for our sins. A sacrifice to God only provides atonement if it accepted by God. So Jesus was predicting that God (the Father) would accept the sacrifice. Secondly, the Resurrection provided a partial fulfilment of Jesus' prediction that all humans would be raised from the dead by showing that one human (Jesus) was raised. Thirdly, the resurrection of Jesus was a resurrection in which Jesus had supernatural powers (to pass through doors etc.).[29]

Jesus Will Bring Everything into Submission to God

Ibrahim: I would like to return to 1 Corinthians 15, where Paul pictures Jesus as the man who is raised ahead of everyone else:

> But in fact Christ has been raised from the dead, the first fruits of those who have died. 21 For since death came through a human being, the resurrection of the dead has also come through a human being; 22 for as all die in Adam, so all will be made alive in Christ. . . . 24 Then comes the end, when he hands over the kingdom to God the Father, after he has destroyed every ruler and every authority and power. . . . 28 When all things are subjected to him, then the Son himself will also be subjected to the one who put all things in subjection under him, so that God may be all in all.

Paul sees Jesus as the first human to be raised, the first fruits of the resurrection of humanity. But look at what he says will happen when the end comes. Then Jesus will submit to the rule of God his Father, who alone will be in control. The role of Jesus is to gather human beings under God's rule, and once his task is complete then he will be one of those human beings who acknowledge the rule of God. Whatever Paul wrote about Jesus being exalted to God's right hand, he sees being at the right hand as a *subordinate* position in the final analysis. There is no equality of status here between the Son and the Father. If Jesus is honored and venerated by Paul as Lord, then that does not imply that Paul gives Jesus the same honor and veneration as he gives to God.

Paul: I think that in Philippians 2:6-11, Paul saw Jesus as the Son of God who emptied himself of his equality with the Father to become human and die on the cross and was raised up to his former position of

---

29. Swinburne, *Was Jesus God?* 124-25.

equality by being raised up by the Father. In Colossians 1:15–19, Paul calls Jesus the image of the invisible God, and says that everything in this created world was made through the Son and for him, and that God was pleased to have his fullness dwell in Jesus. So I don't think that we can isolate the picture in 1 Corinthians from other statements of Paul. When Paul called Jesus, "Lord" he meant the same as when he called God "Lord." There is an equality of status even if the tasks of the Father and Son are different. It is the supreme task of the Father to rule the universe. It is the supreme task of the Son to reconcile that universe to the Father. Paul puts it clearly in Colossians 1:20, where he states that "through him God was pleased to reconcile to himself all things, whether on earth or in heaven, by making peace through the blood of his cross." The Father and Son work in harmony for the good of the world. The resurrection of Jesus from the dead is a sign that God will renew everything.

Ibrahim: What happens at the end of time should be our next discussion. But I still hold that the equality of status between God the Father and the Son is not proven by these quotations from Paul. You argue that they have equality of status but different tasks. However, the task of Jesus is to reconcile humanity to God. He does not reconcile humanity to himself. He points away from himself to God. The very nature of the task given to Jesus by God is one that reflects away from his death and resurrection to the Creator himself. If Paul thinks of the Son being a participant in the creation of the world, then surely, he does so by invitation from God. This is ultimately why he hands over the world to God at the end. Jesus aims to glorify God in everything he does.

Paul: The mystery of the relationship between the Father and the Son lies in this submission of the Son to the will of the Father. But you must reckon with the fact that the only human being who is in this relationship is Jesus. No other person is the image of God and has the fullness of God. The resurrection is the sign of this for the rest of humanity. We have not met the human Jesus like his disciples. But if we are convinced that God raised Jesus from the dead then we can be sure that God is planning for our resurrection to eternal life in his presence. Yet we are dependent on faith rather than sight. Wolfhart Pannenberg has noticed this dependency, even if we are sure that Jesus was raised from the dead:

> Assertion of the historicity of an event does not mean that its facticity is so sure that there can no longer be any dispute regarding it. . . . In the case of the resurrection of Jesus, all Christians must realize that the facticity of the event will be contested right

up to the eschatological consummation of the world because its uniqueness transcends an understanding of reality that is oriented only to this passing world and because the new reality that has come in the resurrection of Jesus has not yet universally and definitively manifested itself.[30]

We live by faith rather than sight. But the day will surely come when we will see clearly that Jesus has been raised to the highest place and every knee will bow to confess that he is Lord.

Ibrahim: From my perspective, Jesus is an example of right living, and devotion to God. I have no problem seeing him vindicated after his martyrdom for proclaiming love of God and neighbor. God raised him to himself because he was more closely aligned with God's cause than any other man. One day he will return to once more bring people to God, and he will continue to be highly honored in this world and the next. Q3:45, is concerned with the announcement of Jesus' conception to Mary. "The angels said, 'Mary, God announces the news of a word from Him: his name is the Messiah, Jesus, the son of Mary: he will be honored in this world and in the next life, and he will be among those who are near to God.'"

Paul: Let us then consider how Jesus will return from heaven to earth to fulfill the plans that God has made for the reconciliation of the world to himself.

---

30. Pannenberg, *Systematic Theology*, 2:361.

ten

Returning in Power

PAUL OPENS THE DISCUSSION of the return of Jesus from heaven, which was central to the teaching of the early church. Ibrahim suggests that the first Christians had different views of the results of Jesus' coming. The apostle Paul speaks of Jesus gathering his followers in heaven, while the Revelation of John sees Jesus reigning on earth. Paul believes that the latter is also taught by the apostle Paul. Ibrahim describes the hope of eternal life in the Qur'an as centered on the rule of God, but Paul insists that the Christian view has Jesus sharing rule with the Father. Ibrahim challenges Paul over the role of Jesus, since the Qur'an teaches that he is only a messenger of God and the Prophet Muhammad said that Jesus would return to break crosses and kill pigs. Paul suggests that this tradition of Jesus breaking crosses only developed in the ninth century, but Ibrahim defends the authenticity of the saying. Ibrahim raises the question of the authenticity of the sayings of Jesus about the future coming of the Son of Man. Paul acknowledges that there are different interpretations, but that he believes Jesus really did speak of his future return to judge humanity. Certainly, the apostolic writers were sure that he would come back as judge.

Ibrahim interprets the Parable of the Sheep and the Goats in Matthew 25 to reflect Jesus teaching about love for neighbor. He agrees that judgment will take note of how we have cared for the needy, but he questions whether Jesus would have ignored love for God. Paul interprets the parable to teach that love for Jesus motivates love for neighbor. He argues that the main difference between the teaching of the New Testament and the Qur'an about judgment and eternal life is the attitude of people to Jesus the judge, which is at the heart of the New Testament but is absent from the Qur'an. Ibrahim questions this emphasis on Jesus as judge. He points out how Jesus in John's Gospel seeks for faith in himself when in the Synoptic Gospels he seeks for faith in God. How could the early Christians have so quickly placed faith in Jesus at the center of their life? He hopes that modern Christians may follow the example of John Hick and Stanley Samartha who have moved away from placing Jesus at the center to realizing that living at peace with people of other faiths means putting God at the center. Paul counters with the conviction that Jesus will be confessed as Lord when he comes, and that people will come to see that he is on the throne alongside his Father.

Ibrahim turns to the nature of judgment. He believes that the intention of the heart will be the focus on the Day of Resurrection. He holds out the hope that God will forgive out of his mercy and compassion even those who have been raised in cultures that worship many gods, but who worship a creating deity according to the light they have. They may need to spend time in the Fire to have their wrongdoing purged, but eventually they may be brought out into the bliss of eternal life with God in the Garden. Paul does not believe in a purgatorial fire, but holds that the New Testament teaches that some may be excluded from God's presence. He looks forward to the new city presented in Revelation 22, where God will share his throne with Jesus and believers will enjoy a life without pain or suffering.

The Return of Jesus in the New Testament

Paul: The return of Jesus after his ascension to the right hand of the Father is a theme shared by the apostolic writers. It is obviously a real concern to the Thessalonian Christians to whom Paul writes in the early fifties of the first century. They were anxious about the condition of members of the church who had died although Jesus had not yet returned. Would they be able to experience life with Jesus? Paul reassures them that they are already with Jesus in 1 Thessalonians 4:13–18:

> But we do not want you to be uninformed, brothers and sisters, about those who have died, so that you may not grieve as others do who have no hope. **14** For since we believe that Jesus died and rose again, even so, through Jesus, God will bring with him those who have died. **15** For this we declare to you by the word of the Lord, that we who are alive, who are left until the coming of the Lord, will by no means precede those who have died. **16** For the Lord himself, with a cry of command, with the archangel's

call and with the sound of God's trumpet, will descend from heaven, and the dead in Christ will rise first. 17 Then we who are alive, who are left, will be caught up in the clouds together with them to meet the Lord in the air; and so we will be with the Lord forever. 18 Therefore encourage one another with these words.

Paul must have taught these Christians when he was with them about the return of Jesus from heaven to gather both the dead and living believers to live with him. Notice that his emphasis is on sharing life with Jesus where he reigns as Lord. The details of this new life with Jesus are not given here. Gordon Fee points out that "Paul has almost no interest whatever in our final eschatological 'geography'; rather, his interest is altogether personal, having to do with their being 'with the Lord.'"[1]

Ibrahim: Paul seems to believe that Jesus will come to collect his followers and take them to heaven. However, the Book of Revelation has a vision of Jesus coming to rule the world and destroy the enemies of truth. There appear to be two quite different ideas about the return of Jesus in the early church. Revelation 20:4–6 speaks of martyrs being raised to life and reigning on earth for a thousand years:

> They came to life and reigned with Christ a thousand years. 5 (The rest of the dead did not come to life until the thousand years were ended.) This is the first resurrection. 6 Blessed and holy are those who share in the first resurrection. Over these the second death has no power, but they will be priests of God and of Christ, and they will reign with him a thousand years.

Lots of Christians are eagerly expecting Jesus to come back so that they can rule the world. They believe the establishment of the State of Israel is a major sign of the arrival of Jesus, and they see Muslims as Jesus' enemies because Muslims oppose Jewish occupation of Muslim territory. John Hagee represents many conservative Christians when he sees hordes of Muslims intent on attacking Israel and her Western supporters.

> America is stumbling in the fog of political correctness, lacking the intellectual honesty to admit that radical Islam has every intention of conquering Western civilization. . . . The Islamic religion is a rapidly growing religion that is often controlled by militants who want to impose their beliefs on the rest of the world. Their three main goals are to:
>
> 1. Drive all westerners out of the Middle East.

---

1. Fee, *Thessalonians*, 181.

2. Exterminate Christians and Jews.
3. Establish a one-world Islamic government.²

Paul: There are Palestinian Christians whose ancestors were among the earliest Christians and who see the modern State of Israel as opposing Jesus. According to Yohanna Katancho, "Several Palestinian liberation theologians affirm that the Palestinian Jesus is again facing Herod, but this time it is an Israeli Herod."³ So there are different opinions about the significance of the State of Israel. Perhaps those who are least affected by everyday life in that part of the world can see the return of the Jews to the land promised to Abraham as a fulfillment of that original promise. When we read the New Testament, the emphasis is on the rule of Jesus with those who trust him. Paul has a vision in Romans 11:26–29 for his fellow Jews to finally acknowledge Jesus as Lord, so their contribution to life on earth would be a part of the whole scheme of Jesus' return to rule.

Christians have interpreted the rule of Jesus in a variety of ways. Augustine thought that the picture of Jesus ruling for a thousand years was symbolic of his *current* reign through the church. "The church even now is the kingdom of Christ, and the kingdom of heaven. And so even now his saints reign with him."⁴ My own view is that the picture of the New Jerusalem in Revelation 21 is central to the visions of John. The city comes down to earth, not just for a thousand years, but forever, and therefore the thousand-year reign of the martyrs is eclipsed by the eternal life of the believers in the city. While many Christians have looked to the millennial period, John in Revelation 21 wants us to see beyond this to a new earth:

> And I saw the holy city, the new Jerusalem, coming down out of heaven from God, prepared as a bride adorned for her husband. 3 And I heard a loud voice from the throne saying, "See, the home of God is among mortals. He will dwell with them; they will be his peoples, and God himself will be with them; 4 he will wipe every tear from their eyes. Death will be no more; mourning and crying and pain will be no more, for the first things have passed away."

In the end, the vision of Jesus being at the heart of the New Jerusalem, removing all suffering from those who are with him, is similar to the

---

2. Hagee, *Jerusalem Countdown*, 1.
3. Katancho, "Reading the Gospel of John through Palestinian eyes," 104.
4. Augustine, *The City of God*, Book 10:9, Vol 6:307–9.

teaching of Paul that believers will live with Jesus. Steve Motyer believes that Paul visualized Jesus coming to reign on earth from heaven. "It is to the *earth* that he 'descends', to take up his kingship. . . . The *vision* [in 1 Thessalonians 4] is of a whole earth touched and transformed by the return of its Lord, greeted by dead and by living alike who rise to welcome him back."[5] This scene is something that I look forward to witnessing, and it motivates me to keep going when things get difficult.

Eternal Life in the Qur'an and the Role of Jesus, according to the Prophet Muhammad

Ibrahim: Yes, the reward of future life in God's presence is highly motivational. For me, life without suffering and evil is a prospect that outweighs any pain that I experience now. The Qur'an repeatedly holds out the prospect of eternal life for the believers, which will be a glorious reward. Q15:45–48, emphasizes the wellbeing of life in the gardens that God has prepared:

> The righteous will be in Gardens with springs of water. **46** "Enter them in peace and security." **47** We will remove any hatred from their hearts as brothers, sitting on thrones, face each other. **48** exhaustion will not touch them. They will never be evicted from that place.

This is a vision of peace and security which never descends into dispute or trouble as so often happens in this life. How wonderful to experience that complete tranquility and harmony among people in the future world!

Paul: The New Testament vision of the new life centers on Jesus, but the Qur'an has no role for him apart from being one of God's messengers who is highly regarded for his testimony.

Ibrahim: Jesus is given the reward due to his faithful witness to the One who sent him. However, Christians are in danger of missing out on the reward of eternal bliss through their false assessment of Jesus' role as Q5:65–66 points out:

> If only the People of the Book had believed and feared God, We would have forgiven their wrongdoing and would have brought them into the peaceful Gardens. **66** If they had kept the Torah

---

5. Motyer, *Come, Lord Jesus!*, 240.

and the Gospel and what was sent down to them from their Lord, they would have been fed from above and from beneath their feet. A group of them are on the right path, but as for many of them, evil is what they do.

The wrongdoing of the Christians is outlined a few verses later in Q5:72:

> Those who say, "God is the Messiah, son of Mary," do not believe. The Messiah said, "Children of Israel, worship God, my Lord and your Lord." Whoever makes an associate for God, God will forbid him from the Garden, and the Fire will be his home. There will be ho helpers for the evildoers.

Entry to the Garden of peace and security is dependent on right belief that produces right behavior. Wrong belief takes a person away from the path to eternal life and leads to eternal death.

The proper attitude to Jesus is so important to the future welfare of Christians. This is confirmed by the Prophet Muhammad, who taught that Jesus would return from heaven to earth to proclaim the truth of Islam and lead his followers to a right worship of the One True God. Abu Hurayra, one of the companions of the Prophet, reported the following:

> I am the closest among humans to Jesus, Mary's son, because there is no prophet between us. He will descend, so recognize him when you see him. . . . He will break the crosses, kill the pigs, and abolish the poll tax. . . . He will die and the Muslims will pray over him and bury him.[6]

According to the Prophet Muhammad, Jesus will return to challenge Christian veneration of the cross and their flouting of the Torah, which prohibits the consumption of pork. Jesus appears at the end of time to warn those who take his name that they must give up their deviant beliefs and practices if they want to find eternal security.

Paul: If Jesus really is returning to denounce veneration of the cross then it is surprising that this idea is not found in eighth-century Muslim accounts of the return of Jesus. Muqatil ibn Sulayman says that God will raise Jesus to himself and cause him to die after he has returned from heaven to wage war on the antichrist [al-dajjal],[7] but he does not mention

---

6. Tabari, *Jamiʿal-Bayan*, on Surah 4:157–59.

7. Muqatil, *Tafsir*, 1:279 and 1:420, in Reynolds, "The Muslim Jesus: Dead or Alive?" 245.

any attack by Jesus on veneration of the cross or of eating pork. Ibn Ishaq says that Christian leaders from Najran were informed by the Prophet Muhammad during their meeting that God took Jesus to himself when people wanted to kill him.[8] Ibn Ishaq says nothing about Jesus returning to confront veneration of the cross and consumption of pork. Mathias Zahniser has argued that the account in Ibn Ishaq is more authentic than the later tradition attached to Abu Hurayra:

> Since the biography of Muhammad developed partly through explanation of the Qur'an, it would seem strange that a story such as Jesus' return to break crosses and slay the antichrist did not turn up in it, if it were in fact something Muhammad had stressed.[9]

There seems to have been a process of adding data to an original basic story. By the eighth century, Q4:157 was understood to teach that Jesus was raised to heaven alive and that he would return to earth to die to fulfill what he said about his death in Q19:33. However, during the ninth century, accounts of what Jesus would do after his return to earth were added. According to Nu'aym ibn Hammad al-Marwazi (d. 844), Jesus will return to Jerusalem, marry, and be buried in the Prophet's house at Medina alongside the Prophet Muhammad.[10] The collectors of the Prophetic sayings, Muslim ibn al-Hajjaj (d. 875) and Muhammad ibn Isma'il al-Bukhari (d. 870) have the version of Abu Hurayra recorded by Tabari, but they do not refer to Jesus dying, being buried, and then resurrected. Their interest was in recording what Jesus would do when he returned—breaking crosses, killing pigs, abolishing the poll tax, and providing great wealth for everyone.[11] It is obvious that there are a variety of accounts of what the Prophet Muhammad said, and the concerns of different people in various situations have influenced the way these stories have been reported. My own opinion is that Muslims felt the need to respond to Christian teaching about the return of Jesus to establish the kingdom of God by developing their own interpretation of his return, which emphatically excluded any possible reference to his coming to rule.

---

8. Ibn Ishaq, *Life of Muhammad*, 276.

9. Zahniser, *The Mission & Death of Jesus*, 56.

10. Nu'aym, *Kitab al-fitan*, 346 and 354, in Cook, *Studies in Muslim Apocalyptic*, 173 and 177.

11. *Sahih Muslim*, 1:72, and *Sahih al-Bukhari*, 3:425, 4:657.

Ibrahim: Just because there are different sayings of the Prophet does not mean that some of them were invented later. You only have to think about the way the sayings of Jesus have been reported in the Gospels to realize that different reporters emphasize different things that he said. The same applies to Muhammad. What struck Muslims as important in the eighth century may well have changed in the following century. In any case, Abu Hurayra was a companion of the Prophet and if the two respected collectors of sayings included his report about Jesus returning to destroy crosses and kill pigs, then there is no reason to doubt that this is a true teaching about the return of Jesus.

The Son of Man Coming to Judge Humanity

Ibrahim: We can have the same kind of discussion about whether Jesus said he would return in the Gospels. Earlier we noted that Dominic Crossan does not think that Jesus spoke about his death as a ransom for sinners or about his resurrection from the dead. Likewise, Crossan believes that Jesus did not expect to return. He represents a good number of Christian scholars. Rudolf Bultmann thought that Jesus referred to a Son of Man figure coming in the future, but that this person was someone other than Jesus.[12] His view has also had a significant following. In Mark 13:26-27 Jesus speaks of the Son of Man coming to gather his followers: "Then they will see 'the Son of Man coming in clouds' with great power and glory. 27 Then he will send out the angels, and gather his elect from the four winds, from the ends of the earth to the ends of heaven." There is simply no consensus among interpreters about whether Jesus actually said this. You can find many who hold that the early church put these words on Jesus' lips because they were eagerly expecting Jesus to return to earth, as you have shown from Paul's letters, and they therefore wanted to have Jesus prophesy his return before he died.

Paul: I recognize that there is controversy about the future coming of the Son of Man. N. T. Wright thinks Jesus was speaking about his vindication by God after his death and not about his return to earth:

> When Jesus speaks of "the Son of Man coming on the clouds," he is not talking about the second coming, but, in line with the

---

12. Bultmann, *History*, 112.

Daniel 7 text he is quoting, about his vindication after suffering. The "coming" is an upward, not a downward, movement.[13]

Craig Evans holds that Jesus could not have been speaking about the return of the Son of Man at the time of the destruction of Jerusalem mentioned in verses 2–23. It is only after the tribulation of an antichrist figure standing in the temple that the Son of Man will come "meting out judgment and salvation on earth. . . . Verse 26 is drawn from Daniel 7:13 and apparently was the key to Jesus' messianic self-understanding."[14] He understands Jesus predicting his own future return as judge and redeemer. This is certainly the belief of the early church as we have seen. Tom Wright does not hesitate to admit this. "As soon as Jesus had been vindicated, raised, and exalted, the church firmly believed and taught that he would return. . . . Paul's letters are full of the future coming or appearing of Jesus."[15] But how did the early church come to such a strong conviction of Jesus returning to earth from heaven if Jesus had not taught this about his own future? As far as I am concerned, this question must be answered in a historically meaningful way. The followers of Jesus did not make up a story from their collective imagination about a future coming of Jesus. It was given to them by Jesus himself.

Ibrahim: There is no doubt that the New Testament writers saw Jesus returning to judge humanity, and to separate the righteous from the wrongdoers. Matthew is particularly concerned to tell stories in his Gospel about the Son of Man separating people into two groups. Perhaps he invented them to promote an idea that Jesus himself did not teach, but that the early Christians firmly and enthusiastically believed about the return of Jesus from heaven to earth. In Matthew 25:1–13 there is a story of five foolish girls who are excluded from a wedding feast after turning up late because they went back to fetch oil for their lamps. I suppose they are punished for lack of preparation for the big event. An even more frightening story is told in Matthew 25:31–46:

> When the Son of Man comes in his glory, and all the angels with him, then he will sit on the throne of his glory. 32 All the nations will be gathered before him, and he will separate people one from another as a shepherd separates the sheep from the goats, 33 and he will put the sheep at his right hand and the goats at the

---

13. Wright, *Surprised by Hope*, 137.
14. Evans, *Mark 8:27—16:20*, 328.
15. Wright, *Surprised by Hope*, 140.

left. 34 Then the king will say to those at his right hand, "Come, you that are blessed by my Father, inherit the kingdom prepared for you from the foundation of the world; 35 for I was hungry and you gave me food, I was thirsty and you gave me something to drink, I was a stranger and you welcomed me, 36 I was naked and you gave me clothing, I was sick and you took care of me, I was in prison and you visited me."

They ask Jesus when they saw him hungry or thirsty, a stranger, naked or in prison and he says:

> "Truly I tell you, just as you did it to one of the least of these who are members of my family, you did it to me." 41 Then he will say to those at his left hand, "You that are accursed, depart from me into the eternal fire prepared for the devil and his angels; 42 for I was hungry and you gave me no food, I was thirsty and you gave me nothing to drink, 43 I was a stranger and you did not welcome me, naked and you did not give me clothing, sick and in prison and you did not visit me."

When they ask Jesus when they saw him in need he says:

> "Truly I tell you, just as you did not do it to one of the least of these, you did not do it to me." 46 And these will go away into eternal punishment, but the righteous into eternal life.

Jesus is alleged to have taught that he will return to sit on a throne as king and judge all the nations. Eternal life is granted to those who gave food and drink to those who lacked the basics, and who tended the sick and those in prison. Eternal punishment is the lot of those who failed to pay attention to needy people. There is nothing here about idolatry, failure to worship the One True God, which is characteristic of his teaching, when he said, "Love the LORD your God with all your heart and strength." There is only the emphasis of his statement, "Love your neighbor as yourself." As it stands, this story presents a one-sided view of righteous living, and it would be dangerous to read it as truly representative of Jesus' message.

Paul: I think that the separation of the righteous and the ungodly is a common enough theme in the parables of Jesus. It is not necessary to think that Matthew invented these stories. Luke 13:22–30 records sayings of Jesus that are found in Matthew 7:13–14 and 21–23:

> Jesus went through one town and village after another, teaching as he made his way to Jerusalem. **23** Someone asked him, "Lord, will only a few be saved?" He said to them, **24** "Strive to enter through the narrow door; for many, I tell you, will try to enter and will not be able. **25** When once the owner of the house has got up and shut the door, and you begin to stand outside and to knock at the door, saying, 'Lord, open to us,' then in reply he will say to you, 'I do not know where you come from.' **26** Then you will begin to say, 'We ate and drank with you, and you taught in our streets.' **27** But he will say, 'I do not know where you come from; go away from me, all you evildoers!' **28** There will be weeping and gnashing of teeth when you see Abraham and Isaac and Jacob and all the prophets in the kingdom of God, and you yourselves thrown out. **29** Then people will come from east and west, from north and south, and will eat in the kingdom of God. **30** Indeed, some are last who will be first, and some are first who will be last."

Luke records the exclusion of people from hospitality just like the five foolish girls who were shut out of the wedding feast. He also has the division of people into the righteous and the evildoers, just as Matthew has. In other words, there are good grounds for holding that Jesus really did teach these themes. In fact, he is teaching that love for God is inextricably bound up with love for neighbor. They cannot be separated. These stories show what love for God looks like. David Wenham interprets the significance of the separation of the sheep and goats as a warning to Christians to live appropriately:

> The parable is a severe warning to those who see the revolution of God as something purely spiritual and to do with "my personal relationship with God," and who fail to see that the kingdom is a practical down-to-earth revolution and that no amount of spiritual gifts, or fervour in calling Jesus Lord, will be persuasive on judgement day. Jesus calls his followers to be a revolutionary, caring community, not comfortable conservationists protecting the status quo.[16]

In other words, my love for God has to be seen in the way I love my neighbor. I cannot claim to love God if I disregard the needs of my fellow humans.

---

16. Wenham, *Parables*, 93.

Ibrahim: This takes us back to our discussion of love for God and neighbor. Certainly, there has to be a balance between them. This is taught in the Qur'an in Q3:133–36:

> Hasten to forgiveness from your Lord and to a Garden that is as spacious as the heavens and the earth prepared for the righteous: **134** those who provide for others out of prosperity or adversity, who restrain their anger and pardon people. God loves those who do good. **135** When they have committed a shameful act or harmed themselves they remember God and ask Him to forgive their sins. Who forgives sins except God? They do not persist in what they have done wrong because they are aware of it. **136** Their reward is forgiveness from their Lord, and Gardens with rivers flowing below them where they will live forever, an excellent wage for those who work.

Notice how love for God is expressed in love for neighbor. Those who are forgiven by God also forgive others. Perhaps the opposite is sadly the case, that unwillingness to forgive others is a sign of ignoring God. Too often we think that believing in God is separate from treating others with respect and patience. Our relationships with our neighbors reflect how we relate to God. Q50:31–35 shows that this is so:

> The Garden will be brought near to the righteous and will not be far away. **32** "This is what you were promised. It is for everyone who returned to, remained with, **33** and feared the Most Merciful, who is hidden, and who came with a repentant heart. **34** Enter it in peace. This is the Day of eternal life." **35** There they will have what they want, and in our presence much more.

In order to maintain right relationships with neighbors we need to maintain a right relationship with God.

Q51:15–19 spells out the intimate connection between love for God and neighbor that is rewarded by eternal life:

> The righteous will be in Gardens with springs of water. **16** They will receive what their Lord has given them because they had done good deeds before that. **17** They slept only a little at night, **18** asked for forgiveness at dawn, **19** and gave of their wealth for the need of the beggar and the destitute person.

We look at the needy with compassion when we spend time at dawn seeking the forgiveness of God for our faults. Instead of condemning those who have fallen on hard times we seek to lift them up, just as God has lifted us from our foolishness and failure.

Jesus as Judge in the Apostolic Writings

Paul: I reckon that the major difference between these accounts of eternal life after death and those found in the New Testament is the focus on Jesus in the latter. In the story of the sheep and the goats, Jesus indicates that those who visited prisoners and fed the hungry were already believers in him. In fact, Jesus is warning his followers not to separate faith in him from love for others, as Stephen Travis argues:

> Their deeds of love express a relationship with Jesus, hidden and unconscious though it may be. . . . Those who have a relationship to Jesus expressed in deeds of love are welcomed into the kingdom-presence of God. Those whose lack of positive deeds betrays their lack of relationship to Jesus are excluded from his presence.[17]

Peter opens his first letter to Christians in Asia Minor by encouraging them to fix their eyes on Jesus when they are persecuted for their faith in him. 1 Peter 1:1–9 is full of hope in eternal life guaranteed by God the Father for those who trust in his Son:

> Peter, an apostle of Jesus Christ, To the exiles of the Dispersion in Pontus, Galatia, Cappadocia, Asia, and Bithynia, **2** who have been chosen and destined by God the Father and sanctified by the Spirit to be obedient to Jesus Christ and to be sprinkled with his blood: May grace and peace be yours in abundance. **3** Blessed be the God and Father of our Lord Jesus Christ! By his great mercy he has given us a new birth into a living hope through the resurrection of Jesus Christ from the dead, **4** and into an inheritance that is imperishable, undefiled, and unfading, kept in heaven for you, **5** who are being protected by the power of God through faith for a salvation ready to be revealed in the last time. **6** In this you rejoice, even if now for a little while you have had to suffer various trials, **7** so that the genuineness of your faith—being more precious than gold that, though perishable, is tested by fire—may be found to result in praise and glory and honor when Jesus Christ is revealed. **8** Although you have not seen him, you love him; and even though you do not see

---

17. Travis, *Christ and the Judgement of God*, 226.

him now, you believe in him and rejoice with an indescribable and glorious joy, **9** for you are receiving the outcome of your faith, the salvation of your souls.

The return of Jesus is the moment of revelation of the reality of faith in him. Peter exhorts the believers to focus on Jesus, to be ready for his coming, and to maintain the joy that arises from the expectation of meeting him. So, he goes on to remind them that they should behave toward other people in the light of the arrival of Jesus in 1:13–16:

> Therefore prepare your minds for action; discipline yourselves; set all your hope on the grace that Jesus Christ will bring you when he is revealed. **14** Like obedient children, do not be conformed to the desires that you formerly had in ignorance. **15** Instead, as he who called you is holy, be holy yourselves in all your conduct; **16** for it is written, "You shall be holy, for I am holy."

Self-centeredness should be replaced by love for Jesus, which will be expressed in love for others. Peter spells this out: "Rid yourselves, therefore, of all malice, and all guile, insincerity, envy, and all slander" (2:1). Therefore, the expectation of the return of Jesus was at the heart of the early church's teaching about eternal life. The coming back of Jesus would be the beginning of that new life.

This is the conviction of John in his first letter. 1 John 3:1–3 shows that God the Father loves his children who have come to him through faith in his Son. Their love for Jesus will affect their lifestyle among their neighbors:

> See what love the Father has given us, that we should be called children of God; and that is what we are. The reason the world does not know us is that it did not know him. **2** Beloved, we are God's children now; what we will be has not yet been revealed. What we do know is this: when he is revealed, we will be like him, for we will see him as he is. **3** And all who have this hope in him purify themselves, just as he is pure.

The revelation of Jesus governs John's thinking here. Jesus was revealed in the past to take away sin and when he is revealed in the future, the children of God will become like Jesus, pure and spotless. In the present time of waiting for Jesus to come, those who love him will seek to be like him. The driving force behind the advice given by the apostles, whether Paul or Peter or John, was the eager expectation that Jesus would return from heaven to be Lord of his community. While they waited for him they should live as he would want them to. He set an example of laying down his life for others, so they should do likewise.

Ibrahim: This emphasis on Jesus returning to judge humanity means that only those who believe in him will find the security of eternal life. Instead of focusing on right belief in the One True God the early church shifted attention to faith in Jesus, when he himself had called for people to turn to God. It is this development in the apostolic period that concerns me as a Muslim whose whole attention is taken up with loving God with heart, mind, and strength, to quote Jesus in Mark 12:30. Muslims appreciate the Jesus of the first three Gospels who points to God rather than himself. They find the Fourth Gospel reflecting the apostolic enthusiasm for exalting Jesus to a place of equality with God, so that he draws attention to himself as one to believe in. According to John 9:7 Jesus gave sight to a man born blind. Here is the conversation between them in John 9:35-39:

> Jesus said, "Do you believe in the Son of Man?" 36 He answered, "And who is he, sir? Tell me, so that I may believe in him." 37 Jesus said to him, "You have seen him, and the one speaking with you is he." 38 He said, "Lord, I believe." And he worshiped him. 39 Jesus said, "I came into this world for judgment so that those who do not see may see, and those who do see may become blind."

Therefore, John's view of Jesus is that he should be worshiped and that anyone who fails to do so is spiritually blind. This is followed in John 14:6-9 with Jesus claiming to be the exclusive pathway to God because he is the very embodiment of God:

> Jesus said to him [Thomas], "I am the way, and the truth, and the life. No one comes to the Father except through me. 7 If you know me, you will know my Father also. From now on you do know him and have seen him." 8 Philip said to him, "Lord, show us the Father, and we will be satisfied." 9 Jesus said to him, "Have I been with you all this time, Philip, and you still do not know me? Whoever has seen me has seen the Father. How can you say, "Show us the Father'?

Just look at the language here, completely different from the way Jesus speaks in the other Gospels. I find it incredible that Jesus could be so misrepresented so soon after his life. But then the apostolic writings show us that this "deification" of Jesus took place very quickly and that the early

Christians gave titles and roles to Jesus that were originally given to God in the Hebrew Scriptures. God the judge who holds humans accountable for their actions becomes Jesus the judge who grants eternal life to those who worship him as God.

Paul: The apostolic witness is to Jesus being Lord of all. In Acts 4:10–12, Peter told the members of the Jewish Council in Jerusalem who had brought Peter for questioning about his proclamation of the resurrected Jesus and his healing a crippled man in the name of Jesus:

> Let it be known to all of you, and to all the people of Israel, that this man is standing before you in good health by the name of Jesus Christ of Nazareth, whom you crucified, whom God raised from the dead. **11** This Jesus is "the stone that was rejected by you, the builders; it has become the cornerstone." **12** There is salvation in no one else, for there is no other name under heaven given among mortals by which we must be saved.

Peter challenges the Jewish leaders to acknowledge that Jesus is appointed by God as the means of salvation. Paul agrees in Romans 10:9–13:

> because if you confess with your lips that Jesus is Lord and believe in your heart that God raised him from the dead, you will be saved. **10** For one believes with the heart and so is justified, and one confesses with the mouth and so is saved. **11** The scripture says, "No one who believes in him will be put to shame." **12** For there is no distinction between Jew and Greek; the same Lord is Lord of all and is generous to all who call on him. **13** For, "Everyone who calls on the name of the Lord shall be saved."

The apostle Paul quotes from the prophets Isaiah and Joel and applies their statements about God the Lord to Jesus the Lord.

Modern Christian Approaches to Jesus as Judge

Ibrahim: It is altogether unfortunate that the church developed such a narrow view of salvation. I believe that Islam was revealed to challenge this exclusive focus on Jesus because it had taken many people away from the truth of the need to give God his rightful place. There needed to be a corrective after centuries of drift away from the unity of God, and the elevation of Jesus to a place of equality with him. This is clear in the way that Christians are warned in the Qur'an not to rate Jesus more highly than they should, since he was only a messenger of God.

At least in our time there are Christians who appreciate the urgent necessity to broaden the whole story of salvation in the name of Jesus to salvation by God in terms more in keeping with the truth that God is Creator and Lord of humanity. John Hick came to see that the Qur'an confirms the portrait of Jesus in the first three Gospels, apart from the crucifixion, and that Islam is a means of the salvation of Muslims despite the denial of the crucifixion:

> I suggest that differences of historical judgment, although having their own proper importance, do not prevent the different traditions from being effective, and so far as we can tell, more or less effective, contexts of salvation. Evidently, then, it is not necessary for salvation that we should have correct historical information.[18]

He is reflecting the view of Stanley Samartha, the first director of the Dialogue Program of the World Council of Churches, who urges Christians to avoid exclusive claims for Jesus:

> Elevating Jesus to the status of God or limiting Christ to Jesus of Nazareth are both temptations to be avoided.... A Theocentric Christology avoids these dangers and becomes more helpful in establishing new relationships with neighbors of other faiths.[19]

If you insist on holding onto New Testament concepts of Jesus as co-equal with God, sitting on a throne alongside him, judging humanity on his behalf, and selecting for eternal life only those who have faith in Jesus, then there is no hope for Muslims, let alone Jews or anyone else who believes in the Creator of the world. They will all fail the final test of not believing in Jesus as Lord. Samartha is right to argue that such narrowness will never encourage harmony among the peoples who share the same planet.

Paul: Hick and Samartha received a response from Wolfhart Pannenberg in a collection of essays published to provide a more mainstream position on the role of Jesus in the salvation of humanity. He argues that Christians cannot forsake the New Testament teaching, which claims "[t]hat the transcendent God is present in Jesus' activity, not that God

---

18. Hick, *The Metaphor of God Incarnate*, 145.
19. Samartha, "The Cross and the Rainbow," 80.

is some transcendent reality which human beings may experience and respond to in different ways."[20] This sounds very much like an exclusive position on the revelation of God in Jesus. Pannenberg then puts flesh on this statement by asking the question, "When a Hindu or Sikh prays to God, how can we know that in his intention it is the same God we worship."[21] The answer is that "The Christian has the promise of God in Christ. The other religious traditions do not provide that particular promise."[22] Pannenberg believes that salvation comes through Jesus even for those who have never trusted in him. "Even in the case of those who will participate in the Kingdom of God without having encountered Jesus in their earthly life, Jesus will be their Saviour, no matter what form of religion they were following."[23] The decision for the salvation of those without explicit knowledge of Jesus will be made based on "the affinity of their lives to Jesus' mission and proclamation."[24] But then how is that affinity understood? Pannenberg looks to the Parable of the Sheep and the Goats in Matthew 25, which "implies that many will be admitted to the Kingdom on the basis of their works although they did not know Jesus."[25]

In other words, those who love their neighbor reflect the way of Jesus even if they do not consciously believe in him. But the judgment is made by Jesus, as in the Parable of the Sheep and the Goats, and their salvation is a gift from him. Rather than promoting an exclusive and narrow view that depends on people believing in Jesus before they meet him at the Day of Judgment, Pannenberg visualizes them being surprised that they were serving Jesus without realizing it, as is the case in the parable Jesus told in Matthew 25. From my perspective, there is a lot of wisdom in this proposal, since the final encounter with Jesus on the great day of reckoning will most likely produce the stunning realization among many that Jesus is indeed Lord of Creation. The apostle Paul, in Philippians 2:11, looks forward to the time when "Every tongue should confess that Jesus Christ is Lord, to the glory of God the Father." In Romans 11:30–32, Paul holds out the hope that Jews and non-Jews will receive God's mercy. He writes to the mainly non-Jewish church in Romans 11:

20. Pannenberg, "Religious Pluralism and Conflicting Truth Claims," 102.
21. Ibid., 103.
22. Ibid., 104.
23. Ibid., 100.
24. Ibid., 98.
25. Ibid.

> Just as you [gentiles] were once disobedient to God but have now received mercy because of their disobedience, 31 so they [Israel] have now been disobedient in order that, by the mercy shown to you, they too may now receive mercy. 32 For God has imprisoned all in disobedience so that he may be merciful to all.

The Day of Judgment may turn out to be a wonderful day of reversals.

The Results of the Day of Judgment

Ibrahim: I take the view that the intention of the heart will be central to the proceedings on the Day of Judgment. Since humans are born with a natural inclination to worship their Creator, they continue to develop in awareness of his oversight. Sometimes they wander from him in self-indulgence, but as in the story of the lost son told by Jesus, they come to their senses and return home to the one who waits for them. The Almighty has the power to draw everyone to himself, even those steeped in cultures that worship many gods. I too believe that God will look at the secret thoughts of each person, and will judge according to the light they have received, even in very dark places. Therefore, those who worship many deities may acknowledge a creating power among them, and by attending to the creating god they reach out to the Creator of the world who they will meet on the Day of Judgment. He will demonstrate to them how they have been led astray to give worship to that which is not him, but out of his mercy he may forgive them for what they did not realize in the cultural setting in which they were raised. Judgment belongs to him and we must not assume ahead of time what decisions he will make.

On the Day of Resurrection, according to Q17:13–14, every human being will find their actions recorded in a book which will be opened and read. There will be a division based on the record, according to Q69:18–37:

> On that Day you will be examined and your secrets will not be kept secret. 19 Whoever is given his book in his right hand will say, "Here, read my book. 20 I believed I would receive my account." 21 He will have a delightful life 22 in an elevated Garden, 23 that has fruit nearby. 24 "Eat and drink to your enjoyment because of what you did in the past days." 25 Whoever is given his book in his left hand will say, "If only I had not been given my book 26 and had not become aware of my account. 27 If only it was the end. 28 My wealth has no value for me 29 and my

power has collapsed before me." 30 "Take him and bind him. 31 Then burn him in the Fire 32 tied with a chain measuring seventy cubits. 33 He did not believe in God the Almighty, 34 and he did not advocate making provision for the poor. 35 On this Day he is without a friend. 36 He has no provision except dirty water 37 that only sinners consume."

This division into two kinds of people does not necessarily mean that the rejected ones are lost forever. I believe that the Prophet Muhammad intercedes for those who are not in a condition to be granted immediate access to the Garden, and who can be restored after a period of purgation in the fire to burn up their wrongdoing. I also agree with Ghazali who believes this permission to intercede is extended to others. "When certain of the faithful enter hell deservedly, God shall through His grace accept the Intercession made on their behalf by the Prophets, the Saints, the Divines and the Righteous."[26] I believe that Jews and Christians, who worship the Creator, albeit imperfectly, may be taken out of Hell once their purification has been completed.

Paul: I am not drawn to the notion of a purgation of wrongdoing before entrance to eternal life. Even though this has been the belief of the Catholic Church, I do not find the New Testament teaching that those who are granted life after death may need to spend time being cleaned up in hell. Jesus' threat of hell appears to be a complete separation from life with God. Nowhere does he imply that there is an escape to life after exclusion to a condition of complete darkness where there will be weeping and gnashing of teeth, as he puts it in Matthew 25:30. Nor do any of the apostolic writings offer this suggestion. Perhaps it is best to think of all humanity meeting Jesus on the Day of Resurrection and leaving Jesus to decide who has truly rejected him. Anthony Thiselton makes the case for some being so opposed to the values of Jesus that they will not wish to live with him:

> On one side, it is difficult to imagine obstinate resistance in the light of God's love; on the other, it is hard to imagine forces of ingrained self-absorption and narcissism choosing to yield control of their lives. For some, stubborn self-will is bound up with their very identity.[27]

---

26. al-Ghazali, *The Remembrance of Death*, 210.
27. Thiselton, *Life after Death*, 158.

I reckon that those who have no interest in life after death may well be in the latter category. What kind of existence they might have is hard to imagine. The picture of punishment that never ends may in the end be part of the warning to sort out a life of rebellion against God. I tend to think that there is no experience of life outside of the presence of God.

Ibrahim: From my perspective, Hell may finally not be needed once everyone sent there has been purified for eternal life. According to Q78:21-23, "Hell is a trap; 22 for oppressors a destination 23 to remain in for a long time." Q11:106-7 says, "Those who are condemned will be in the Fire, moaning and groaning. 107 They will remain there as long as the heavens and the earth last, unless your Lord wills otherwise. Surely your Lord does what He wills." People may spend time in Hell but it is not certain that they remain there forever. God may grant them release out of his abundant mercy and compassion.

On a more positive note, Q56:28-37 shows the joy of eternal life in the Garden where the inhabitants live

> ... among lotus trees without thorns, 29 and acacia trees with tiers of flowers 30 giving extensive shade; 31 beside flowing water, 32 with fruit in abundance 33 that does not come to an end and is not forbidden; 34 and on elevated thrones. 35 For them We have specially created female companions 36 who we made pure, 37 loving, and equal in age.

Male believers are granted relationships with virgins equal in age. Some traditions suggest that the number of perpetual virgins granted to male believers can be as many as a hundred. Jane Smith and Yvonne Haddad point out that female believers will continue to be married to their earthly husband, but there is no mention of partners for unmarried women. Children of the faithful who die before puberty also share eternal life.[28]

However, the most significant aspect of the experience of the Garden is seeing God, according to Q75:22-23: "On that Day glowing faces 23 will gaze on their Lord." Some Muslims have thought that humans will not be able to see God since the essence of God has no physical form. But I agree with Ghazali, who recognized that some believers may live eternally on a rather sensual level, but believed that "the vision of the Divine

---

28. Smith and Haddad, *The Islamic Understanding of Death*, 165.

Countenance" would cause others to be "quite oblivious of the pleasures of the people of heaven."[29]

Paul: Christians have understood eternal life to be an experience in which marriage and reproduction has no place. Jesus taught this in Mark 12:25: "For when they rise from the dead, they neither marry nor are given in marriage, but are like angels in heaven." The most important experience is life with God as Revelation 22:1–5 indicates:

> Then the angel showed me the river of the water of life, bright as crystal, flowing from the throne of God and of the Lamb 2 through the middle of the street of the city. On either side of the river is the tree of life with its twelve kinds of fruit, producing its fruit each month; and the leaves of the tree are for the healing of the nations. 3 Nothing accursed will be found there anymore. But the throne of God and of the Lamb will be in it, and his servants will worship him; 4 they will see his face, and his name will be on their foreheads. 5 And there will be no more night; they need no light of lamp or sun, for the Lord God will be their light, and they will reign forever and ever.

This picture of a new life in a new city in the presence of God who sits on his throne along with the Lamb who was slain to wipe out all wrongdoing is the motivation for Christians in this life to persevere when darkness seems to eclipse light. Steve Motyer ends his treatment of the coming of Jesus with these encouraging words:

> We can only truly know him if we renounce the world's values and let the story of Jesus be written into our lives—the story of joy in the midst of weakness, love in the face of rejection and persecution, hope in darkness, peace in the storm, and faith as we live embedded in our lost and perplexed world. That truly is to let the light of his dawn shine already in the darkness of this world's old night—until heaven opens, the trumpet sounds and the whole form of creation is changed by the gladness of his coming.[30]

Jesus will return in power to rule with the Father in a world that is free from pain and suffering, and I am looking forward to being there with all those who eagerly expect his coming.

---

29. al-Ghazali, *The Remembrance of Death*, 250.
30. Motyer, *Come, Lord Jesus!* 332.

Bibliography

Abdel Haleem, M. A. S. *The Qurʾan*. Oxford: Oxford University Press, 2011.
Allison, Dale C. *Constructing Jesus: Memory, Imagination, and History*. Grand Rapids: Baker, 2010.
———. *Resurrecting Jesus: The Earliest Christian Tradition and Its Interpreters*. London: T. & T. Clark, 2005.
ʿAmmar al-Basri, "*Kitab al-masaʾil w-al-ajwiba*." In, *ʿAmmar al-Basri: Apologie et Controverses*, edited by Michel Hayek, 91–266. Beirut: Dar al-Machreq, 1977.
Anawati George C., and Louis Gardet. *Mystique Musulmane*. Paris: Vrin, 1961.
The Apocryphal New Testament, edited and translated by John K. Elliott. Oxford: Clarendon, 1993.
The Arabic Infancy Gospel. In *The Apocryphal New Testament*, edited and translated by John K. Elliott, 104–7. Oxford: Clarendon, 1993.
Assfy, Z. H. *Islam and Christianity*. York: Sessions, 1977.
Augustine. *The City of God against the Pagans*. Edited and translated by William Chase Greene. 7 vols. Cambridge: Harvard University Press, 1957–72.
———. *Confessions*. Translated by Henry Chadwick. Oxford: Oxford University Press, 1991.
Ayoub, Mahmoud. "The Idea of Redemption in Christianity and Islam." In *A Muslim View of Christianity: Essays on Dialogue by Mahmoud Ayoub*, edited by Irfan A. Omar, 90–97. New York: Orbis, 2007.
———. "Toward an Islamic Christology II." In *A Muslim View of Christianity: Essays on Dialogue by Mahmoud Ayoub*, edited by Irfan A. Omar, 156–83. New York: Orbis, 2007.
Bahaʾ al-Din, *Life of Salah ad-Din*. Edited by Claude R. Conder. London: Committee of the Palestine Exploration Fund, 1897.
Bailey, Kenneth E. *Jesus through Middle Eastern Eyes*. London: SPCK, 2008.
Baljon, J. M. S. *Modern Muslim Koran Interpretation (1808–1960)*. Leiden: Brill, 1961.
Beasley-Murray, George R. *John*. Word Biblical Commentary. Dallas: Word, 1991.
The Holy Bible. New Revised Standard Version. Oxford: Oxford University Press, 1989.
Bock, Darrell, L. "Son of Man." In *Dictionary of Jesus and the Gospels*, Second Edition, edited by Joel B. Green, Jeannine K. Brown, and Nicholas Perrin. Downers Grove, IL: IVP, 2013.
Bultmann, Rudolf. *The History of the Synoptic Tradition*. Oxford: Blackwell, 1963.
———. "The Primitive Christian Kerygma and the Historical Jesus." In *The Historical Jesus and the Kerygmatic Christ: Essays on the New Quest of the Historical Jesus*, edited by Carl A. Braaten and Roy A. Harrisville. New York: Abingdon, 1964.
Collins, Adela Y. *Mark: A Commentary*. Hermeneia. Minneapolis: Fortress, 2007.

A Common Word between Us and You (Summary and Abridgement). Jordan: The Royal Aal al-Bayt Institute for Islamic Thought, Jordan, 2007 C.E., 1428 A.H.

Cook, David. *Studies in Muslim Apocalyptic*. Princeton: Darwen, 2002.

Craig, William Lane. "John Dominic Crossan and the Resurrection." In *The Resurrection*, edited by Stephen Davis, Daniel Kendall SJ and Gerald O'Collins SJ. Oxford: Oxford University Press, 1998.

Crossan, John Dominic. *The Historical Jesus: The Life of a Mediterranean Jewish Peasant*. San Francisco: Harper, 1991.

Crossan, John Dominic, and Jonathan L. Reed. *Excavating Jesus*. London: SPCK, 2001.

Davis, Stephen T. "'Seeing' the Risen Jesus." In *The Resurrection*, edited by Stephen Davis, Daniel Kendall SJ, and Gerald O'Collins SJ. Oxford: Oxford University Press, 1998.

Dennis, John. "Death of Jesus." In *Dictionary of Jesus and the Gospels*, edited by Joel B. Green, Jeannine K. Brown and Nicholas Perrin, 172–93. Downers Grove, IL: IVP Academic, 2013.

Dunn, James D. G. *The Christ and the Spirit, Vol. 1: Christology*. Edinburgh: T. & T. Clark, 1998.

———. *Jesus Remembered*. Grand Rapids: Eerdmans, 2003.

———. *Romans 1–8*. Word Biblical Commentary. Dallas: Word, 1991.

al-Dunya, Abu Bakr ibn Abi. *Kitab al-Ikhwan*. Edited by Mustafa ʿAta. Beirut: Dar al-Kutub al-ʿIlmiyya, 1988.

Esack, Farid. *Qurʾan Liberation & Pluralism: An Islamic Perspective of Interreligious Solidarity against Oppression*. Oxford: Oneworld, 1997.

Evans, Craig A. *Mark 8:27—16:20*. Word Biblical Commentary. Nashville: Thomas Nelson, 2010.

Fee, Gordon D. *The First and Second Letters to the Thessalonians*. Grand Rapids: Eerdmans, 2009.

al-Firuzabadi, Abu Tahir Muhammad ibn Yaʿqub. *Tanwir al-miqbas min tafsir ibn ʿAbbas*. Cairo: al-Babi al-Tabari, 1951.

France, Richard T. *The Gospel of Matthew*. Grand Rapids: Eerdmans, 2007.

Gabrieli, Francesco. *Arab Historians of the Crusades*. London: Routledge, 1969.

al-Ghazali, Abu Hamid. *Ihyaʾ ʿulum al-din*. Cairo: al-Matbaʿa al-Husayniyya, 1954.

———. *Kitab Dhikr al-Mawt wa-ma baʿdahu. The Remembrance of Death and the Afterlife*. Translated by Timothy. J. Winter. Cambridge: The Islamic Texts Society, 1995.

Goldingay, John. *Psalms*. 3 Volumes. Baker Commentary on the Old Testament Wisdom and Psalms. Grand Rapids: Baker, 2006–2008.

The Gospel of Pseudo-Matthew. In *The Apocryphal New Testament*, edited and translated by John K. Elliott. Oxford: Clarendon, 1993.

Gregory of Nyssa. *Catechetical Oration*. In *The Later Christian Fathers*, edited and translated by Henry Bettenson. Oxford: Oxford University Press, 1970.

Gutiérrez, Gustavo. *The God of Life*. New York: Orbis, 1991.

———. *The Power of the Poor in History*. New York: Orbis, 1983.

Hagee, John. *Jerusalem Countdown*. Lake Mary, FL: Frontline, 2007.

Hartmann, Florence, and Ed Vulliamy. "How Britain and the US Decided to Abandon Srebrenica to Its Fate." *The Observer*, Saturday 4 July 2015.

Hick, John. *The Metaphor of God Incarnate*. London: SCM, 1993.

———. *The Rainbow of Faiths*. London: SCM, 1995.

———. "A Recent Development within Christian Monotheism." In *Christians, Muslims and Jews,* edited by David Kerr and Daniel Cohn-Sherbock. Birmingham, UK: Conference of Christians, Muslims and Jews, 1982.
Hooker, Morna. *The Gospel according to St Mark.* London: A & C Black, 1991.
Hultgren, Arland J. *Christ and His Benefits: Christology and Redemption in the New Testament.* Philadelphia: Fortress, 1987.
Hurtado, Larry W. *Lord Jesus Christ: Devotion to Jesus in Earliest Christianity.* Grand Rapids: Eerdmans, 2003.
Ibn al-ʿArabi. *The Bezels of Wisdom.* Translated by R. W. J. Austin, London: SPCK, 1980.
Ibn Hanbal, Ahmad. *Kitab al-Zuhd.* Edited by Muhammad Zaghlul. Cairo: Dar al-Kitab al-ʿArabi, 1988.
Ibn Ishaq. *The Life of Muhammad.* Translated by Alfred Guillaume. Oxford: Oxford University Press, 1955.
Ibn Kathir, Ismaʾil. *Qisas al-anbiyaʾ.* Edited by Mustafa Abd al-Wahid. Cairo: Dar al-Kutub al-haditha, 1968.
———. *Tafsir al-Qurʾan.* Cairo: Dar ihyaʾ al-kutub al-ʿarabiyya, n.d.
Ibn al-Mubarak, ʿAbdallah. *Kitab al-Zuhd.* Edited by Habib al-Rahman al-ʿAzami. Beirut: Dar al-Kutub al-ʿIlmiyya, n.d.
The Infancy Gospel of Thomas. In *The Apocryphal New Testament,* edited and translated by John K. Elliott. Oxford: Clarendon, 1993.
Irenaeus. *Against Heresies.* In *The Early Christian Fathers,* edited and translated by Henry Bettenson. Oxford: Oxford University Press, 1969.
Katancho, Yohanna. "Reading the Gospel of John through Palestinian eyes." In *Jesus without Borders: Christology in the Majority World,* edited by Gene L. Green, Stephen T. Pardue and K. K. Yeo. Grand Rapids: Eerdmans, 2014.
Keener, Craig. *Miracles.* Grand Rapids: Eerdmans, 2011.
Khalidi, Tarif. *The Muslim Jesus.* Cambridge: Harvard University Press, 2001.
Kropp, Manfred. "Beyond Single Words. *Maʾida–shaytan–jibt* and *taghut.* Mechanisms of Transmission into the Ethiopic (Geʾez) Bible and the Qurʾanic text." In *The Qurʾan in Its Historical Context,* edited by Gabriel Said Reynolds. London: Routledge, 2008.
Küng, Hans. *Islam.* Oxford: Oneworld, 2007.
Lawson, Todd. *The Crucifixion and the Qurʾan: A Study in the History of Muslim Thought.* Oxford: Oneworld, 2009.
"Lecture of the Holy Father—Faith, Reason and the University Memories and Reflections." Rome: Libreria Editrice Vaticana, 12 September 2006.
Letters of the Brethren of Purity. *Rasaʾil ikhwan al-safaʾ wa-khullan al-wafaʾ.* Edited by Khayr al-Din al-Zirikli. Cairo: al-Maktaba al-Tijariya al-Kubra, 1928.
Licona, Michael R. *The Resurrection of Jesus: A New Historiographical Approach.* Downers Grove, IL: IVP, 2010.
Lumbard, Joseph. "What of the Word is Common?" In *Muslim and Christian Understanding: Theory and Application of "A Common Word,"* edited by Waleed El-Ansary and David K. Linnan. New York: Palgrave Macmillan, 2010.
Maimela, Simon. "Archbishop Desmond Tutu: A Revolutionary Political Priest or Man of Peace." In *Hammering Swords into Ploughshares: Essays in Honour of Archbishop Desmond Tutu,* edited by Itumeleng Mosala and Buti Tlhagale, 41–60. Basingstoke, UK: Marshall Pickering, 1987.
Maqsood, Ruqaiyyah. *The Mysteries of Jesus.* Oxford: Sakina, 2000.

Marshall, I. Howard. *New Testament Theology*. Downers Grove, IL: IVP, 2004.
Marx, Karl. *Economic and Philosophical Manuscripts*. In *Early Writings*. London: Penguin, 1975.
Moltmann, Jürgen. *The Crucified God*. London: SCM, 1974.
Morris, Leon. *Galatians: Paul's Charter of Christian Freedom*. Leicester, UK: IVP, 1996.
Motyer, Stephen. *Come, Lord Jesus! A Biblical Theology of the Second Coming of Christ*. London: Apollos, 2016.
Muqatil, Ibn Sulayman. *Tafsir al-Qurʾan*. Cairo: 1969.
Nasr, Seyyed Hossein. "Comments on a Few Theological Issues in the Islamic-Christian Dialogue." In *Christian-Muslim Encounters*, edited by Yvonne Y. Haddad and Wadi Z. Haddad, 458–65. Gainesville, FL: University of Florida Press, 1995.
———. *Islamic Life and Thought*. London: George, Allen and Unwin, 1981.
———. "The Word of God: The Bridge between Him, You, and Us." In *A Common Word: Muslims and Christians on Loving God and Neighbor*, edited by Miroslav Volf and Prince Ghazi bin Muhammad bin Talal, 110–17. Grand Rapids: Eerdmans, 2010.
Nuʿaym ibn Hammad al-Marwazi, *Kitab al-fitan*. Edited by Suhayl Zakkar. Beirut: Dar al-fikr, 1993.
O'Collins, Gerald. *Christology*. Oxford: Oxford University Press, 1995.
Omar, Irfan A. *A Muslim View of Christianity: Essays on Dialogue by Mahmoud Ayoub*. New York: Orbis, 2007.
Origen. *Against Celsus*. Translated by Henry Chadwick. Cambridge: Cambridge University Press, 1986.
Pannenberg, Wolfhart. "Religious Pluralism and Conflicting Truth Claims: The Problem of a Theology of the World Religions." In *Christian Uniqueness Reconsidered: The Myth of a Pluralistic Theology of Religions*, edited by Gavin D'Costa, 96–106. New York: Orbis, 1990.
———. *Systematic Theology*, 3 Volumes. Grand Rapids: Eerdmans, 1994.
Parrinder, Geoffrey. *Jesus in the Qurʾan*. London: Sheldon, 1965.
Perrin, Nicholas. "Last Supper." In *Dictionary of Jesus and the Gospels*, edited by Joel B. Green, Jeannine K. Brown, and Nicholas Perrin. Downers Grove, IL: IVP Academic, 2013.
Petri, H. "Devotion to Mary." In *Encyclopedia of Christianity*. Leiden: Brill, 2003.
"Pope apologises to Muslims." Reuters, 16 September 2006.
The Protevangelium of James. In *The Apocryphal New Testament*, edited and translated by John K. Elliott, 48–67. Oxford: Clarendon, 1993.
Pullinger, Jackie. *Chasing the Dragon*. London: Hodder, 1980.
al-Razi, Fakhr al-Din. *Al-Tafsir al-Kabir*. Cairo: al-Matbaʾa al-bahiyya al-misriyya, 1934–62.
Reynolds, Gabriel Said. "The Muslim Jesus: Dead or Alive?" *Bulletin of the School of Oriental and African Studies* 72 (2009) 237–58.
Robinson, Neal. *Christ in Islam and Christianity*. Basingstoke, UK: Macmillan, 1991.
———. "Jesus." In *Encyclopaedia of the Qurʾan*, 3:7–21. Leiden: Brill, 2003.
Salahi, Adil. *Muhammad: Man and Prophet*. Markfield, UK: The Islamic Foundation, 2005.
Sahih al-Bukhari. Edited and translated by M. M. Khan. New Delhi: Kitab Bhavan, 1987.
Sahih Muslim. Translated by A. H. Siddiqi, New Delhi: Kitab Bhavan, 2000.

Samartha, Stanley J. "The Cross and the Rainbow: Christ in a Multireligious Culture." In *The Myth of Christian Uniqueness: Towards a Pluralistic Theology of Religions*, edited by John Hick and Leonard Swidler. New York: Orbis, 1987.
Samir, Samir K. "The Theological Christian Influence on the Qurʾan. A Reflection." In *The Qurʾan in Its Historical Context*, edited by Gabriel S. Reynolds. London: Routledge, 2008.
Siddiqui, Mona. *Christians, Muslims & Jesus*. New Haven: Yale University Press, 2013.
Smalley, Stephen S. *1, 2, 3 John*. Word Biblical Commentary. Dallas: Word, 1984.
Smith, Jane I., and Yvonne Y. Haddad. *The Islamic Understanding of Death and Resurrection*. Albany, NY: State University of New York Press, 1981.
Smith, Margaret. *Rabiʿa the Mystic and Her Fellow-Saints in Islam*. Cambridge: Cambridge University Press, 1928.
Spencer, Richard. "Armenian Massacres." *The Telegraph*, 24 April 2015.
Stowasser, Barbara F. "Mary." In *Encyclopaedia of the Qurʾan*. Leiden: Brill, 2003.
———. *Women in the Qurʾan, Traditions, and Interpretation*. Oxford: Oxford University Press, 1994.
Strauss, David F. *The Life of Jesus, Critically Examined*. New York: Blanchard, 1860.
Swinburne, Richard. *Was Jesus God?* Oxford: Oxford University Press, 2008.
al-Tabari, Abu Jaʿfar. *Jamiʿ al-Bayan ʿan Taʾwil al-Qurʾan*. Beirut: Dar al-maʿrifa, 1972.
Thiselton, Anthony C. *The First Epistle to the Corinthians*. New International Greek Testament Commentary. Grand Rapids: Eerdmans, 2000.
———. *Life after Death: A New Approach to the Last Things*. Grand Rapids: Eerdmans, 2012.
Timothy I. "Dialogue between the Caliph al-Mahdī and Timothy I, Patriarch of the East Syrian Church." In Hans Putman, *L'Église sous Timothée I*, appendix. Beirut: Dar el-Machreq, 1975.
Torrance, Thomas F. *Incarnation: The Person and Life of Christ*. Milton Keynes, UK: Paternoster, 2008.
Travis, Stephen H. *Christ and the Judgement of God*. Peabody, MA: Hendrickson, 2009.
A Treatise on the Triune Nature of God. Edited and translated by Margaret D. Gibson. London: Cambridge University Press, 1899.
Tutu, Desmond. *General Secretary's Report*. South African Council of Churches, 1984.
von Wahlde, Urban C. *The Gospel and Letters of John. Volume 2, Commentary on the Gospel of John*. Grand Rapids: Eerdmans, 2010.
Watt, William Montgomery. *Muhammad Prophet and Statesman*. Oxford: Oxford University Press, 1961.
Welker, Michael. *God the Revealed: Christology*. Grand Rapids: Eerdmans, 2013.
Wenham, David. *The Parables of Jesus*. London: Hodder and Stoughton, 1989.
Wright, N. T. *Pauline Perspectives*. London: SPCK, 2013.
———. *The Resurrection of the Son of God*. London: SPCK, 2003.
———. *Surprised by Hope*. London: SPCK, 2007.
Yunus, M. *Letter to Grameen Bank Members*. 15 May 2011. www.grameen.com.
Zahniser, A. H. Mathias. *The Mission & Death of Jesus in Islam and Christianity*. New York: Orbis, 2008.
al-Zamakhshari, *Al-Kashshaf ʿan Haqaʾiq al-Tanzil*. Edited by Mustafa Husayn Ahmad. Cairo: Matbaʿat al-istiqama, 1953.

General Index

Aaron, 3, 9, 25, 56, 81, 91, 182
Abdel Haleem, M. A. S., 183
ʿAbduh, Muhammad, 162
Abraham, 2, 55–57, 68, 73–74, 91–93, 111, 182, 195, 202
Abu Hurayra, 121, 197–99
Adam, 4, 13, 16, 18, 140, 154, 189
Allison, Dale, 176, 178, 185–86, 188
ʿAmmar al-Basri, 104–5
Anawati, Georges, 58
Angel, angels, 2–6, 8–13, 15–16, 67, 70, 79, 88, 90–91, 94, 101, 108, 120, 131–32, 150, 174, 176, 182, 191, 193, 199–201, 213
Anna, 4, 7–8
Antichrist, 200
Arabia, 64, 80–81, 100, 138, 145, 173
The Arabic Infancy Gospel, 14–15, 111
Arab, 20, 80, 82, 131–33, 138
Armenian, 84–85
Ascension of Jesus to Heaven, 180–81, 186, 188, 193, 198
Assfy, Z. H., 160
Augustine, 58–61, 195
Augustus, 11, 187
Ayoub, Mahmoud, 139, 163–64

Baha' al-Din, 84
Bailey, Kenneth, 54
Baljon, J.M.S., 4n
BBC, 20, 85n
Beasley-Murray, George, 97–98, 127
Bethlehem, 10–11, 151

Bin Laden, Osama, 85
Birth of Jesus, 6, 9–12, 15, 17, 21, 33, 100, 108
Bock, Darrell, 116–17, 125
Brethren of Purity, 187
al-Bukhari, Muhammad ibn Isma'il, 198
Bultmann, Rudolf, 32, 51–52, 199
Byzantine Emperor Manuel II Paleologus, 62–63

Catholic, 7, 17, 19–21, 39, 61, 118, 211
Children of Israel, 2, 11, 24–26, 33–34, 45–46, 49, 55–56, 73–74, 81–82, 87, 90, 92, 97, 100–101, 104, 108–11, 122–23, 150–51, 157, 159, 187, 197, 207, 210
Collins, Adela, 78, 117, 156
Common Word Document, 45–47, 57, 61, 140, 146, 160
Conception of Jesus, 2–6, 8, 12–13, 16–21, 24, 91, 101, 108–10, 138, 168
Cook, David, 198n
Craig, William Lane, 175
Cross, 14, 50–52, 80, 112, 117, 121, 126, 130, 133, 137, 148, 156–70, 172–73, 178, 180–81, 184, 186–90, 197–99, 204–8, 213
Crossan, Dominic, 50, 52, 76, 78, 117, 135, 156, 161, 175, 187–88, 199

GENERAL INDEX

al-Dajjal, 163, 197–98
David, 2, 5–6, 91, 122, 151–52, 180
Davis, Stephen, 176, 178
Day of Judgment, 49, 55, 72, 83, 88, 110, 112–13, 120, 126, 183, 210–11
Death of Jesus, 37, 77, 117–18, 121, 124, 126, 133, 136–37, 140, 143, 148, 150, 153–70, 172–73, 176, 178, 180–84, 186, 188–90, 193, 197–99, 204–6, 213
Dennis, John, 157–58
Disciples of Jesus, 26, 29, 31, 35–37, 49, 51, 54, 57, 62, 69–72, 74, 77, 79, 85, 89, 99–100, 103, 109, 111–13, 115, 125–26, 129, 133, 136–37, 145, 152–53, 155–57, 160, 166, 172–79, 186–90, 194, 200, 202, 206–7
Dunn, James, 36, 66–67, 89, 116, 134, 143–44, 158
al-Dunya, Abu Bakr ibn Abi, 113

Egypt, 10, 12–14, 25, 28, 33–34, 39, 55–56, 83, 123, 137, 157
Elliot, John, 14–15, 31, 111
Elijah, 87–88, 90–91, 185–87
Elisha, 91
Elizabeth, 17
Emmanuel, 6, 18, 100
Enoch, 185–87
Esack, Farid, 123–24, 145–46
Eternal Life, 71–73, 74, 78, 91–93, 97, 99, 125–27, 183–85, 190, 193–97, 201, 204–8, 211–13
Ethiopia, 19, 33, 138
Eucharist, 33, 162
Evangelical, 18, 39
Evans, Craig, 200
Evil spirits, 29, 35–36, 130
Exorcism, 32, 35–36, 115

Fee, Gordon, 194
France, Richard, 76, 79, 142, 155

Gabriel, 4–6, 101, 182

Galilee, 5, 37, 68, 176–78
Gaurdet, Louis, 58n
Ghazali, Abu Hamid, 114–15, 166, 211–13
Ghulam Ahmed Parwez, 4
God the Almighty, 25, 35, 210–11
God the Father, 14, 18, 35, 48, 50–51, 60–61, 70, 95–96, 99–100, 105, 112, 126, 133–34, 137–38, 140–43, 146–48, 151, 166–67, 169–70, 189–90, 193, 201, 204–5, 209, 213
God the Merciful, 9, 25, 56, 78, 101, 131, 144, 203
Goldingay, John, 74
The Gospel of Pseudo-Matthew, 13, 15
Grameen Bank, 42–43
Gregory of Nyssa, 32, 35
Gutiérrez, Gustavo, 118–19, 123

Haddad, Yvonne, 212
Hagee, John, 194
Hasan al-Basri, 181
Healing, 11, 20–22, 24, 26, 28–31, 34–36, 39–41, 55, 57–58, 68, 74, 87, 102, 115, 165, 206–7
Heaven, 33, 35–36, 51, 59, 70, 73–74, 79, 87, 92, 125–27, 134, 137, 141–42, 154, 176–77, 179–80, 182–83, 185–87, 194–97, 199–200, 203–4, 213
Hell, 58, 72–73, 78, 132, 197, 201, 211–12
Herod, 75, 87–89, 195
Hick, John, 36, 135, 208
Holy Spirit, 5–6, 17–18, 20, 40–41, 67, 79, 101–4, 112–15, 119, 122, 133–34, 138, 141–44, 147–48, 169–70, 180, 204
Hooker, Morna, 75, 82, 156
Hultgren, Arland, 184
Hurtado, Larry, 136, 153
Husayn, 164

Ibn ʿAbbas, 160

Ibn Adham, 58
Ibn al-ʿArabi, 38, 61
Ibn Hanbal, Ahmad, 153–54
Ibn Ishaq, Abu ʿAbdallah, 13, 15–16, 19, 26–27, 77, 80, 112, 182–83, 198
Ibn Kathir, Ismaʾil, 4n, 7–8n, 10, 28
Ibn al-Mubarak, ʿAbdallah, 113
Ibn Munabbih, Wahb, 160, 186–87
Idolatry, 55–56
Idris, 182
ʿImran, 7–8
Incarnation, 32, 36, 98–100, 105, 109, 127, 135–36, 138–39, 142, 147–48, 168, 179
The Infancy Gospel of Thomas, 30
Irenaeus of Lyons, 100
Isaac, 73–74, 91, 202
Ishmael, 91

Jacob, 5, 73–74, 91, 202
James the disciple of Jesus, 129,
James the brother of Jesus, 173–74
Jerusalem 10, 31, 37, 57, 74–75, 79, 83–84, 88, 90, 103, 122, 141, 150, 152, 156, 168, 173–75, 179, 183, 186, 195, 198, 200, 202, 207, 213
Jesus as King, 5, 12, 79, 194–96, 198, 200–201, 208, 213
Jesus as Lamb of God, 88–89, 163, 213
Jesus as Lord, 10, 12, 17–18, 31, 57, 79, 109, 111, 135–38, 158, 177–78, 180, 189–91, 193–96, 202, 205, 207–9
Jesus as Mediator, 18, 60
Jesus as Seal of the Saints, 38, 61, 135
Jesus' divine nature, 15–19, 21–22, 26–28, 32, 34–36, 109–10, 126–27, 129, 135–41, 146, 148, 164, 167–69, 178–81, 190, 206–8
The Jesus Seminar, 50–52, 135
Jesus speaking as an infant, 9–10, 12–15, 38, 67, 92, 110, 181

Jews, 10, 14, 28, 31, 35, 37, 45, 47–49, 54, 57, 62, 66, 68–71, 74–77, 80–83, 87, 91, 93–98, 109, 121–23, 126, 130, 132, 134, 136–37, 140–41, 144–45, 150–54, 156, 160–61, 173, 175–76, 179–81, 185–87, 194–95, 207–9, 211
Job, 91
John the Baptist, 4, 16, 66–69, 87–92, 102, 113–15, 181–82
John the disciple of Jesus, 31, 95, 99, 129, 175
Jonah, 91
Joseph, 4–6, 8, 10–14, 17, 31
Joseph of Arimathea, 175
Joseph, prophet, 91, 182
Judas Iscariot, 62, 160
Judgment of God, 26, 49–50, 55–56, 68, 70, 72, 78–79, 83, 88–90, 110, 112–13, 120, 126, 144, 164, 169, 185, 200–201, 204, 206–11

Kaʿba, 19, 49
Katancho, Yohanna, 195
Keener, Craig, 32
Khalidi, Tarif, 113–14, 154n, 166
Kingdom of God, 54, 61–63, 66, 69–76, 78, 82–83, 88, 96, 102, 115, 117–18, 153, 189, 198, 201–2, 204, 209, 213
Kropp, Manfred, 33n
Küng, Hans, 17

The Last Supper, 126, 156–59
Lawson, Todd, 161, 186n–87n
Lazarus, 29, 35
Levi, 81–82
Licona, Michael, 179–80
Lot, 91
Lourdes, 7, 20–21
Lumbard, Joseph, 146–47
Luther, Martin, 18

Maccabean Martyrs, 156–57, 164
Al-Mahdi, Caliph, 168
Maimela, Simon, 120n

Maqsood, Ruquiyyah Waris, 179, 183
Marshall, Howard, 124–25, 180, 184
Marx, Karl, 184–85
Mary, 2–21, 38–39, 60–61, 67, 90, 98, 101, 108–13, 121, 139, 145–46, 175, 186–87, 191
Mary Magdalene, 176, 186–87
Mecca, 19, 49–50, 69, 72, 77 -78, 82–83, 122, 131–32, 183
Medina, 13, 49, 70, 77, 80–82, 108, 123, 131–32, 198
Messiah, 2, 10, 17, 31, 60, 67, 90, 97, 104, 108–9, 122, 130, 137, 148, 150–57, 159, 168, 179, 180, 187, 191, 197, 200
Methodist, 17, 59
Miracles, 17, 19, 24–42, 57, 96–97, 108–10, 119, 138, 164, 168, 206
Moltmann, Jürgen, 169
Morris, Leon, 133
Moses, 2, 25–26, 28, 33–34, 38, 45, 49, 55, 81–82, 91–95, 97–101, 109, 122–23, 125, 182
Motyer, Steve, 196, 213
Muhammad, 13, 15–16, 19–22, 26–27, 38, 47, 49–50, 56–58, 60, 62, 64, 69–72, 77–78, 80–83, 91–94, 110–12, 121–23, 131–32, 153, 164, 180–83, 197–99, 211
Muqatil ibn Sulayman, 186–87, 197
Muslim ibn al-Hajjaj, 198

Najran, 13, 15–16, 138–139, 198
Nasr, Seyyed Hossein, 146, 160–61
Nazareth, 5, 31, 98, 111, 119, 163, 207–8
Nero, 165
Nicodemus, 96–97, 102, 127
Noah, 56–57, 91, 93
Nuʿaym ibn Hammad al-Marwazi, 198

The Observer Newspaper, 84
O'Collins, Gerald, 17
Omar, Irfan, 139, 163–64

Origen, 32
Orthodox, 19, 39, 61, 84

Palestine, 99, 195
Pannenberg, Wolfhart, 190–91, 208–9
Paradise, 14, 58, 71, 77, 177, 182, 197, 203, 210–12
Parrinder, Geoffrey, 17
Pentecostal, 39
Perpetual Virginity of Mary, 6, 11–12, 18
Perrin, Nicholas, 159
Peter, 31–32, 37, 64, 71, 129, 141, 157, 164–66, 172–76, 207
Petri, H., 7, 18
Pharaoh, 25, 33, 49
Pharisee/s, 35, 54, 75, 116, 136, 186
Philip, disciple of Jesus, 206
Philip, King of France, 83
Polytheist/s, 49, 55, 59, 62, 77, 80, 82–83, 88, 131–33, 138–39, 146–47, 210
Pope Benedict XVI, 20, 45, 61–63
Pope John Paul II, 17
Pope Pius IX, 7
Pope Pius XII, 7
Prayer, 4, 6–7, 9, 18–20, 26, 33, 39–43, 48, 50–52, 55–56, 58–59, 61, 67, 74, 76, 112, 115, 121, 132, 133–38, 140, 159, 166, 197, 209, 211
Priest, priests, 75, 90, 117, 121–22, 130, 137, 154, 174, 194
Prophet, prophets, 2, 5, 9, 12–13, 15–16, 18, 25–29, 32, 34, 38, 45, 47, 49, 56, 60, 66, 69–71, 77, 79, 82, 85, 87–88, 91–94, 98, 100–1, 104, 108–12, 116–17, 119–21, 130, 144, 150–52, 156, 158–59, 164, 179–83, 187, 196–99, 202, 207–8, 211
Protestant, 17–18
The Protevangelium of James, 7–9, 11–12
Pullinger, Jackie, 39–41
Purgatory, 20

GENERAL INDEX 225

al-Qaeda, 85
Quraysh, 19, 49–50, 77

Rabiʿa al-ʿAdawiyya, 58
Razi, Fakhr al-Din, 4n, 27–29, 38, 160–62
Reed, Jonathan, 51n, 76n, 78n
Resurrection, 55, 61, 126, 131, 143, 167, 177, 180–83, 186, 188–89, 194, 196, 210–11, 213
Resurrection of Jesus, 36–37, 117–18, 143, 148, 155–56, 167–70, 172–80, 182–91, 193, 199–200, 204, 207
Reynolds, Gabriel, 197n
Richard I, King of England, 83–84
Rida, Rashid, 162
Robinson, Neal, 15, 29, 181n–82
Roman, 32, 35, 48–49, 62, 73–79, 96, 130, 134–35, 151–53, 161, 163, 165

Saints, 39, 41, 61
Salah al-Din, 83–84
Salahi, Adil, 81
Salome, 11
Salvation, 6, 10, 12, 59, 69, 169, 181, 200, 202, 204–5, 207–9
Samaria, 97–98
Samartha, Stanley, 208
Samir, Samir Khalil, 33
Satan, 4, 7, 102, 114–15, 153, 201
Sayyid Ahmed Khan, 4
Scribes, 46–47, 75, 93, 116–17
Second Coming of Jesus, 121, 180–81, 185, 191, 193–99, 204–6, 213
Shiʿa, 45–46, 164
Siddiqui, Mona, 162–63, 180
Smalley, Stephen, 99
Smith, Jane, 212
Smith, Margaret, 58n
Solomon, 91
Son of God, 5–6, 13, 17–18, 32, 36, 60–61, 88, 95–96, 104, 109, 127, 129–34, 136, 138–42, 144, 147–48, 150, 152, 169, 173, 179–80, 184–85, 189–90, 204
Son of Man, 60, 106, 113, 116–17, 120–21, 124–27, 129, 153–54, 157–58, 179, 199–200, 206
Son of Mary, 3, 9, 19, 26, 47, 56, 60, 67, 90, 92–93, 104, 106, 108–13, 121, 130, 137, 150, 153, 159, 182, 191, 197
Stephen, 179–80
Stowasser, Barbara, 4n–5n, 13
Strauss, David, 51
Sufi, 58, 114–16, 135, 153–54, 166, 187
Sunni, 45–46, 85, 114, 164
Swinburne, Richard, 147–48, 188–89

Tabari, Abu Jaʾfar, 5n, 121, 181, 186n, 197n–98
Tacitus, 161
The Telegraph Newspaper, 85
Temple, 4, 8, 16, 57, 67, 75–76, 88, 122, 156, 200
Thiselton, Anthony, 158–59, 211
Thomas, 37, 178, 206
Timothy, Patriarch, 168–69
Torah, 38, 45–49, 55, 57, 92–95, 97–98, 101, 109–10, 116, 123, 196–97
Torrance, Thomas, 105, 142, 169
Travis, Stephen, 204
Trinity, 18, 36, 103–5, 108, 130, 141–47, 169–70
Tutu, Desmond, 119–20

von Wahlde, Urban, 98

Watt, William Montgomery, 80
Welker, Michael, 169
Wenham, David, 54, 202
Wesley, Charles, 59–60
Wesley, John, 59
Word of God, 2, 36, 60, 79, 85, 89–90, 94–96, 98–100, 104–5, 126–27, 138–40, 147, 163
Wright, N. T., 168, 185, 199–200

Yunus, Muhammad, 42–43

Zahniser, Mathias, 198
Zamakhshari, 4n, 10, 27
Zechariah, 4, 7–8, 16–17, 67, 90–91, 113

Bible Index

OLD TESTAMENT

Genesis
1:1–3	94–95
5:24	185–87
12:2–3	68–69
17:8	195

Exodus
20:2–3	137
32:25–29	81–82

Leviticus
19:18	46

Deuteronomy
6:4–5	46
19:21	47

2 Samuel
7:16	5

2 Kings
2:11	185–87

Psalm
2:1–12	152–53
47:2	58
47:7–9	74
79:18	60
110:1	121–22, 179
146:5	58

Isaiah
7:14	6
9:6–7	151–52
28:16	207
40:3	90
45:23	137
53:3–12	154–55, 157–58, 165
61:1–2	119

Daniel
7:13–14	116–17, 120–22, 125, 157, 200

Joel
2:32	207
3:14–15	120

Micah
5:2–5	100, 151

Malachi
3:1	87–88
4:5–6	88

NEW TESTAMENT

Matthew
1:18–25	6, 12

Matthew (continued)

1:23	18, 36, 100
2:1–12	10
5:3	70
5:39	51
5:42	51
5:43–48	48–49, 51–52, 64
6:1–4	70
6:9	35, 134
6:14	134
6:18	134
6:19–20	70
6:24	70–71
6:26	134
7:11	134
7:13–14	201–2
7:21–23	201–2
8:5–13	73–74
9:9	49
10:1	35
10:8	35
11:1–19	87–88
11:19	114
19:25–26	133
22:37–40	57, 201
25:1–13	72–73, 200
25:30	211
25:31–46	200–201, 204, 209
26:52	152–53
26:69–75	165
27:46	50
27:57–61	175
28:1–10	176
28:16–17	177–78
28:17	37
28:18–19	141–42
28:20	178

Mark

1:1	129, 150
1:4	66
1:4–6	114
1:7	67
1:9–11	88
1:10	102
1:11	129
1:12	102
1:15	66
1:21–28	29
1:40–45	28
2:1–12	29–30
2:5	36, 116
2:10–11	116, 124
2:14	49
2:28	116
3:11	130
3:31–35	112
4:41	37
5:1–20	57
5:6–8	130
5:35–41	30
6:2–3	111
6:12	36
6:14–29	88
6:30–34	30
6:45–52	30
6:41	33
7:31–37	29
8:22–26	28
8:29	153
8:31	117, 153–54
8:32–33	153
9:7	129
9:31	117, 154
9:42–48	71–72
10:23–27	69
10:29–30	71
10:33–34	117, 154
10:45	153–54, 156
10:46–52	28
11:15–18	75–76
12:13–17	75
12:25	213
12:28–31	46, 57, 201
12:36–37	122
12:43–44	57
13:2–23	200
13:24–27	120, 199–200
14:22–24	157
14:34–36	166
14:35–36	133
14:62	121
14:63–64	122
14:66–72	165

BIBLE INDEX   229

15:34	50
15:39	130
15:43–47	175
16:1–8	176

Luke

1:5–25	17
1:26–38	5–6, 17
1:46–55	6
2:1–21	10
2:11	18
3:7–14	68–69, 88
3:23	6
4:1	115
4:14	102
4:16–21	102, 118–19
4:32	115
4:35	115
5:15–16	115
5:27	49
6:27–35	51–52, 64
6:28	50
7:11–17	29
9:1	35
9:1–2	115
9:6	115
10:1	62
13:22–30	201–2
15:11–32	52–54, 96
17:11–19	28
18:9–14	54
22:56–62	165
23:34	50
23:34–35	133
23:50–56	175
24:1–12	176
24:26	155–56
24:36–51	176
24:37	175

John

1:1–5	95
1:6–9	90
1:10–13	95–96
1:14	36, 89, 96, 98, 139
1:15	90
1:17–18	95–96
1:21	88
1:23	90
1:26–27	90
1:29	88
1:31	90
1:32–33	102
1:34	88
2:1–11	30
2:23	34
3:1–12	96–97, 102
3:13–15	125
3:15–16	127
4:3–30	97–98
4:54	35
5:1–18	29
5:25	127
5:28–29	126–27
6:35	37
6:53–54	126
6:58	37
6:62	126
6:68–69	37
8:28	126
9:35–39	206
10:30–39	35
11:1–45	29
12:10–11	29
12:18–19	35
12:47–48	35
13:21–30	95
14:6–9	206
15:15–18	95
15:26	112–13
17:11	134
17:21	134–35
18:11	165
18:15–18	165
18:25–27	165
19:25	112
19:26–27	95, 176
19:38–42	175
20:1–18	176
20:19	175
20:25	37
20:26–29	177
20:26	175
20:28	37
21:7	95
21:20	95

Acts

2:4	103
2:14–36	31
2:38	141
3:1–10	31–32
4:10–12	207
7:56	179
9:1–8	174
9:34	32

Romans

1:1–4	151–52, 179
1:3	6
4:24–25	184
8:9–11	142–44
8:14–17	133–34, 143–44
8:34	60
10:9–13	207
10:20	60
11:26–29	195
11:30–32	209–10

1 Corinthians

9:1	177
11:23–26	158–59
15:3–9	172–74
15:17–19	184
15:20–28	189
15:34	185
15:42–44	177
16:22	136

2 Corinthians

4:10	58–59
5:17	18
12:2–4	177

Galatians

1:13–19	173–74
4:4	180
4:5	60
4:6	133

Philippians

2:5–11	136–37, 168, 189, 209

Colossians

1:15–20	190

1 Thessalonians

4:13–18	193–94, 196

Hebrews

12:1–2	167

1 Peter

1:1–9	204–5
1:3–4	167
1:13–16	205
2:1	205
2:13–15	164–65
2:18–25	165
5:5	59

1 John

1:1	89
1:1–3	99
3:1–3	205–6

Revelation

5:6–7	89
19:11–21	79–80, 163–64, 194
19:13	89
20:4–6	194
21:1–4	195
22:1–5	213

Qur'an Index

Reference	Pages
2:87	108
2:111–12	71
2:177	70
2:216–18	78
2:256	62
3:35–46	67
3:35–42	9
3:35–37	7–8
3:37–40	16, 90
3:40	4
3:42	8
3:45–47	2–4, 90, 94, 98, 100,
3:45	108, 140, 150, 191
3:46	13
3:47	139–40
3:49	24, 27, 32, 34, 37–38
3:50–51	140
3:55	181
3:59	16, 140
3:61–63	140–41
3:64	140
3:133–36	203
4:157–59	121, 182, 197
4:157	150, 159–63, 198
4:158	182
4:159	121, 183
4:164	98–99
4:171–73	146
4:171	20, 60–61, 90, 94, 98, 100–101, 103–4, 108–9, 115, 130–31, 139–40, 144, 150
5:17	109
5:44–47	47, 93
5:45	48
5:46–47	93
5:46	92
5:47	109
5:48	94
5:51	123
5:65–66	92, 196–97
5:72–73	103, 146
5:72	109, 150, 197
5:73–74	144
5:75–76	109–10
5:109–11	110
5:110	13, 34, 37–38
5:112–15	26, 33
5:116–17	19, 60–61, 109, 144
5:116	112
6:83–89	91
7:142–47	55
7:148–53	56
9:29	83
9:30–31	130
9:31	137–38
11:69–83	57
11:106–7	212
15:45–48	196
16:102	103–4
17:1	183
17:13–14	210
17:111	132
19:15	181
19:16–17	3
19:17–22	101
19:19	4
19:20–22	3
19:23–34	9, 11–12
19:24–26	15

19:27–28	3–4	51:15–19	203
19:30–33	12–13	53:19	131
19:30	92	53:36–54	9
19:33	181–82, 198	56:28–37	212
21:26–29	131–32	57:26–28	56
21:91	5	61:6	110, 112
22:39–40	77	61:14	110–11
23:91	132	69:18–37	210–11
25:2–3	131	71:1–25	57
26:10–68	25, 33, 49	72:3	133
26:69–90	55	73:8	47
33:26–27	80	75:22–23	212–13
35:40	132–33	78:21–23	212
37:149–58	131	87:19	91
42:13	92–93	89:17–20	69–70
42:15	93	90:4–20	72
48:29	93	112:1–2	47
50:31–35	203		

www.ingramcontent.com/pod-product-compliance
Lightning Source LLC
Chambersburg PA
CBHW020407230426
43664CB00009B/1220